Essays on Pedagogy

Pedagogy is at last gaining the attention in English-speaking countries that it has long enjoyed elsewhere. But is it the right kind of attention? Do we still tend to equate pedagogy with teaching technique and little more? Now that governments, too, have become interested in it, is pedagogy a proper matter for public policy and official prescription?

In *Essays on Pedagogy*, Robin Alexander brings together some of his most powerful recent writing, drawing on research undertaken in Britain and other countries, to illustrate his view that to engage properly with pedagogy we need to apply cultural, historical and international perspectives, as well as evidence on how children most effectively learn and teachers most productively teach.

The book includes chapters on a number of themes, expertly woven together:

- the politicisation of school and classroom life and the trend towards a pedagogy of compliance;
- the benefits and hazards of international comparison;
- pedagogical dichotomies old and new, and how to avoid them;
- the centrality of talk to development, learning and teaching and the empowering potential of classroom dialogue;
- how education and pedagogy might respond to a world in peril;
- the rare and special chemistry of the personal and the professional which produces outstanding teaching;
- the scope and character of pedagogy itself, as a field of enquiry and action.

For those who see teachers as thinking professionals, rather than as technicians who merely comply with received views of best practice, this book will open minds while maintaining a practical focus. For student teachers it will provide a framework for their development. Its strong and consistent international perspective will be of interest to educational comparativists, but is also an essential response to globalisation and the predicaments now facing humanity as a whole.

Robin Alexander is Fellow of Wolfson College at Cambridge University, UK, Professor of Education Emeritus at Warwick University, UK, and Director of the Primary Rev... ...01) won the Outstanding Book Award of th... ...ssociation.

Essays on Pedagogy

Robin Alexander

Routledge
Taylor & Francis Group

LONDON AND NEW YORK

First published 2008
by Routledge
2 Park Square, Milton Park, Abingdon, Oxon, OX14 4RN

Simultaneously published in the USA and Canada
by Routledge
270 Madison Avenue, New York, NY 10016

Routledge is an imprint of the Taylor & Francis Group, an informa business

© 2008 Robin Alexander

Typeset in Palatino by
Florence Production Ltd, Stoodleigh, Devon

British Library Cataloguing in Publication Data
A catalogue record for this book is available from the British Library

Library of Congress Cataloguing in Publication Data
Alexander, Robin J.
  Essays on pedagogy / Robin Alexander.
    p. cm.
  Includes bibliographical references and index.
  1. Teaching. 2. Learning. I. Title.
  LB1028.A417 2008
  371.102 – dc22   2008003199

ISBN10: 0–415–45482–4 (hbk)
ISBN10: 0–415–45483–2 (pbk)

ISBN13: 978–0–415–45482–7 (hbk)
ISBN13: 978–0–415–45483–4 (pbk)

For Karen

Contents

Acknowledgements

It is not possible to list all those to whom debts of gratitude are owed for their contributions to the various projects on which this book draws; and, as always, the ethics of educational research prevent one from naming the children and teachers to whom in a sense one owes most – for without engaging directly with them and their worlds there is little on the subject of pedagogy that one can say. However, I must acknowledge those institutions and organisations that provided platforms for what started as lectures or conference papers: Warwick University Institute of Education, Cambridge University Faculty of Education, the Hong Kong Institute of Education, the American Educational Research Association and the International Association for Cognitive Education and Psychology. I also thank the bodies that awarded grants for the work on which the papers draw: the Economic and Social Research Council, the Leverhulme Trust, the British Council and the Sir Edward Youde Memorial Fund. Thanks for permission to reproduce copyright material are due to Routledge (Chapter 3), Oxford University Press (Chapter 4) and the Governors of the Perse School (Chapter 7).

My debt to fellow-toilers in the fields of education and pedagogy is apparent in the References, and I trust that they will take their appearance there as a mark of thanks rather than mere convention. I could try to single out those of the many cited there to whom I owe most, but instead I would rather name two people who have influenced and inspired me over several decades: not just in the undertaking of particular pieces of research or writing, but by setting standards of scholarship and insight that the rest of us rarely, if ever, achieve, and by imbuing these with wisdom and humanity of a kind which the current politico-educational ascendancy seems unable to comprehend, let alone value. They are Jerome Bruner and the late and much-missed Brian Simon.

Finally, for her companionship and collaboration on journeys to distant parts armed with cameras, audio recorder, video recorder, film, tape, notebooks, schedules and other apparatus of ethnographic research, for assistance in making sense of the resulting data, for support during the lengthy and difficult process of writing and much more besides, I thank, above all, this book's dedicatee, my wife Karen.

Abbreviations

ACI	American Competitiveness Initiative
AERA	American Educational Research Association
BERA	British Educational Research Association
BICSE	Board on International Comparative Studies in Education
CACE	Central Advisory Council for Education
CATE	Council for the Accreditation of Teacher Education
CBI	Confederation of British Industry
CDC	Curriculum Development Council
CfBT	Centre for British Teachers
CICADA	Changes in Discourse and Pedagogy in the Primary School
DCSF	Department for Children, Schools and Families
DES	Department of Education and Science
DfEE	Department for Education and Employment
DfES	Department for Education and Skills
DfID	Department for International Development
DPEP	District Primary Education Programme
EDI	Education for All Development Index
ESRC	Economic and Social Research Council
Eurydice	Education Information Network of the European Union
FIMS	First International Mathematics and Science Study
FISS	First International Science Study
GDP	Gross Domestic Product
GTCE	General Teaching Council for England
HMCI	Her Majesty's Chief Inspector of Schools
HMI	Her Majesty's Inspector/Inspectorate
HMSCI	Her Majesty's Senior Chief Inspector of Schools
IAEP	International Assessment of Educational Progress
ICCS	International Civic and Citizenship Education Study
IEA	International Association for the Evaluation of Educational Achievement
IR	Initiation-response
IRF	Initiation-response-feedback

ISERP	International School Effectiveness Research Project
KLAs	Key Learning Areas
KS	Key Stage
LATE	London Association for the Teaching of English
MDGs	Millennium Development Goals
NATE	National Association for the Teaching of English
NCC	National Curriculum Council
NCEE	National Center on Education and the Economy
NFER	National Foundation for Educational Research
NGO	Non-governmental organisation
OECD	Organisation for Economic Cooperation and Development
Ofsted	Office for Standards in Education
OISE	Ontario Institute for Studies in Education
ORACLE	Observational Research and Classroom Learning Evaluation
PIRLS	Progress in International Reading Literacy Study
PISA	Programme for International Student Assessment
PRINDEP	Primary Needs Independent Evaluation Project
QCA	Qualifications and Curriculum Authority
RSA	Royal Society for the Encouragement of Arts, Manufactures and Commerce
SCAA	School Curriculum and Assessment Authority
SCDC	School Curriculum Development Committee
SEAC	School Examinations and Assessment Council
SIMS	Second International Mathematics and Science Study
SISS	Second International Science Study
SITES	Second Information on Technology in Education Study
SSA	Sarva Shiksha Abhiyan (Education for All)
SSAT	Specialist Schools and Academies Trust
TDA	Training and Development Agency for Schools
TEDS-M	Teacher Education and Development Study – Mathematics
TIMSS	Trends in International Mathematics and Science Study
TLRP	Teaching and Learning Research Programme
TTA	Teacher Training Agency
UNESCO	United Nations Educational, Scientific and Cultural Organization
WEA	Workers' Educational Association

Chapter 1

Introduction

If 'the bigger picture' were not such a cliché, it might have been used in this book's title, for 'Teaching: the bigger picture' is what the book is about.

The word that does the same job is 'pedagogy'. However, for many people 'pedagogy' means teaching *without* the bigger picture, or what teachers do in classrooms but not why they do it: action, that is to say, divested of its justifications, values, theories, evidence and – especially – divested of that relationship with the wider world that makes teaching an educative process rather than a merely technical one. So 'pedagogy' it has to be, but accompanied by due discussion of its meanings.

At the time of his sudden and premature death in October 2007, Donald McIntyre was working on a project that was as significant as it was ambitious. Since the early 1970s and his seminal study *Teachers and Teaching* (Morrison and McIntyre 1973), McIntyre had explored teachers' thinking and craft knowledge, their practice, training and status. Latterly he had sought to extend the boundaries not just of teaching as a research field but of classroom learning itself, by celebrating the work of those teachers who have abandoned fixed notions of human ability (Hart *et al.* 2004), and who respect and act on what students have to say (Rudduck and McIntyre 2007).

Now, supported by the British Educational Research Association (BERA) and the General Teaching Council for England (GTCE), McIntyre was attempting to provide a comprehensive and coherent response to Brian Simon's famous question-cum-challenge of a quarter of a century earlier: 'Why no pedagogy in England?' (Simon 1981). McIntyre's response would concentrate on remedying rather than explaining the problem, for Simon had already done that (for the 1980s, anyway), and his remedy would provide both a map of the territory of pedagogy and an appropriate discourse for exploring it.

At the time of his death, McIntyre's map had not proceeded much beyond the setting out of possible perspectives – psychological, sociological, comparative, radical, neuroscientific – and themes: effective teaching, teaching expertise, pedagogy as art, classroom ecology, inclusion and so on (McIntyre 2007a). To these he wanted to apply the tests of *rigour, balance, integration* and *practicality* so that the new discourse might make a difference in classrooms rather than confine itself to well-intentioned conversation (McIntyre 2007b).

I mention Donald McIntyre's unfinished project not just to pay tribute to a colleague who was also one of Scotland's – and Britain's – finest educational researchers of the past few decades, but because it reminds us that pedagogy is still very much work in progress. Unlike those who work in education in many other European countries, in Britain we remain unsure what 'pedagogy' means, let alone what it encompasses and how it should be transacted. Or, rather, this was the case until in 1997 the UK government stepped in and replaced enquiry and debate by prescription.

That prescription, as illustrated in the various national 'strategies' for literacy and numeracy and for early years, primary and secondary education that have been promulgated since 1997, meets the last of McIntyre's criteria (practicality) but the other three only fleetingly and, one senses, rather reluctantly. Failure at the levels of evidential rigour and balance therefore compromises the undoubted practical focus of the prescriptions, to the extent that one might suggest that the official response to 'Why no pedagogy?' amounts less to an answer than to a more urgent re-statement of the question.

The party-political takeover of pedagogy compromises the considerable progress towards both a coherent pedagogical discourse and the improvement of teaching which in fact has been made since Brian Simon asked his question in 1981. For while pedagogical research has vastly improved our understanding of learning, teaching and the conditions by which both can be advanced, and while the transformative possibilities of some of this research have been realised, they tend to be countered and countermanded by the culture of compliance. Compliance closes down debate. It cannot secure its objective unless it does so.

I shall have more to say about the culture of compliance in the pages that follow. Meanwhile, there are other indicators of how far we have advanced towards McIntyre's goal of mapping pedagogy yet how much remains to be done.

One is the magisterial succession of editions of the American Educational Research Association's (AERA) *Handbook of Research on Teaching*. The first edition (Gage 1967) was essentially a handbook of process–product research, a quasi-experimental procedure for measuring gains in student learning in relation to such teacher, student, classroom and environmental variables as could also be measured. The current edition at the time of writing (Richardson 2001) is vastly more comprehensive in its thematic and methodological coverage. Process–product research and its offshoot school-effectiveness research take their places alongside qualitative analysis, social inquiry, narrative research, practitioner research and classroom ethnography. In other words, measurement is supplemented by the prior and essential task of understanding what actually happens in classrooms and inside the heads of those who inhabit them. Then there is extensive exploration of the curriculum context of teaching and learning, and the relationship between knowledge 'out there' in its culturally evolved forms (mathematics, science, history and so on) and ways that learners engage and might most successfully engage with them and reach their own understandings of the world that the subjects seek to explore and map. The learner, too, gains from this growing plurality of focus, for in place of the impersonality of generalised all-purpose student input variables we now have an emphasis on *difference* – in gender, ethnicity, language, class and educational need – and what this implies for teaching. To this complex mixture are added policy, teaching as work and above all the context and influence of *culture*.

Yet – and hence again work in progress – the AERA collection is at the same time enthralling and incoherent. Process–product research made a kind of sense. The current *Handbook* is a compendium of possible elements in a theory of teaching lacking any hint as to how they might fit together, and indeed the field is now so vast and diverse that its members talk what are essentially different languages. Many do not even accept that pedagogy is the field in which they are working.

This book seeks to make its own modest contribution to the task of defining, explicating and exploring pedagogy. Noting the muddle over definitions, it offers its own, distinguishing between the act of teaching and pedagogy as the act of teaching together with its attendant discourse about learning, teaching, curriculum and much else. Like the AERA *Handbook*, though of course without that compendium's scale or scope, it tries to show something of the necessary complexity of a field that must encompass culture and classroom, policy and practice, teacher and learner, knowledge both public and personal; and which is open to analysis in many different ways.

The book contains six essays, framed by this introduction and a brief conclusion. The essays are revised and updated versions of pieces written during the decade 1997–2007, and are presented more or less in the chronological order of their first appearance. This, as British readers know well, was the decade of New Labour and Tony Blair, the man who will probably be remembered only for his obsequious alliance with US President George W. Bush in pursuit of a disastrous invasion of Iraq, but who also presided over a programme of intervention in England's system of public education that sought to raise standards and extend the marketisation of education, as of other public services, initiated by his Conservative predecessors. Policy, then, and the politics of centralisation and control, provide an inescapable backdrop for the chapters that follow.

But the decade 1997–2007 was significant in other ways, and I would certainly not wish either to overstate the educational hegemony of New Labour or to set this book up as a political riposte. There are much more important tasks. This was the decade during which in Britain, as in many other countries, fundamental questions about personal and collective identity in a fast-changing world were provoked by the information revolution, affluence, migration, the retreat of old values and certainties and their replacement by a starker polarisation of religion and political creed, of wealth and poverty, and of the declining West and the newly empowered East. All this was superlatively and presciently captured in Manual Castells' remarkable trilogy *The Information Age: economy, society and culture* (Castells 1996, 1997, 1998), which I discuss in greater detail elsewhere (Alexander 2001a: 21–2). It was also – less prominent in Castells but inescapable since his books appeared – the decade during which climate change and global warming, allied to an exponential rate of population growth, were at last accepted as placing humanity as a whole in a predicament of unprecedented severity and urgency.

If pedagogy – as I argue in this book – is the act of teaching together with the ideas, values and beliefs by which that act is informed, sustained and justified, then in any book seeking to do something approaching justice to the complexities of pedagogy this wider context matters no less than what goes on in classrooms. That indeed, was the rationale for a more personal venture during the decade in question; the intellectual and geographical journey represented by the study *Culture and Pedagogy* (Alexander 2001a) and the avenues that in turn it opened up. This was a comparative exploration of the relationship between culture, policy, schooling and pedagogy in five countries – England, France, India, Russia and the United States – and its international perspectives in the sphere of education mirrored the growing internationalisation of Britain's economic and cultural life. The study also assisted me greatly in the task of making a much more than parochial sense of pedagogy, both as a domain of enquiry and as practical classroom action, for while the study started with national educational histories it culminated in a close-grained international comparative analysis of that classroom talk through which, quintessentially, both culture and learning are mediated.

Now to the essays themselves. The word 'essays' is used, incidentally, both to signal that they are freestanding reflections on the theme of pedagogy rather than a unitary sequence of chapters, and to indicate their flavour. Though most are grounded in empirical research, they reflect on the implications of that research rather than replicate the formal accounts of it that are available elsewhere. Their purpose is to use research evidence to lift the discourse of pedagogy out of mere reportage into critique, speculation and conceptual re-framing. These, the essays insist, are some of the important matters that pedagogical discourse in our kind of world really must encompass. One of the essays (Chapter 7) stands somewhat apart from the rest by being grounded less in research evidence than personal experience.

'Pedagogy goes East' (Chapter 2) was first presented as the 1996 W.A.L. Blyth Lecture and was subsequently published as an occasional paper by the University of Warwick (Alexander 1996, rev. edn 2000). Its particular spur was the publication by the Office for Standards in Education (Ofsted) of an analysis of the pedagogical implications of the international surveys of educational achievement (Reynolds and Farrell 1996). The chapter explores the possibilities and pitfalls of the growing internationalisation of the debate about pedagogy, and the uses and abuses of international comparison, giving particular attention to the deceptively simple nostrums of school effectiveness research and the fundamental naivety of the campaign to make 'interactive whole class teaching' the new default in England's primary school classrooms. That campaign was central to the National Literacy and Numeracy Strategies introduced by New Labour in 1998 and 1999. The chapter has been extensively revised to take account of recent developments, especially the international student achievement surveys, the latest of which is published as this book goes to press and makes depressing reading for English and American educators (Twist *et al.* 2007).

'Principle, pragmatism and compliance' (Chapter 3) also responds to an official document, this time the slim but bountifully illustrated *Excellence and Enjoyment*, a picture book for teachers with which the UK government launched its national strategy for primary education in 2003 (DfES 2003a). The essay examines – and strongly criticises – the evidential basis of the confident claims and prescriptions contained in this further and critical stage in the government's takeover of pedagogy. It looks behind these claims and prescriptions, at the political culture that gives rise to them and at the hubris of their architects, who presume their own political omniscience and the teaching profession's ignorance (Barber 2001). The essay also uses the entire episode to reflect on the progress that may or may not have been achieved since Simon first asked 'Why no pedagogy in England?' (Simon 1981). In doing so, the essay starts to map out the scope of pedagogy itself, a process which continues in the chapters that follow. Like 'Pedagogy goes East', this chapter started as a public lecture, in Cambridge, this time, rather than Warwick. It was later published as a journal article (Alexander 2004a).

'Beyond dichotomous pedagogies' (Chapter 4) began as an invited paper for the 2002 conference of the American Educational Research Association in New Orleans and was later revised for publication in the reader *Education, Globalization and Social Change* (Alexander 2006a). Drawing strongly on the *Culture and Pedagogy* research, it pursues and updates a preoccupation or frustration with which I have lived for several decades: the reduction of complex pedagogical questions and practical classroom choices to the discourse of dichotomy and mutual exclusion (see, for example, Alexander 1984, Chapters 1–3). This tendency I first charted as a feature of the relatively benign discourse of primary education during the 1970s and 1980s, though its much older pedigree and dangers are illustrated in the Hadow Report's highly influential assertion that 'The curriculum is to be thought of in terms of activity and experience rather than knowledge to be acquired and facts to be stored' (Board of Education 1931). With the growing politicisation of education during the 1990s, and especially since 1997, dichotomous discourse acquired a harsher, cruder, more moralistic and vituperative edge, and in 2008 it remains one of the biggest obstacles to sane and rounded debate about the most important educational questions with which we are confronted. It was partly to escape or transcend this condition that I embarked on the *Culture and Pedagogy* research, and in this essay I try to show the enriching possibilities of a discourse that is inclusive rather than exclusive, and pluralist rather than dualist.

With 'Talking, teaching, learning' (Chapter 5) we come to pedagogy in its most intimate and perhaps influential sense, the talk that takes place in classrooms between teachers and students and among students themselves. The essay is a revised version of a keynote paper given at the 2005 conference of the International Association for Cognitive Education and Psychology, unpublished elsewhere until now. The work that it summarises, which I call 'dialogic teaching', grew in large measure out of the *Culture and Pedagogy* comparative analysis of classroom interaction and discourse. This enabled me to extend the repertoires and possibilities of talk for learning and teaching beyond the boundaries of recitation and 'pseudo-enquiry' within which they remained confined by history and habit in many British and American classrooms, and which had been charted in two earlier projects (Alexander 1995; Alexander *et al.* 1996). All three projects made extensive use of transcribed video and audio data. Space in the present publication does not allow this to be reproduced, so I refer readers to the numerous analysed transcript examples in Alexander 1995: 103–219 (from England) and Alexander 2001a: 427–528 (from England and four other countries). The rationale and framework for dialogic teaching, and the considerable body of psychological, linguistic and pedagogical research by which it is informed, are set out more fully in Alexander 2006b. Also available is a DVD/CD pack containing 24 lesson extracts from schools in North Yorkshire, one of an increasing number of British local authorities in which this approach is being developed and evaluated (North Yorkshire County Council 2006).

'Pedagogy for a runaway world' (Chapter 6) is the most explicitly international of all these essays, the one that most obviously gives point to 'the bigger picture'. It started, like most of the others, as a public lecture, later published as a monograph (Alexander 2006c). On this occasion the venue was Hong Kong, where in 2005–6 I held a Sir Edward Youde Visiting Professorship. The essay took the idea and principles of dialogue that frame the approach to talk reform discussed in Chapter 5, and expanded them into the wider territory of educational discourse as a whole. The essay advances a version of dialogue that owes much to the work of Mikhail Bakhtin, and his ideas are applied in the contexts of educational policy, teaching and curriculum. But the essay also brings together ideas from some of the other chapters: the imperative – no longer an option – of a truly international and global perspective on national education questions; the importance and pedagogical power – sadly an under-exploited power – of classroom talk; the need to break away from the impoverishment of a dichotomising curriculum discourse that remains locked into crude and unhelpful polarities such as 'knowledge versus skills' and 'teaching versus learning'. Dialogue in this essay is argued for as indivisible. It is not merely a feature of cognitively productive classroom talk; it is a basic condition for tackling the daunting educational and social questions that confront educators everywhere.

'Words and music' (Chapter 7) is utterly different from the essays that precede it, though it retains the focus on pedagogy. It does so by considering what makes teaching exceptional rather than merely competent ('merely' here does not belittle competence but differentiates it both from excellence and the more restricted repertoire of the novice). In *Culture and Pedagogy* I venture to nominate, from the lesson transcripts analysed towards the end of the book, those teachers who appear to have achieved most conspicuously and securely that central and sometimes miraculous pedagogical moment of scaffolding children's understanding from partial to fuller understanding, or from existing knowledge to new. Yet in Chapter 7 I accept that the perspective of the outsider, even one who works forensically on the fine detail of classroom transactions, misses an all-important ingredient: what it feels like to experience teaching of this quality. Owing much to the pioneering work of Jean Rudduck (Rudduck and Flutter 2003; Flutter and Rudduck 2004; Rudduck and McIntyre 2007), 'student voice' has become an important focus for educational enquiry and professional action in Britain. It features prominently in the 2006–8 Review of Primary Education in England (the Primary Review) which is referred to in this book's closing pages (Alexander and Hargreaves 2007; Robinson and Fielding 2007). However, students' accounts of outstanding teaching are usually presented as lists of generalised characteristics aggregated from different children and teachers, or they rely on the observer's or researcher's judgement that what is deemed to be excellent really is.

It was for all these reasons, and because I and others who were his pupils believed that the teacher in question was indeed truly exceptional, that I departed from the professional habit of a lifetime and introduced an element of autobiography. For Douglas Brown, the teacher in question, taught me. This is what it felt like, and – contradicting the assumption that to be taught in a way that challenges and advances understanding is unalloyed bliss – it was not always a comfortable experience. Though it is stylistically and experientially different from the other chapters, Chapter 7 shares some of their themes: the power of dialogue (in the Bakhtinian rather than narrower conversational sense); the centrality of the teacher's mastery of the subject and his or her depth of engagement with it (this teacher achieved that rare double of combining teaching in a school with lecturing at a university); the likelihood that teachers such as this will not flourish in a culture of compliance; and the deadening impact of that culture on truly creative and inspirational teaching. Especially, the account drives home the point that 'it may well be impossible to be a teacher of the kind that stretches minds and fires imaginations unless one is also a rather special person.' The chapter first appeared in a limited-circulation collection of essays by 25 or so of Douglas's former pupils to mark the fortieth anniversary of his death (Loades 2005) and has been revised for publication here.

Chapter 2

Pedagogy goes East

Look East for new ideas, say education researchers. The English education establishment should take a leaf out of the motor industry's book and look East for new ideas, says a new report. It is necessary to draw on educational ideas and practices from overseas if the gap in achievement between English schoolchildren and their counterparts is to be bridged.

(Ofsted 1996: 1)

This essay reflects on a phenomenon that is as old as schooling itself: the international traffic in educational ideas, or what some misleadingly call 'policy borrowing'. (Are the policies returned to their owners? In what condition?)

The trade is an ancient one: we might recall the pan-European impact of the *trivium* and *quadrivium* up to and well beyond the Renaissance, or of the outward spread of the monitorial system from its base in 1790s Madras (now once again Chennai), or of the influence in both obvious and surprising places of Comenius, Rousseau, Locke, Froebel, Herbart, Montessori, Spencer, Dewey, Piaget and Vygotsky. (A romp through the pantheon of such 'great educators' used to be standard fare in teacher training courses.) Yet each generation learns from educational comparison in different ways and for different purposes.

So there was nothing intrinsically remarkable or novel in the injunction to 'Look East for new ideas' with which Ofsted chose to launch their report *Worlds Apart?* (Reynolds and Farrell 1996). Less venerable, though thoroughly of their time, were the political and media hype with which the report was greeted.

Worlds Apart? reviewed international surveys of educational achievement from 1964 to 1990, offered explanations for the relatively poor showing in these surveys of pupils in English schools, and proposed classroom solutions to halt the decline and raise standards. The accompanying press release, quoted above, set the tone for the ensuing media coverage and political response. According to *Worlds Apart?*, the countries from which England had most to learn were Germany, the Netherlands, Switzerland and Hungary (at that stage Finland had not achieved its later dominance of the international league tables), and the so-called 'Pacific Rim' countries, especially Korea and Taiwan. Top of the list of practices to be imported was 'interactive whole class teaching'.

Meanwhile, the UK's Conservative government of Margaret Thatcher and her successor John Major was approaching the end of its fourth successive term and an unbroken 18 years in office, and was being strongly challenged by Tony Blair's New Labour. Both main political parties had made education a prominent election issue – or in Blair's case, lest anyone should blink and miss it, 'education, education, education' – and each aimed to beat the drum of 'standards' more loudly than the other. One of their principal targets was primary education, especially – indeed exclusively, for the rest of the primary curriculum had all but disappeared – the standards of pupils' performance in literacy and numeracy. There was much scapegoating of teachers, teacher trainers and researchers, and of the supposedly progressive legacy of the Plowden Report (CACE 1967), which these supposed ideologues had apparently imposed on a hapless generation of the nation's children. It was a time for which Kenway's phrase 'discourse of derision' was especially suited.[1]

The political assault was fuelled by evidence of declining economic competitiveness, the UK's mixed showing in the international league tables of educational performance, and – as summarised in *Worlds Apart?* – accounts of classroom practices in some of the European and Asian countries whose performance had outstripped that of Britain. The urge to claim causal links between pedagogy, educational attainment and economic performance proved irresistible.

Then came New Labour's landslide election victory of May 1997. Having to their satisfaction defined the educational problem and identified its causes and culprits, the incoming government uncorked the authoritarian instinct that is never far from the surface of British politics and tightened the screws of central control, thus greatly accelerating a process of centralisation which the Conservatives had initiated during the 1980s and which at the time (Old) Labour had vigorously opposed – as parties in opposition invariably do, but only when in opposition.[2] Looking back, we may well nominate 1988 and 1998 as the decisive moments in this process. Indeed, 1988 saw the introduction of a National Curriculum under the Conservatives, while in 1998 New Labour broke through the final barrier and, through its National Literacy and Numeracy Strategies, began to prescribe exactly how teachers should teach (DfEE, 1998a, 1999a).

The analysis I offered in 1996 in response to these developments remains, in my view, relevant, and in a centralised education system the relationship between pedagogy and policy is no less important than that between pedagogy and research. (Policy, research and pedagogy have a complicated triangular relationship, though each line is to a degree skewed by the context of overt political power.) The onward march of centralisation continues, though a decade later governments are less dismissive of the hostility it provokes and try to sound more supportive of teachers. International educational comparison, borrowing, lending, piracy, plagiarism or imperialism – call them what you will, and in any case the traffic doesn't just go one way – have become thoroughly institutionalised adjuncts of a policy process which is ever more sharply attuned to the global market place; and policies that were once merely 'flagship' are now 'world class'. Here, an imperialist metaphor replaces the antiquated Nelsonian one, but both – along with the attendant talk of 'task forces', 'step changes' and 'standards drives', which are either 'rolled out' or 'hit the ground running' – speak to a distinctly macho, not to say militaristic mindset. Above all, every New Labour policy and initiative was not only 'new' but 'tough'. That being so, 'the onward march of centralisation' hardly overstates the position, though we should probably resist the temptation to take the metaphor a jackboot too far.

Further allusions in what follows need to be briefly explained. Given the considerable media and political interest provoked by the Ofsted *Worlds Apart?* report, and exercising a certain licence, I compare below this episode to the fuss surrounding first the publication of the 1991 research report on primary education in Leeds (Alexander and Willcocks 1991; Alexander 1997a) and to the still greater furore that attended its sequel, the discussion paper on primary education at Key Stage 2 (Alexander *et al.* 1992) commissioned by Secretary of State Kenneth Clarke just before Christmas 1991 (hence the journalistic inevitability of 'three wise men'). At that time Woodhead was Chief Executive of the National Curriculum Council (NCC), one of the precursors of the current Qualifications and Curriculum Authority (QCA). Three years later he became an increasingly controversial Chief Inspector of Schools (HMCI) and head of Ofsted and in that capacity commissioned *Worlds Apart?* from Reynolds and Farrell.

At this time too, Sig Prais from the National Institute of Economic and Social Research was working with inspectors and teachers in the London Borough of Barking and Dagenham to encourage greater awareness of the possibilities of continental teaching methods. Their pioneering programme involved taking groups of teachers to schools in Germany and Switzerland, and the introduction of a distinct and principled version of whole class teaching (Luxton and Last 1997; Luxton 2000) that was subsequently widely copied, though regrettably without its initiators' understanding of the underlying principles.

To Prais and Luxton, the most prominent advocates of interactive whole class teaching, the character of the interaction was at least as important as the organisational arrangement we call 'whole class teaching'. This basic point was missed time and time again, for this particular piece of policy appropriation was more one of domestication to an existing agenda: nostalgia for the supposed virtues of 1950s 'chalk and talk' whole class instruction and the standards of attainment and behaviour that this kind of teaching was held to have secured in a lost world of village greens, warm beer, cricket, deference and character-building levels of post-war deprivation. Here is Prime Minister Major, stiffening the sinews of the Conservatives at their last party conference before the 1992 general election:

> We will take no lectures from those who led the long march of mediocrity through our schools. I will fight for my belief. My belief is a return to the basics in education. The progressive theorists have had their say and, Mr President, they've had their day.
>
> (Major 1991)

And onward to Harfleur in a grey suit. Such heroic talk was sustained throughout the years of the 1992–7 Major government and well into the three Blair administrations of 1997–2007, when phoney wars were replaced by the real thing, with catastrophic consequences for the people of Iraq.

However, in Barking and Dagenham 'interactive whole class teaching' was no mere fad, and its proponents looked out to continental Europe rather than back to 1950s England. We shall see in Chapter 5 how this one local authority has sustained and deepened its belief in the pedagogical power of well-founded pupil–teacher and pupil–pupil interaction, most recently by exploring the potential of dialogic teaching, which also has a continental pedigree.

In a very real sense, then, 1996 is the right year to start this sequence of essays. The debate about educational problems and solutions has gone international; a new government is in the wings, desperate for power after 18 years in Margaret Thatcher's strident wilderness and relishing its chance to impose its own will on the nation's schools in place of hers; and pedagogy is at last beginning to gain a prominence in British educational research and debate that is commensurate with its importance.

HISTORY REPEATS ITSELF?

So: summer 1996. Much like 1991, really. A general election in the offing; a convenient report on the condition of education; shock/horror headlines; a *Panorama* programme to provide media gravitas; and a government initiative to stop the rot.

In 1991 it was the Leeds report (Alexander and Willcocks 1991; Alexander 1997a), while the ensuing government initiative was the so-called 'three wise men' primary discussion paper (Alexander *et al.* 1992). In 1996 it was the Ofsted report on international standards in primary education (Reynolds and Farrell 1996) and the rot-stopping government initiative was a national curriculum for the training of teachers. Otherwise the scenario was pretty well the same. Even the headlines appeared to have been recycled: 'Government attacks trendy teachers'. . . . 'Happiness but little learning' . . . 'Back to basics' . . . 'Back to tried and tested methods' . . . 'Back to the blackboard at primaries'. . . . 'Teachers get a caning from Ken' . . . For Ken, however, read Chris.[3]

There were differences, of course. In 1996 there were three studies, not one: alongside the Ofsted report we had the findings from Taiwan of the International School Effectiveness Research Project (ISERP) (Reynolds and Teddlie 1995; Creemers *et al.* 1996), together with the Gatsby-funded action research project on primary mathematics teaching in Switzerland, Germany and Britain, led by the National Institute for Economic and Social Research in partnership with the London Borough of Barking and Dagenham (Prais 1997; Luxton and Last 1997).

More critically, whereas in 1991–2 the Opposition had little to say on primary education, by 1996 they were very much in on the act. Indeed, by then an intriguing consensus had emerged, as political right and left jockeyed for control of territory hitherto held uncontested by the far right – 'progressive' teaching methods, incompetent teachers, back to basics, irrelevant and ideologically suspect teacher training. It was an early indicator of a battle for the right-of-centre vote that was to be sustained throughout the Blair years, 1997–2007. In 1996, speaking almost as one, the Secretary of State, the Shadow Secretary of State and the Chief Inspector instructed primary teachers to modify or even abandon their existing practices and adopt the 'interactive whole class teaching' successfully used in Taiwan, Switzerland, Germany and the Netherlands. The HMCI even put a figure on it – whole class teaching for 60 per cent of mathematics lessons teaching and 50 per cent of the rest of the curriculum (Woodhead 1996). Each made the obligatory pilgrimage to Barking and Dagenham to applaud schools' use of the required procedure. Gillian Shepherd and David Blunkett[4] accused teacher trainers of neglecting both the basics and whole class teaching, and Gillian Shepherd announced a national teacher training curriculum that was impressive not so much for its radicalism as for its amnesia, since there had been a national teacher training curriculum in England since 1984 (DES 1984).

But the big difference between 1991–2 and 1996–7 was that although the political rhetoric and posturing hadn't changed, its context had become global rather than national. Britain's position in the international league tables of economic performance and competitiveness continued to slide downwards, especially in relation to certain countries in Europe and the Pacific Rim. So too did students' educational performance, at least as judged by the tests in mathematics and science that were conducted for the International Association for the Evaluation of Educational

Achievement (IEA) and the International Assessment of Educational Progress (IAEP); and this performance gap had apparently increased over the 30 years since the IEA and IAEP testing programmes started (Keys *et al.* 1996; Harris *et al.* 1997). Adding to the gloom, a government-commissioned skills audit unfavourably compared the skill levels of Britain's new employees with those of Japan, Singapore, Germany, France and the USA (Green and Steedman 1997).

At the same time, we were told that there was a conclusive causal relationship between these measures of national decline and the teaching methods used in the country's primary schools. Hence Taiwan, Switzerland, Barking and Dagenham, interactive whole class teaching and Chief Inspector Woodhead's 60 per cent.

INTERNATIONAL COMPARISONS OLD AND NEW

It has become almost obligatory for academic comparativists to quote Edwardian administrator and university vice-chancellor Michael Sadler:

> In studying foreign systems of education we should not forget that the things outside the schools matter even more than the things inside the schools, and govern and interpret the things inside . . . The practical value of studying in a right spirit and with scholarly accuracy the working of foreign systems of education is that it will result in our being better fitted to study and understand our own . . . No other nation, by imitating a little bit of German organisation, can thus hope to achieve a true reproduction of the spirit of German institutions. The fabric of an organisation practically forms one whole. That is its merits, and its danger. It must either be taken in all, or left unimitated . . . All good and true education is an expression of national life and character.
>
> (Sadler 1900, 1902)

These lines were written over a century ago, in the context of anxiety about how Britain's education system should counter Germany's growing industrial and commercial supremacy. With our millennial multicultural consciousness we might balk at Sadler's assumption of national cultural homogeneity. And swept along on the tide of globalisation as we now are, we might find his purist rejection of cultural borrowing rather quaint. Nevertheless, there are important challenges to any educator, in any time or place, in what Sadler asserts. Is the primary purpose of comparative study to understand other education systems or to extrapolate from them? Do we analyse education elsewhere in order better to understand our own practices, or in order to change them?

At first sight the implied distinction on the basis of purpose is valid. On the one hand there is the long-established and somewhat cosy academic community of educational comparativists, harking back, in Britain at least, to Sadler, Arnold and Jullien.[5] Though with the next university research assessment exercise always in view they attend to the real or imagined requirements of 'user groups', they remain more or less united in the conviction that comparative study is pursued primarily for its own sake; that pursuit of understanding comes first and policy applications second.

In contrast, the new comparers, headed by the proud standard-bearers of 'school effectiveness' and 'school improvement', are user-directed from the outset. Indeed, their impatient labels make it clear that the priority is to *change* schools and classrooms rather than to understand them. Schools, then, are by their nature in need of such intervention. The new comparers' endeavour is quantitative, quasi-scientific and pragmatic. They seek out policy-makers and are sought by them. Eschewing academic problematising, ignoring history and cutting to the chase, their talisman is 'what works'. They are the academic community's jet-setting, high-tech, professional go-getters, the Essex men and women of educational research.

This demarcation seems to be acknowledged by those on either side of it. Altbach and Kelly (1986) identify several traditions, or theoretical/methodological standpoints, that have shaped the discipline of comparative education: idiosyncratic 'travellers' tales', the more normative and policy-directed 'educational lending and borrowing', which Michael Sadler (quoted above) was keen to resist, historical and cultural analysis, the social sciences, economics (with a strong dose of human capital theory, especially in studies of developing countries), and psychometrics. However, though this might be regarded as a continuum, an invitation to interdisciplinarity and eclecticism, others see it more in terms of opposing paradigms. Thus, writing before the current vogue for school effectiveness research but in the early context of the IEA and OECD achievement studies that have sustained it, comparativist Edmund King saw this emergent tradition as 'positivist, determinist and manipulative' (King 1979: 23).

From their side of the line, Reynolds and Farrell blame comparativists such as King for the fact that there are so few convincing explanations for the poor showing of English pupils in international comparisons of achievement. They write despairingly of:

> ... the frankly inept contribution which the comparative education discipline has made over time ... the presence of a large body of theories, without any apparent empirical backing ... a large range of descriptive case studies of individual schools which it is impossible to synchronise together because there are no common measures of outcomes or processes utilised ... descriptions of the range of educational, political, economic and cultural phenomena within different

countries, with no attempt ever made to assess the contribution of the educational system as against that of other factors.

(Reynolds and Farrell 1996: 53)

Quite apart from the cavalier inaccuracy of most of these claims, this stance is problematic in other respects, for Reynolds in essence contends that there is no place for speculative theory in our attempts to understand other cultures and how education is conceived of and undertaken within them; that unless individual researchers in different traditions and different countries co-ordinate their activities within a common analytical framework they might as well go home; that educational phenomena can validly be compared only in terms of measurable processes and outcomes; and that political, cultural, economic and educational aspects of a society are not worth studying unless they can be factor-analysed.

In other words, Reynolds does not make a case against mainstream comparative education so much as parody it to press his political case to have provided a more useful alternative. On this basis he can dismiss as academic niceties the problems that vex comparativists and to which his own study is no less immune than theirs: misinterpretation or over-interpretation of results in a research field whose inherent frailties are compounded by barriers of culture and language; ethnocentrism; selective borrowing (Holmes 1981; Noah 1986).

However, the most fundamental weakness in Reynolds' approach, and in the way international educational comparison was being used more generally in the 1990s UK policy context, is his – and its – handling of culture. He and Farrell say (the italics are mine):

We do not . . . know yet what is the exact contribution of the *educational* system and of the *cultural* and *social* systems to the very high levels of educational success enjoyed by other societies, although most observers would credit the system at least as much as the society.

(Reynolds and Farrell 1996: 28)

Separating the cultural, educational and social into three apparently independent and freewheeling 'systems', which can then be translated into a collection of factors for the purposes of statistical correlation, is untenable, even supposing that someone could explain the difference between a 'cultural system' and a 'social system'. Life in schools and classrooms is an aspect of our wider society, not separate from it: a culture does not stop at the school gates. The character and dynamics of school life are shaped by the values that shape other aspects of our national life. The strengths of our primary schools are the strengths of our society; their weaknesses are our society's weaknesses. Or, as Ernest Boyer put it: 'A report card on public education is a report card on the nation. Schools can rise no higher than the communities that serve them' (quoted in Noah 1986). Culture, in comparative analysis and understanding, and certainly in national systems of education, is all.

The compartmentalisation of culture is unsatisfactory not only in a broad conceptual sense. If the argument were only one of how the word 'culture' should be defined it would be hardly worth making, in this context anyway. More important are the educational consequences of this view. At national level it enables governments to press their claim that questions of quality in education can be resolved by attacking pedagogy while ignoring structure and resources. It allows them to deny that a government's broader social and economic policies impact in any way on what teachers do, or can do, in the classroom. Conversely, it allows teachers to excuse or underplay their own agency and to blame government policy or resourcing levels for matters of which they have more control than they may be prepared to admit. At classroom level it encourages the view that pedagogy carries no educational messages or values of itself, but is merely a value-neutral vehicle for transmitting curricular content; and it discourages vital questions about the importance of 'fit' between pedagogy, the children being taught, and the knowledge domains from which curriculum experiences are drawn. Effective teaching arises from attention to cultural, psychological, epistemological and situational considerations, not merely organisational and technical ones.

Most of all, treating culture as an independent variable in a statistical calculation encourages the assumption that you can detach an educational strategy from the values and conditions that give it meaning and ensure its success, transpose it to a context where these may be diametrically opposed, and yet expect it to deliver the same results.

Part of the problem is Reynolds' somewhat polarised view of the options in comparative study itself. On the one hand there is policy-directed comparison of the kind he advocates, deploying a methodology that yields what he believes is a definitive account of educational cause and effect; on the other hand there is . . . everything else. The Board on International Comparative Studies in Education (BICSE) of the United States National Academy of Sciences find this dichotomy unhelpful. Instead, they identify three types of international comparative education study according to their primary purpose:

> Type I studies typically include large-scale surveys that aim to compare educational outcomes at various levels . . . Type II studies are designed to inform one or more particular . . . education policies by studying specific topics relevant to those policies and their implementation in other countries. Type III studies are not designed to make direct comparisons . . . in terms of specific policies or educational outcomes.

Rather, they aim to further understanding of educational processes in different cultural and national contexts.

(National Research Council 2003: 13)

Type I includes the large-scale international student achievement studies of IEA and OECD (TIMSS, PISA, PIRLS and so on).[6] Type II covers the policy-directed studies, outside the context of achievement testing, commissioned by OECD, and indeed, as in the case of *Worlds Apart?*, by Ofsted. Type III includes the majority of academic comparative studies. Classics of this genre include King's seven-nation historical and comparative study of education systems and policies (King 1979) and the three-nation ethnographic study of pre-school education in China, Japan and the United States by Joseph Tobin, David Wu and Dana Davidson (Tobin *et al.* 1989).

However, BICSE note that though their typology 'avoids false dichotomies in educational research – large-scale versus small-scale, qualitative versus quantitative – it is not without its difficulties' (National Research Council 2003: 13) in that there is blurring at the boundaries of methodology and outcome, if not of initial purpose. So, for example, the later TIMSS studies included, as a contribution to understanding what lies behind national differences in student achievement, case studies and videotape-based analysis of a kind which is more typical of Type III. On the other hand, BICSE has no doubt where the power and perceived policy relevance lies, for while the majority of comparative education studies are Type III, Type I studies receive most of the funding, and the funding difference per study is truly vast. Type I studies are a multi-million dollar business; Type III studies scrape together what they can from hard-pressed funding bodies.

The BICSE report is helpful because, arising in a policy context as it does, and prepared by people who have been directly involved in all three kinds of study, it authoritatively challenges Reynolds' view that exploratory and interpretative comparative studies serve no useful policy purpose. The report argues:

Although they vastly outnumber Type I and Type II studies, Type III studies often do not come to the attention of policy makers or the public. This is a loss, since many are rich in narrative detail and paint a more engaging and provocative portrait of education in other countries than do the summary bar charts and graphs typical of many larger studies. Ethnographic and case studies, in particular, can explore cultural context in depth and, in turn, help elucidate the way education is organised and understood in different cultures.

(National Research Council 2003: 23–4)

In other words, policy-makers stand in as much need of Type III understanding as do ordinary mortals. It is on this basis that BICSE recommend a more balanced approach to the public funding of comparative studies with a view not merely to identifying differences in achievement but also to promoting a better public and political understanding of education in the United States (in this case) and elsewhere. They recommend, specifically, increased investment 'in studies that focus on understanding the education experiences of other countries in their own context . . . to provide a broader context for U.S. experiences and efforts to innovate' (National Research Council 2003: 70).

The Type I/III distinction usefully opens up the policy end of the comparative continuum. However, we might venture a different way of cutting the cake of policy-directed comparative analysis, this time distinguishing between three typical policy requirements or quests: for *facts*, for *indicators* and for *effectiveness*. This allows us to probe more critically the claims made for this kind of activity.

THE QUEST FOR FACTS

First, there is the assembling and collating of comparative factual information about different national systems. One example is the work of Eurydice, the Education Information Network of the European Union (EU). One of their publications is a seemingly helpful compendium of information and statistics relating to pre-school and primary education in the EU, and covers matters such as the ages and stages of education, the distribution of time during the school year, week and day, the aims, content and time requirements for national curricula, and contingent matters such as textbooks and teaching methods (Eurydice 1994). This kind of data is now available online or on CD, and through these formats the range of information is, potentially and actually, vastly increased. Between them, the United Nations, the World Bank and OECD now carry regularly updated educational data on most countries in the world, as do UK agencies such as the National Foundation for Educational Research (NFER) and QCA.

However, what may seem to be the lowest common denominator and least contentious aspect of policy-oriented comparative study – collating information from official documents – is not without its problems and, surprisingly perhaps, needs to be treated with no less caution than more obviously questionable kinds of data. For example, Eurydice tells us this:

> In England, Wales and Northern Ireland, the Secretaries of State
> have proposed the following criteria [for the development of the
> curriculum]: rather than being provided with detailed proposals, schools
> should be given significant opportunities to develop their educational

programme according to their own schemes of work . . . a broad and flexible statutory framework . . . consideration of what has been learned about child development, good educational practice and the results of research.

(1994: 77)

Bearing in mind that this statement was published in 1994, when the National Curriculum was exerting its tightest grip on schools and teachers, and child development had been outlawed from teacher training courses,[7] British readers will recognise it for the travesty that it is. One wonders whether this version of the balance of state and school control over the curriculum was the genuine mistake of an out-of-sorts archivist or a piece of deliberate government misinformation. Either way, it should give us pause for thought. If the status of the educational fact at this most basic level is shaky, how do we judge the higher-stakes empirical studies?

The difficulty for this kind of information-gathering is that it is a long way removed from verifiable practice. It is as reliable as the – usually official – providers of the information wish it to be, and I have found several other examples of statements purporting to represent the truth about a given national education system that are little more than policy-apologists' spin. Indeed, in less polite company they would be called lies. This is especially the case when the data are accounts of policy rather than statistics. On the other hand, both are also good examples of the strengths and limitations of a typical product of the information age. The data are interactive, and they can be corrected, updated and disseminated much more easily and rapidly than can the print equivalents; yet they require contextual knowledge to be properly understood and interpreted, and – no less important – for their veracity to be tested.

Veracity, though, is critical, because it is the *raison d'être* of this kind of material. The national statistical data on which international comparisons are also based may be less secure than they seem. The 2006–8 Primary Review had, as one of its four evidential strands, the collection and assessment of official data on primary education in England by government and the national agencies responsible for curriculum, assessment, standards and teacher training (DfES/DCSF, QCA, Ofsted and TDA). It quickly became apparent that the data collected by these agencies could sometimes be compromised by frequent methodological changes, for example in national statutory tests and Ofsted inspection arrangements, and that these weakened their value as a basis for tracking trends over time, and certainly for making grand and empirically unverifiable claims – as ministers and national agencies frequently did from 2001 onwards – that England's teachers were the 'best-trained ever' (e.g. TTA 2005: 1).

More specifically, in an analysis of measured standards over time in English primary schools using eleven independent measures, Tymms judged that apparent improvements needed to be offset against improved teaching of test technique and indeed teaching to the test, and that 'the use of new tests every year with cut-scores to define levels severely restricts the use of the tests as a tool to monitor standards' (Tymms 2004: 491). He and others also argued that the system was fatally compromised by successive governments' insistence on making one measure – the Key Stage 2 tests – serve three different purposes: individual pupil assessment, the monitoring of national standards, and school accountability (Tymms and Merrill 2007; Harlen 2007). We pursue this latter point in the next section.

THE QUEST FOR INDICATORS

Since 1987, OECD has been developing indicators in respect of what it terms educational inputs, outputs, processes and resources, the latter being both fiscal and human. The organisation has published detailed accounts of ways of defining the quality of schools, teaching and learning (OECD 1994, 1995a, 1995b). By 1995, this endeavour had produced the second edition of the compendium *Education at a Glance* (OECD 1995c) and its linked volume of statistics (OECD 1995d). *Education at a Glance* conceives of education in terms of three broad considerations: 'contexts', 'costs, resources and school processes', and 'results'. The *contexts* include demography, employment, unemployment and per capita gross domestic product (GDP), together with the outcomes of surveys of public opinion on educational purposes and priorities. The *costs, resources and processes* include educational income and expenditure, student numbers, the teaching force and teaching time. The *results* are defined as 'student outcomes', 'system outcomes' (leaving qualifications from secondary and higher education) and 'labour market outcomes' (employment and earnings).

Later volumes in the series factored in a wider array of indicators, though always within the same basic framework, and included findings from the TIMSS and TIMSS-R (the TIMSS mathematics and science repeat), PIRLS (reading literacy) and PISA (scientific, reading and mathematical literacy) achievement studies (OECD 2004a, 2005b, 2006).

There is no denying the value of the OECD volumes as a resource for comparative research, let alone policy. But what you get out of such an exercise depends on what has been put into it. Thus, in the 1995 edition of *Education at a Glance* the wide range of *outcomes* at the primary stage was reduced to a single indicator, reading scores at age nine (education at a glance indeed) while the real-life untidiness of school and classroom *processes* was subjugated by reducing them to just two indicators: 'grouping within classes' and time spent teaching the different subjects. In the 1998 edition the selection of process indicators was no less arbitrary and inadequate: intended teaching time and the availability of computers (OECD 1998). By 2004 instruction time and class size had been added (OECD 2004a). *Education at a Glance* gives us a great deal of information about the financial and demographic context of schooling but precious little insight into schooling itself, let alone pedagogy.

In the volumes dealing in greater detail with indicators of quality for schools, teachers and learning, OECD do go beyond reading scores and the distribution of curriculum time. But because they stay firmly within the bounds of what can be quantified and then measured the focus remains skewed both in terms of what is included and how it is analysed, and this is a particularly serious problem in respect of the content, dynamics and outcomes of teaching and learning, much of which inconveniently resists such treatment. Even time on task, a 'process' indicator much favoured in school effectiveness research as both apparently objective and amenable to calculation, is much more problematic than it may seem. Supposing you can guarantee that when you observe children 'on task' they actually are (who knows what is going on in their heads when their eyes are apparently glued to a book?), how do you effect your calculation of hours per year on task? Like this, perhaps:

$$\text{TIONTA} = \frac{\{\text{SPERLEN} \times \text{SSCHPER} \times \text{SDAYSYR}\}}{60} - \frac{\{\text{TORDERT} \times \text{SDAYSYR}\}}{60} \cdot \frac{5}{5} + \frac{\{\text{YAHWKT} \times \text{SDAYSYR}\}}{5}$$

(OECD 1995a: 27)

Even with knowledge of what the letters in this wonderfully baroque formula signify, one has to recognise that there is a rather tautologous and self-validating character to enterprises of this kind. They start from indicators that have featured in earlier studies, often for no reason other than that such indicators have been shown to be technically feasible. These indicators are then built into new research designs, and thence provide the framework for further research, which in turn consolidates their position. Thus, what happens to be within the bounds of statistical computation comes to define the very nature of teaching itself, and armed with such definitions of 'quality' policy-makers, presumably, can simply touch the relevant input, process or output switch and feel they have the entire system under control. Note the way, incidentally, that all these OECD indicator studies have *quality* on their cover pages but inside are all about *quantity*.

By 2007, international indicators not only summarised trends. They also provided the basis for multi-million-dollar loans and grants from development agencies. Reviewing the literature relating to UN Millennium Development Goal 2 (Universal Primary Education), and examining examples not just from OECD but also from the United Nations, the

World Bank, the European Commission and Britain's Department for International Development, I was not encouraged by what I found. In sum:

- Early indicator models concentrated on input and outcome and ignored process.
- Later models attended to educational process but in an arbitrary and selective fashion, isolating only those aspects which were deemed readily amenable to measurement, regardless of their pedagogical significance.
- Yet the very act of isolating such aspects in effect conferred validity upon them, whether or not validity was merited, so quality was reduced to quantity.
- Some models, attempting to move beyond the crudity of early indicator frameworks, leavened their instrumentalism with the language of affectivity and focused on desired attributes of teachers themselves. However, this introduced unacceptably high levels of ambiguity and inference into an exercise which was ostensibly about achieving the opposite.
- On closer examination, most nominated indicators of process, of whatever persuasion, are really input or contextual variables.
- In general, pedagogy has been made to fit the available measures rather than the other way round.
- Where direct measures are not available, proxies are used, and the proxies for process tend to be, again, outcomes or inputs.
- The framing of educational process indicators is rarely, if at all, justified by reference to research on learning and teaching.

(Alexander 2007a)

Small wonder, then, that the assiduous calculators of time on task as an ostensibly reliable indicator of student engagement and learning haven't come across Gage's bracing objection that time on task is 'a psychologically empty quantitative concept' (Gage 1978: 75). Meanwhile, the United Nations' Education for All Development Index (EDI) reduces 'quality of education' to just one indicator: 'survival rate to grade 5 of primary education' (UNESCO 2007). 'How good was your primary education?' 'I survived to grade 5.'

The context of aid to developing countries provides the least ambiguous application of the input-output approach to shaping policy decisions. It is relevant here partly because we have a moral as well as a financial interest in knowing how 'aid' is conceived, calculated and distributed on our behalf – Watson (1993) of course argues a familiar case when he writes of aid as a 'two-edged sword' that assists developing countries while maintaining the gap between donor and recipient nations and benefiting the former in tied purchasing of equipment and training by as much as 70 per cent – but more particularly because the aid scenario illustrates in an extreme form some of the problems under consideration in this chapter.

In the aid literature, education inputs, processes and outcomes are reduced to their barest essentials as a basis for calculating the cost-effectiveness of particular kinds of intervention. Thus, Lockheed and Verspoor's much-cited World Bank study of primary education in developing countries (1991) identifies five main educational variables – curriculum, learning materials, teaching time, teaching quality and teachability – and divides aid options under these headings into 'promising avenues' for investment and 'blind alleys'.

The 'blind alleys' included 'Provide school lunches ($12)'. The danger in this kind of calculation becomes apparent when we contrast that deletion from the list of viable policies with the strong prima facie evidence from one of the world's biggest programmes for universalising primary education, India's Sarva Shiksha Abhiyan (SSA). In the poorer rural areas where educational need is greatest, those working in the field have found that there is a direct and positive relationship between the provision of free midday meals, children's enrolment and retention in school and their engagement in the classroom (IndianNGOs.com 1997).

As for indicators of output – typically measured through tests of student attainment at different ages, most commonly in reading, mathematics and science, this is now such a vast and complex field that it demands a book in its own right. To the early IEA studies of the 1960s have been added a succession of international achievement studies, each one more ambitious than its predecessor, and generating a veritable blitz of acronyms (the earlier trio was a mere shot over the bows) – FIMS and SIMS (First and Second International Mathematics and Science Studies), FISS and SISS (ditto for science), TIMSS, TIMSS-R (the subsequent repeat of TIMSS), PIRLS, ICCS (International Civic and Citizenship Education Study), TIMSS Advanced, SITES (Second Information on Technology in Education Study), TEDS-M (Teacher Education and Development Study – Mathematics); and, outside the IEA framework, PISA (OECD's Programme for International Student Assessment, in mathematical, reading and scientific literacy).

IEA originated at a UNESCO meeting in 1958 and was legally incorporated in 1967. Yet it is only in the past decade that its work has become compulsory reading for researchers and policy-makers. The 1991–2 'three wise men' enquiry surveyed the then available IEA and IAEP reports for evidence on how the attainment of English primary pupils compared with that from other countries, but found the data sparse, inconclusive and marred by methodological difficulties (Alexander et al. 1992: 11–17). The process seems to have entered a new and more reliable phase (Ruddock et al. 2006) with PISA (2000, 2003, 2007) and TIMSS (1999, 2003, 2007).

Now the acronym league tables are eagerly scanned for what they say not just about student achievement but also the national psyche.

However, though Whetton *et al.* (2007) believe that forty years into the game international achievement surveys now have a reasonably robust methodology, the extent to which earlier studies were marred by sampling and psychometric problems, translation inconsistencies and cultural bias cannot be understated (Steedman 1999; Robinson 1999; Broadfoot 1999). Even now, newspapers regularly carry dark reports of 'coaching to the tests' on an industrial scale in some Asian countries, not to mention cheating. By 2007, the stakes were such that teachers in England, too, were being accused of these misdemeanours.

In an overview prepared for the Washington-based National Center on Education and the Economy (NCEE), Ruzzi summarises the results of the PISA, TIMSS and PIRLS studies from 1995 to 2003. The NCEE overall ranking is shown in Figure 2.1.

Finland's strong showing has attracted much attention, as has the apparently more modest performance of what in 2007 was the world's only superpower, the United States. It does not feature at all in Figure 2.1, and in PISA 2003 it was ranked 33 out of the 41 participating countries in mathematics, 23 in reading, 22 in science and 34 in problem-solving.

Finland's pre-eminence in these studies is now consistent, though it was not always so. During the 1960s Finland was ranked below average.

Ranking	Top in reading	Top in mathematics	Top in science
1	Finland	Singapore	Taiwan
2	Canada	Hong Kong	Singapore
3	Australia	Korea	Japan
4	Korea	Taiwan	Korea
5	New Zealand	Japan	Hong Kong
6	Ireland	Flemish Belgium	Finland
7	Hong Kong	Netherlands	Hungary
8	Sweden	Finland	Czech Republic
9	Japan	Canada	Netherlands
10	Netherlands	Switzerland	England
11	Liechtenstein	Slovak Republic	Australia
12	Belgium	Australia	Canada

Figure 2.1 Ranking of countries participating in international education assessments, grade 8 and above, 1995–2003

Source: Adapted from Ruzzi 2006

By 1980 it had climbed to average, forging ahead during the 1990s. Fredriksson (2006) explains this trend as a combination of factors:

- the 1970s comprehensive school reforms, which 'substantially reduced the heterogeneity of schooling across the country and across family backgrounds';
- 'favourable family background' characteristics: relative cultural homogeneity and low rates of immigration;
- a teaching force which is highly motivated, well qualified and skilled.

To these, Lyytinen (2002) adds:

- exceptionally high levels of student interest and engagement in reading outside school;
- a unified system of schooling based on equity and which minimises low achievement.

Meanwhile, the Ofsted comparative study of the education of six-year-olds in England, Denmark and Finland, in which I was involved, noted the following distinctive and possibly contributory features (Ofsted 2003a):

- universal entitlement to high-quality pre-school education;
- a relatively late start to formal schooling (age seven);
- an emphasis in early learning on personal and social development;
- a high degree of decentralisation, with concomitantly high levels of autonomy at the level of the school;
- relative linguistic as well as cultural homogeneity;
- an exceptionally high value placed, throughout Finnish society, on active as well as functioning literacy (valuing and enjoying reading as well as being able to do it).

Putting all these together, it is clear that cultural, structural and professional factors combine in a distinctive and productive way. It must, however, be noted that the international league tables are disproportionately headed by city states and wealthy countries with homogeneous cultures and small populations (Finland has 5.2 million inhabitants and even the largest in the 'top two' group in Figure 2.1, Canada, has only 33 million). In contrast, Britain has a population of 60.2 million occupying a country considerably smaller than Finland – the relative population densities are 635 (UK) and 38 (Finland) persons per square mile – and to put this striking difference in further perspective, Britain's population since the 1981 census has increased by as much as Finland's total population. Culturally, too, the countries are worlds apart: Finland has few immigrants while London, with some 300 languages regularly spoken, is reckoned to be the world's most diverse capital city.

On this basis, the modest showing of the US, too, is unsurprising: this is a country that is highly decentralised and culturally very diverse. It has a large population (302 million in 2007), massive disparities in the wealth, health and prospects of its citizens, and considerable divergence in matters of value and identity. Indeed, it is reasonable to suggest, the ostensible advantage of high GDP notwithstanding, that the larger and more complex a country in terms such as these, the less likely it is to be found near the top of the IEA/OECD educational achievement league tables. Conversely, if achieving the winner's podium is an indicator of the successful teaching of mathematics, reading and science, it isn't necessarily an indicator of cultural vitality.

In the context of this essay's references to the relationship between pedagogy and power, it is also salutary to note, as OECD records, that:

> In most of the countries that performed well, local authorities and schools ... have substantial responsibility for educational content and/or the use of resources, and many set out to teach heterogeneous groups of learners.
>
> (OECD 2004b)

In his detailed analysis of the impact of Britain's current culture of testing, Mansell argues this point much more strongly. He believes that the post-1997 culture of 'hyper-accountability' has not raised standards, and after examining UK national tests results, international surveys such as PISA and the consistently unflattering claims of declining standards of basic skills emanating from universities and employers, he concludes:

> Pursuing results almost as ends in themselves has been forced on schools, in their desperation to fulfil the requirements of hyper-accountability. But this grades race is ultimately self-defeating. It does not guarantee better-educated pupils, just better statistics for schools and government.
>
> (Mansell 2007: 199)

In her survey of alternative assessment regimes for the 2006–8 independent Review of Primary Education in England (the Primary Review) Harlen reaches a similar conclusion:

> Evidence of changes in standards of achievement over the years does not support the claim that testing 'drives up standards.'
>
> (Harlen 2007)

What makes the conclusions of analysts such as Mansell and Harlen noteworthy is that they are based not on suspect international comparisons – 'centralisation' and 'decentralisation' are among those concepts that do not travel well across international boundaries – but on analysis of the UK government's own data.

Perhaps the most disturbing and consistent finding about England's schooling that emerges from the international surveys, to be set squarely against the country's apparent successes in reading and science (Whetton *et al.* 2007; Twist *et al.* 2007) is the exceptionally wide spread of scores. The gap in attainment in English schools between the highest- and lowest-performing students is far wider than in many other participating countries. With 'world class' performance by some students goes a long and stubbornly persisting tail of underachievement by many others. In terms of outcome, England's system of education is an exceptionally unequal one.

The reasons for this are complex. Culture and pedagogy both play a central part, but high-stakes testing is unlikely to offer any assistance to those who are already struggling, for what is most striking about the attainment gap is the precision with which it maps onto other gaps: the gap between rich and poor; the gap of social class, still in a supposedly classless society, a significant indicator of social prospects; the gap in parental aspirations; the gap in the quality of under-five care; the gaps of gender, race and disability; the gap of social exclusion (Joseph Rowntree Foundation 2007; Madge and Barker 2007; Sammons *et al.* 2007; Equalities Review 2007). England is in every sense a deeply divided society.

THE QUEST FOR EFFECTIVENESS

The distinct possibility that centralised decision-making combined with high-stakes testing might be educationally counter-productive cut no ice with New Labour, and from 1997 'school effectiveness' became a further adjunct to its pursuit of higher educational standards. The government appointed a Standards Minister and a Standards Task Force, and established within the DfEE (precursor to DfES and today's DCSF) a Standards and Effectiveness Unit. At the same time, school effectiveness researchers were making large claims about their ability to deliver answers to the question of what kinds of schooling and teaching have the greatest impact on children's learning. Their research would cut through the methodological qualifications and caveats that characterised previous school and classroom research and would thus appeal directly and unambiguously to policy-makers and practitioners.

Thus, by little more than a terminological sleight of hand, two agendas merged: a government's wholly laudable wish to raise educational standards, and the ambitions of a particular group of academics. The result was a degree of intellectual hegemony that, underpinned by tight central political control, frustrated rather than enhanced the development of pedagogy as practice and field of enquiry.

The first wave of school effectiveness research was largely non-empirical. It consisted of territory demarcation and the collating of those few empirical studies that, as defined by school effectiveness researchers themselves, were deemed relevant to the endeavour (Reynolds et al. 1994). 'Effectiveness' was defined very simply, as a statistical calculation of the gain in output over input:

> We define effectiveness in two dimensions [graph shows axes of input and output] . . . The 'quality' dimension is modelled as the average score of each school on output (corrected for input) and is represented by the intercept (each school has a different intercept). The 'equity' dimension encompasses the compensatory power or selective quality of schools. Some schools can better compensate for input characteristics than others. This dimension is represented by the slopes of the within school regression of input on output.
>
> (Creemers, in Reynolds et al. 1994: 10–11)

Those studies that conformed to this statistical paradigm, but only those studies, were extensively reviewed in the publications of the school effectiveness group that established itself in the UK and then networked across several other countries. In a parallel venture, Ofsted commissioned an extrapolation of the 'key characteristics of effective schools' from school effectiveness research through a group at London University's Institute of Education (Sammons et al. 1995). This came up with eleven factors:

- professional leadership (of head)
- shared vision and goals
- a learning environment
- concentration on teaching and learning
- purposeful teaching
- high expectations
- positive reinforcement
- monitoring progress
- pupil rights and responsibilities
- home–school partnership
- a learning organisation.

Each of these was subdivided. Thus 'professional leadership' included 'firm and purposeful', 'a participative approach' and 'the leading professional', while 'purposeful teaching' was explicated as 'efficient organisation', 'clarity of purpose', 'structured lessons' and 'adaptive practice'.

Hamilton's pretty devastating critique of this exercise sees it as predicated on a pathological view of schools as sick institutions in need of clear policy prescriptions presented as 'magic bullets or smart missiles'; he faults the methodology of aggregating findings from studies conducted by different methods, at different times and in different countries; and rejects 'the suppositions and conclusions of such research . . . as an ethnocentric pseudo-science that serves merely to mystify anxious administrators and marginalise classroom practitioners' (Hamilton 1995).

In my view, the aggregation is not only indefensible. It yields, for example, a model of an all-powerful but collegial school head, which, whatever its currency in the UK or USA where most of the reviewed studies were undertaken, makes no sense in those countries – France, India and many others – where school heads have more limited jurisdiction. It is also reductionist and banal. And not one of the factors listed above takes us beyond what the commonsense of a layperson would have predicted.

Notwithstanding government patronage, the promise of school effectiveness research as defined by its proponents has yet to be realised. The ambitious nine-nation ISERP has confirmed some of the factors in effective teaching that emerged from other classroom research, notably the importance of organising classroom time and space as economically as possible, maximising childrens' opportunity to learn, and generating challenging and focused pupil–teacher interaction. (Reynolds *et al.* 2002). But alongside confirmation and consolidation of what we already knew we must set the pedagogical acreage about which ISERP says nothing, especially in respect of classroom dynamics, discourse and the content of teaching and learning. We shall return to these matters in our substantive discussions of pedagogy in later chapters. Meanwhile, I would add the following further reservations to Hamilton's.

First, and perhaps most important given its international and comparative claims and my earlier arguments on this score, school effectiveness research does not deal more than cursorily with culture. Culture, indeed, is treated as no more than another variable, having significance no greater than, say, time on task or opportunity to learn.

Second, because it focuses exclusively on behaviours, school effectiveness research is technically unable to engage with the purposes, meanings and messages that elevate pedagogy from mindless technique to considered educational act. Teaching is presented as value-neutral, content-free and entirely devoid of the dilemmas of value and circumstance that confront real teachers daily.

Third, there is a degree of arbitrariness in the variables that the paradigm includes and excludes, as can be seen in Creemers' frequently cited model (Creemers 1997). In fact, most are derived from literature searches, so the model – being merely a representation of what others have chosen to write

about or investigate – is by no means as comprehensive as it app
or claims.

Fourth, there are obvious technical questions to be addressed in ISEl
and related studies: sampling, the use of questionnaires rather than
observation as the basis for identifying effectiveness factors, the highly
mechanistic approach to such classroom observation as is undertaken.

Fifth, there is a spurious absolutism to the terminology of school
effectiveness – 'success', 'failure', 'improvement', and of course 'effective'
itself – which conceals the technical deficiencies of the research and implies
a degree of homogeneity in schools, classrooms and lessons that cannot
be sustained empirically.

Sixth, school effectiveness research is unacceptably exclusive and tacitly
rejects the principle of cumulation, which is vital, in any discipline, to the
advancement of knowledge. Its literature makes little or no reference to
the much longer and more substantial tradition of pedagogic research that
has attempted to address the same question – what teaching makes the
most difference? – but by different means.

INTERACTIVE WHOLE CLASS TEACHING: THE 1990s TOTEM OF EDUCATIONAL EFFECTIVENESS

All of which brings us to whole class teaching, which alongside a
good dose of the basics, was the late 1990s panacea not just for effective
primary education but also, apparently, for a highly trained workforce
and an economy as lean, competitive and successful as any on the Pacific
Rim – before they crashed, that is, as several did soon after the publication of *Worlds Apart?* (BBC 1998). We hope that the events were not
connected.

Consider first these six classroom cameos:

1   In a language lesson in a Russian village school the teacher brings a
    six-year-old child to the front of the classroom, uses probing questions
    to elicit and then test her thinking, sometimes encouraging the child
    to write on the blackboard as an alternative or adjunct to expressing
    an idea orally. At intervals she invites the other pupils to question,
    confirm or qualify what the child has said. Although pupils raise their
    hands to volunteer opinions, the teacher is more likely to nominate
    directly the children from whom she wishes to hear, and to construct
    her questions with them in mind. Her manner is energetic, intense,
    precise, almost operatic, yet inclusive and encouraging. The pupils
    respond with equal energy and precision. The teacher evaluates what
    they say, often at length. The children are seated in rows, facing the
    teacher and the one child who, on this occasion, acts on their behalf.
    Others are given their turn at this extended and public form of

interaction – not all during the same lesson, for the interactions are too long to permit this, but over the next few lessons.

2   A teacher in a downtown school in the United States switches, at regular intervals, between whole class teaching and collaborative group tasks in order to foster her six-year-old pupils' understanding of mathematical sorting by attribute, basing the tasks on the story of 'Corduroy's Button', which she has read earlier. Each group has a number of counters of different colours, shapes and sizes. The teacher challenges the groups to find the button by progressively eliminating the attributes. After each collective problem-solving stint she calls the students together to explain and justify their findings. They do so by raising their hands and bidding for her attention. The teacher's language is studied and exact, yet also laced with humour and evident affection. Her responses to the pupils' contributions combine encouragement with – grounded in what they say – further questions. The pupils are seated in groups of between four and six, so as the procedure changes so they turn outwards to face the teacher or inwards to face each other.

3   The same teacher reaches the end of this lesson and asks the children to re-arrange the tables in a horseshoe. This they do quickly (within 90 seconds) and quietly, for moving the furniture to make the layout consistent with the mode of interaction is something that can happen several times a day in this classroom. The pupils then sit on the outside of the horseshoe, with the teacher at its open end, so that all can see each other. The teacher then opens a class discussion in which she encourages as many pupils as possible to participate. They listen to each other, ask questions, offer comments, and from time to time disagree.

4   The teacher in an Indian village school uses chanted repetition to instil by rote her six-year-old pupils' recognition of numbers between 10 and 100. She speaks, pointing to a number on the blackboard and asking what it is, and they chant their response. The cycle is several times repeated for each number until the teacher judges that most or all children have joined in. She then moves on to the next number. And the next. There is no verbal feedback on what the pupils say, and no questions are asked by way of probing their understanding. The class has 60 pupils, and the children sit cross-legged with their satchels and slates on their laps, facing the teacher.

5   A teacher in an English primary school teaches handwriting to six-year-olds by getting individuals to demonstrate and then the whole class to mime, with grand sweeps of their arms, the movement of the pen as it traces the joined-up letters 'id'. The mime-imitation is repeated several times, the children standing up. At the end, there is a cheery 'Well done' and mutual applause. In a neighbouring

school a teacher opens a lesson with 'Welcome to the Literacy Hour'. The children sit on the floor; the teacher stands at the front with a hand-shaped pointer. On the board is a sequence of pictures underneath each of which is a fragment of a story. The teacher points; the children read aloud in unison; the pointer moves on.

6   In the south of France a teacher of nine-year-olds works through a schematised framework for analysing and constructing a story involving dialogue. He prompts or cues the responses that he wishes them to provide (for they have done this before), and in this way fills in on the blackboard the various stages of the framework from 'initial state' through 'interruption', 'change', 'reaction', 'equilibrium' to 'final state'. Much later in the same lesson, the teacher asks six pupils in turn to read aloud the stories that by then they have drafted. He makes critical comments, gives qualified praise, corrects pronunciation and grammar, but also invites questions from pupils and encourages their comments, which they readily volunteer. The first episode entails recall and instruction; the second, collective critical appraisal.

Which of these is an example of interactive whole class teaching? If by this we mean the practice of teaching the same thing to all the children at the same time, then the answer is clear: all of them are. Moreover, from my own research data alone I can multiply tenfold the diversity hinted at in these six examples even before we consider countries other than those five in which I have worked most concentratedly, England, France, India, Russia and the United States (Alexander 1995: 103–219; Alexander 2001a: 427–528).

'Interactive whole class teaching' sounds precise enough as a category of teaching method, and tough enough as a stick with which to beat teachers and teacher trainers, but actually it covers a very wide variety of practices, takes many different forms and serves many different purposes. In the examples above we find interaction between teachers and pupils and among pupils themselves. Mostly the teacher asks the questions, but sometimes the pupils do. In some cases pupils bid for the teacher's attention by raising their hands. In others the teacher nominates the pupils from whom she or he wishes to hear. Sometimes the teacher gives feedback on pupils' contributions, but the extent and thrust of the feedback varies considerably and sometimes there is none at all. Sometimes the children stand, sometimes they sit, and when they sit they may be in groups, rows, an open horseshoe or a tight cluster on the floor at the teacher's feet. Nor does all this whole class teaching involve talk: there is mime too.

Expressing the matter somewhat more technically, we find, within this one organisational device called 'interactive whole class teaching', the traditional closed discourse structures of IR-IR (repeated teacher initiation/pupil response) and IRF (teacher initiation/pupil response/teacher feedback) which characterise rote and recitation teaching, together with the more open-ended forms of discussion, and the reciprocity of true dialogue. We also find turns taken by hands-up *bidding* and by teacher-chosen *nomination*; and teachers using the contrasting strategies of *rotation* (brief exchanges with one child at a time, aiming to include as many as possible by the end of the lesson) and *extension* (a smaller number of longer cumulative exchange sequences with one child, to which the other children listen and on which they may be invited to comment). I shall say much more about these dimensions of oral pedagogy in Chapter 5.

Yet in the early days, months and years of New Labour's standards drive there were frequent exhortations to make whole class teaching the default pedagogy, on the basis of its claimed correlation not only with high educational standards but also economic success. For in this matter the message of *Worlds Apart?*, certainly as understood by its political advocates, was that the relationship between pedagogic practice, student educational attainment and national economic performance was indeed a linear one, a question of simple cause and effect.

WHOLE CLASS TEACHING AND ECONOMIC PERFORMANCE

Let's consider this extension of the claim for the efficacy of (interactive) whole class teaching by, appropriately, imagining an interactive whole class encounter in typical recitation mode.

Teacher:	What do Hong Kong, Switzerland and Korea have in common?
Student:	They are among the richest and most highly competitive of the world's high-income market economies.
Teacher:	Good. What else?
Student:	They have some of the world's highest graduation rates from secondary and higher education.
Teacher:	What about the teaching in their schools?
Student:	It's mostly whole class teaching.
Teacher:	What do Bangladesh, Malawi and Nigeria have in common?
Student:	They are all low-income, low GDP economies.
Teacher:	Good. What else?
Student:	They have some of the world's lowest secondary and higher graduation rates.
Teacher:	And?

Student: They are in the bottom 15 per cent of the 177 nations listed in the United Nations' Human Development Index.
Teacher: What happens in their classrooms?
Student: It's mostly whole class teaching.
Teacher: What do you deduce from this?

We deduce, of course, that worldwide, whole class teaching can be made to correlate as surely with low or middle GDP/GNP as with economic prosperity and competitiveness; and with educational *under*achievement as convincingly as with high outcome measures such as graduation, qualifications and performance in the IEA achievement studies. For whole class teaching is one of the two near-universals of basic education on this planet, the other being an emphasis on the 3Rs (Benavot *et al.* 1991). The correlational exercise, in short, is meaningless and inadmissible.

If this is so, then three conclusions follow. First, whole class teaching, as such, cannot be defined as the magic ingredient *x* of high educational performance, let alone of economic prosperity. Quite apart from what I've just said, consider the United States, in whose elementary schools there is much group and individual teaching, but which remains economically supreme. Consider economically successful Canada and Finland, whose schools also use a diversity of teaching methods yet whose school students consistently outperform those of the US in the international achievement studies. Consider Russia, which uses whole class teaching extremely effectively to achieve high standards at an early age in the basics, yet whose economy is only now beginning to recover from the disastrous decade that followed the collapse of the Soviet Union. And consider Hong Kong with its dynamic economy and outstanding educational achievement as judged by the PISA tests (OECD 2005a), where the default pedagogy is whole class teaching, yet whose schooling is backed by, and perhaps depends on, a substantial after-school coaching industry into which ambitious parents perforce sink much of their income.

Second, therefore, and surely obvious to all but those whose power over our education system exceeds their understanding of it, educational success, like educational failure, is multi-factorial, and (Sadler again) the things outside the school matter as much as those inside the school.[8]

Third, if we want to understand how whole class teaching contributes both to relative success and relative failure in educational performance, then we need to move beyond the talismanic label and examine its constituents.

WHAT, THEN, *IS* WHOLE CLASS TEACHING?

If we ask ourselves what is going on in the six classroom cameos above, we can identify three simultaneous levels or dimensions of activity.

Organisation

First, the teacher is using a particular organisational device, that of working on a single task with all the pupils at the same time. To facilitate this, desks or tables may be arranged in rows – or not. This is the minimal definition of whole class teaching, and the one on which the political advocates of the method tend to fixate. Even then, they manage to be more minimal still, insisting that the only way to whole class teach is from the front of the room. Fortunately, most teachers feel free to stand at the back, the front or the middle, or even to move around.

Discourse

Second, central in every case is discourse between the teacher and his or her pupils. The teacher deploys a variety of ways of asking questions, handling answers, explaining, instructing, giving feedback, and getting pupils to volunteer and explore their ideas. Such discourse can vary enormously in style, substance, pace and, of course, quality. As any school or university student knows, whole class teaching can be intellectually exhilarating or mind-numbingly boring. Analytically speaking, the discourse *mode* may range from direct instruction to discussion, and its *form* may be interrogatory, expository, evaluative or dialogic (Alexander 2001a: 517).

The discourse also varies in *intention*: on the basic continuum offered by Her Majesty's Inspectorate of Schools (HMI) in the 1978 primary survey (DES 1978), it can be *didactic* or *exploratory*. 'Didactic discourse' on the HMI continuum can be sharpened up into *direct instruction* as defined a year later by Rosenshine. He restricted his definition to 'didactic ends, that is instruction towards rational, specific, analytic goals . . . instruction is defined as structured but not authoritarian . . .', questions are pitched so as to enable pupils to produce a high proportion of correct answers, and feedback '. . . is immediate and academically oriented.' (Rosenshine 1979: 38). Or, in Nystrand's typology, questions may be *test* (directed at getting students to recall or repeat the thinking of others) or *authentic* (directed at getting students to think for themselves) (Nystrand *et al.* 1997).

Or, as another way of looking at pedagogic intention in teacher–pupil discourse we might consider the two clusters that emerged from the ESRC-funded Changes in Discourse and Pedagogy in the Primary School (CICADA) analysis of the discourse in 60 lessons given by English primary teachers in 1986, 1988 and 1992. One group of teachers tended towards discourse that was dominated by directions, commands and judgements, and which involved setting up a learning task, standing back while children undertook it, intervening only where necessary, and providing feedback. The other group tended towards discourse that emphasised explaining, exploring, asking questions and eliciting ideas and information.

In the first ('Cluster 1'), the discourse was essentially a device for managing the learning task; in the second ('Cluster 2') it was intrinsic to it. Neither was associated exclusively with the supposed polarities of whole class teaching or individual attention, though the Cluster 2 teachers had a greater proportion of whole-class interactions than did Cluster 1. The clusters, incidentally, were stable over time, despite the apparently disruptive impact of the National Curriculum (Alexander 1995: 220–69).

Whichever mode we adopt for analysing teacher–pupil discourse in a whole class setting, we need to note that whole class teaching need not exclude other kinds of activity. For instance, in several of the above cameos pupils interacted with each other as well as with the teacher, and in the American example they alternated whole class teaching and working collaboratively in groups. Such collaborative group activity was in this case an adjunct of the whole class teaching, not something apart from it, still less – as is sometimes argued – philosophically opposed to it. Fortunately, this extreme and nonsensical position, though flirted with by ministers and favoured by the tabloids, was not sustained in New Labour's national strategies, which encouraged individual, paired and group interaction alongside particular forms of whole class teaching.

Meaning

The third dimension of whole class teaching is the one least attended to in both public discussion and educational research. Whatever the purpose and manner of his or her interaction, the teacher conveys ideas, information and instructions relating to the learning task together with values and expectations. The latter range from requirements of an instrumental and explicit kind relating to pupils' behaviour and to their progress and attainment in the subjects taught, to the somewhat more subliminal values concerning the nature and worthwhileness of different ways of thinking, knowing and understanding. In their turn, pupils respond. Meanings are exchanged and created.

Moreover, in this matter the teacher is not necessarily autonomous. The method chosen – whether whole class teaching or something else – is a necessary response to the particular circumstances in which teacher and children find themselves. English teachers may complain of the adverse impact on their work of peer culture and parental attitudes, but such anxieties pale into insignificance in comparison with what teachers in many other countries cope with. The particular Indian teacher whose work is briefly captured above was working in a context of limited material resources, a class of 60 children, most of whose families are below the poverty line, and 80 per cent parental illiteracy. The method seems minimalist and repetitive, but her room for manoeuvre is strictly limited.

The American teacher's handling of questions and answers – precise and firm as to substance yet gentle, humorous and accommodating in its manner – is in this particular case a carefully judged response to the unstable backgrounds and dangerous neighbourhoods from which many of her pupils come. The Russian teacher, who started her career in 1945, and was working well into what in Britain would be deemed retirement, told us that she was teaching under Yeltsin much as she did under Gorbachev, Brezhnev, Khrushchev and even Stalin, but in doing so was trying to provide – as needs must for many schools in Russia – a haven of unambiguous values and a model of firm but benign adult authority in a context of traumatic change and insecurity.

These three pedagogic dimensions – *organisation*, *discourse*, and *meaning* – underpin all teaching strategies, not merely whole class teaching. In attempting to evaluate the impact of a teacher's actions, we need to explicate the character of each and assess their congruence. In coining the label 'Class Enquirer' the ORACLE team (Galton *et al*. 1980) presaged this line of analysis in respect of two of the three dimensions (though not the third) arguing the primacy of discourse, and specifically what they called 'higher-order cognitive interaction', an idea that is close to Luxton's version of 'interactive whole class teaching' (Luxton 2000). Thus, in the ORACLE analysis the typology of individual monitor, group instructor and class enquirer includes the dimensions of organisation (individual, group, class) and discourse (monitoring, instructing, enquiring). However, because their observers used pre-coded behavioural categories and did not analyse lesson transcripts, the educational meanings that were being exchanged could not be included.

'Interactive whole class teaching' can also be examined in terms of task demand. In the classic continental version of direct instruction (as used, for example, by the Russian teacher) the learning steps are frequent and shallow, so as to enable all the children to move on together. Thus, overall, the interaction may be 'higher order' but each of its individual segments may have a relatively low level of demand in order to maximise the chances of success for all children in the class. The Indian teacher exemplified an extreme version of this principle.

If we consider the three dimensions further, we observe that discourse and meaning are not exclusive concomitants of a particular pattern of organisation, but are in fact generic aspects of other organisational approaches, too. We could take the ORACLE labels and interchange them to illustrate this point. The ORACLE 'class enquirer' fits the idea of 'interactive whole class teaching', but there are also class instructors and class monitors, just as there are group enquirers and group monitors as well as the ORACLE 'group instructors'.

If, further, we set the three dimensions against what we know about how children learn, it can fairly be concluded that it is the character of the discourse and the meanings that are conveyed and exchanged in teaching that are the more critical ingredients, however important the organisational strategy may appear to be – and this quite apart from matters such as subject matter, task design, assessment and so on, which are equally fundamental to our consideration of the quality and impact of teaching. Certainly, as I consider the international observational and video data from which the six cameos above were taken, I find that although the organisational aspect of whole class teaching varies a certain amount between the lessons observed, the discourse and the meanings vary much more, and with far greater subtlety.

Moreover, this is not just a matter of analytic clarity. There are important moral choices at stake. If the teaching methods of the admired Taiwanese or Swiss classrooms are indeed *manifestations of* cultural values rather than merely – as in ISERP school effectiveness methodology – *responses to* them, then we need to be clear whether, in the proper pursuit of pedagogic efficiency, we wish to import, along with the method, everything else that the method conveys to the pupils who experience it: messages about, for example, the extent to which knowledge is open or bounded, provisional or uncontestable; about how ideas should be handled; about the kinds of authority that teachers and curricula embody and the extent to which they may be questioned; about how individuals and groups should relate to each other; about the balance of individual autonomy and collective responsibility; about what counts as successful learning; and about what it means to be educated.

We should also be alert to the power of pedagogy to deliver messages that may or may not be consistent with the educational goals that we espouse, just as we should understand that in importing a teaching method that we find admirable we may also import values with which we may be rather less comfortable. This is an appeal not to covert xenophobia but to a proper understanding of the relationship between pedagogy and culture.

It is, then, to the *generic properties* of strategies such as whole class teaching that we should be attending in this necessary debate about improving education, and in our wholly proper desire to draw on inter-national comparisons in order to effect such improvements. In shifting focus we might find it necessary to make two observations.

First, 'interactive whole class teaching' is either a meaningless catch-all or a term with highly specific stipulative intent. If the latter, then it needs to be defined. The Barking and Dagenham horseshoe seating arrangement is combined with PowerPoint for explicating and testing pupil understanding, an emphasis on oral projection and clarity, and liberal use of verbal devices to steer towards consensus or at least common ground ('Does everyone agree?', 'I agree, but . . .'). Yet it is but one of the many versions of interactive whole class teaching that are possible. During the countdown to the 1997 general election, the political pilgrims to Barking and Dagenham, in search of a simpler gospel, ignored this. Now, ten years later, I find that the same problem attends what I call 'dialogic teaching'. This is less a specific teaching method than a pedagogic approach that draws on a broad array of organisational and interactive repertoires according to circumstance and need, but is guided and tested by the five core principles of *collectivity, reciprocity, supportiveness, cumulation* and *purposefulness* (see Chapter 5 and Appendix). Thus, in dialogic teaching the organisational and interactive forms of the talk will vary, but the principles are non-negotiable.

The second point to make is that it is easy enough to import the organisational elements of whole class teaching. It is much more difficult to import the discourse with which, at best, the continental tradition of whole class teaching – say – is associated.

At best then, this discourse is brisk, energetic, searching and articulate, and it is informed by the teacher's deep understanding of the subject being taught. And there is an absence – which many teachers in England find surprising – of that special teacherly tone and vocabulary that are such distinctive features of many English primary schools and American elementary schools, especially where early years teaching is concerned: slow, careful, oblique ('somebody's using a big voice'), collective ('we' rather than the more confrontational 'you'), encouraging, patient, euphemistic, self-conscious and, above all, different from the language of the world outside school. What you often hear in continental classrooms is a direct, businesslike quality in the exchanges between teachers and pupils that on the teacher's side some in England or the US would find brusque, even brutal, but which is countered by pupils' readiness to stand up and give a confident account of what they know and how they think.

This matter of congruence or incongruence between the language of the classroom and the language of life outside school is significant. What went on in the French and Russian classrooms in which we collected some of the most thought-provoking examples of classroom interaction in the *Culture and Pedagogy* study was embedded in a culture in which words, reasoning and argument are historically of profound importance, in which the sound and quality of the native language, and the individual's ability to use it, matter a great deal, and in which daily life, whether in the classroom, the family, the restaurant or the street, is in part a celebration of the power and excitement of talk.

In this context it is also pertinent to report that when we analysed the data from all five countries in terms of the 23 'generic activities' through which pupils undertook their prescribed learning tasks, we found that on a simple quantitative measure the ratio of structured talk to writing was very different in the French and Russian classrooms from those in England and the US – much more writing in the English and American classrooms, much more structured talk in the French and Russian ones. Is this significant? I think it is, culturally no less than educationally.

To identify teaching methods as a significant contributor to education standards is reasonable: teaching, fortunately, does make a difference. To identify a single teaching strategy as the solution is, for reasons I have rehearsed, naive. To do so in a climate of blaming and shaming is unsafe in the extreme:

> It is fashionable to blame the Plowden Report for what are perceived as the current ills of primary education. However, if ill-conceived practices have been justified by reference to Plowden, this reflects far more damagingly on those who have used the report in this way than on Plowden itself . . . If things have gone wrong – and the word 'if' is important – then scapegoating is not the answer. All those responsible for administering and delivering our system of primary education need to look carefully at the part they may have played.
>
> (Alexander *et al.* 1992: 10)

It is a mark of the depths to which, by the early 1990s, public educational discourse in Britain had sunk that, when the report containing this clear warning was published, the first thing the government did was to do precisely what the report's authors had cautioned against and blame not just the Plowden Report but Lady Plowden personally for the problems which they had identified.[9] It was not surprising, therefore, that when a few years later *Worlds Apart?* was published, such caveats as Reynolds and Farrell had built into their analysis were also brushed aside in the stampede to go East and replace whatever was going on in British schools with 'interactive whole class teaching'.

NOTES

1   Popularised from Ball (1990b) though used earlier by Jane Kenway in Ball (1990a).

2   In 1987, during the parliamentary debate on the Education Reform Bill which paved the way for a national curriculum, national tests, the transfer of powers from local educational authorities and much more, Labour education shadow, Jack Straw, warned the House of Commons: 'Under the guise of fine phrases like "parental choice" and "decentralisation" the Bill will deny choice and instead centralize power and control over schools, colleges and universities in the hands of the Secretary of State in a manner without parallel in the western world.' What he really ought to have said was 'You ain't seen nothing yet.'

3   Kenneth Clarke, Secretary of State for Education and Science, 1990–2; Chris Woodhead, HM Chief Inspector of Schools, 1994-2000.

4   Gillian Shepherd was Conservative Secretary of State at the time of the 1997 General Election. With New Labour's victory in that election, her shadow David Blunkett took over and held the post until 2001.

5   Matthew Arnold (1822-88), poet, essayist and school inspector, who also wrote influential reports on education in France, Switzerland and Holland; Marc-Antoine Jullien de Paris (1775-1848), credited with the first use of the term 'comparative education', and author of *Esquisse et Vues Préliminaires d'un Ouvrage sur l'Éducation Comparée* (1817).

6   Acronym alert: International Association for the Evaluation of Educational Achievement (IEA), Organisation for Economic Cooperation and Development (OECD), Trends in International Mathematics and Science Study (TIMSS), Programme for International Student Assessment (PISA), Progress in International Reading Literacy Study (PIRLS).

7   Amazing but true. From 1989 to 1994 I was a member of the Council for the Accreditation of Teacher Education (CATE), the national agency responsible for advising the UK government on the content of teacher training courses and then accrediting them, and precursor of TTA and TDA. In drafting the revised content criteria that later became DES Circular 14/93, we were told by DES officials to strike out references to child development because the minister would interpret them as endorsement of a return to Plowdenite progressivism. When we challenged this on the grounds that teachers needed to know how children develop and learn and that this was a matter of research rather than ideology, the official said that if we didn't remove the references, the minister would. The government's claim a year later that the national curriculum was grounded in 'what has been learned about child development' therefore struck those of us in the know as particularly brazen.

8   For discussion of the problems of attempting to trace causal links between educational and economic performance, see Brown and Lauder 1997, Steedman 1999, Robinson 1999 and Bonnet 2002.

9   After the publication of the 1992 'three wise men' report *The Sunday Telegraph* carried a full-page article by Secretary of State Kenneth Clarke with the headline 'The Great Betrayal: after affecting our schools for 25 years, the Plowden Report has been laid to rest without mourners'. Alongside was a photographic rogues gallery of Lady Plowden and leading members of her committee. My protesting in the press that 'Few episodes in recent educational journalism have been more disgraceful than the vilification of Lady Plowden, and our report explicitly distances itself from such behaviour' (Alexander 1992) cut no ice. In private correspondence, Lady Plowden told me that as a result of the combined government and media campaign against her report and 'progressivism' generally, she and her family had to suffer the kind of journalistic harassment that is normally reserved for 'A' list celebrities and suspected paedophiles. (My comparison, her distress.)

Chapter 3

Principle, pragmatism and compliance

STILL NO PEDAGOGY?

In 1981, Brian Simon published 'Why no pedagogy in England?' (Simon 1981). On 20 May 2003 the UK government unveiled *Excellence and Enjoyment: a strategy for primary schools* (DfES 2003a).

'Why no pedagogy?' is an academic critique that commands attention by force of argument and evidence. *Excellence and Enjoyment* relies on large print, homely language, images of smiling children, and populist appeals to teachers' common sense. Substantively, it seeks to secure professional goodwill, and possibly to disarm criticism, by relaxing the pressure of government prescription and targets. But beyond this surface appeal are important statements on learning, teaching, curriculum and assessment, which are arguably the core of that pedagogy whose absence Brian Simon deplored. On these and other matters, *Excellence and Enjoyment* designates itself not just a Primary National Strategy but also a 'blueprint for the future'. It therefore provides an appropriate test of how far, a quarter of a century on, Simon's criticisms remain valid.

Simon believed that pedagogy in England was neither coherent nor systematic, and that English educators had developed nothing comparable to the continental European 'science of teaching'. Consequently, teachers in England tended to conceptualise, plan and justify their teaching by combining pragmatism with ideology but not much else. This approach, he believed, was reinforced in their training, where trainees encountered education theory that they could not readily connect with what they saw and did in schools.

Simon traced this condition back, in part, to the Victorian public-school view that education should be concerned with 'character' rather than the intellect, and partly to the heavily utilitarian mission of the elementary schools that existed at the opposite end of the Victorian educational spectrum – delivering the 3Rs, social conformity, and cheapness with or without efficiency – and from which today's primary schools directly descend. Though Simon readily acknowledged the growing influence of psychology on educational thinking during the later twentieth century, he did not concede, even when he re-visited his 'Why no pedagogy?' article in the 1990s, that it or its cognate disciplines yet offered anything approaching the coherent pedagogy which he could point to elsewhere in Europe (Simon 1994).

Of course, all education is grounded in social and indeed political values of some kind, and necessarily so; and Simon himself was nothing if not ideological in his sustained pursuit of causes such as non-selective secondary education. So his critique is less a rejection of ideology as such than a complaint that the pursuit of social and political goals through the complex activity we call teaching cannot be undertaken on the basis of ideology alone, or even ideology leavened with pragmatism. Ideology may define the ends in teaching and hint at aspects of its conduct, but it cannot specify the precise means. Professional knowledge grounded in different kinds of evidence, together with principles that have been distilled from collective understanding and experience, are also called for, in order that – as Paul Hirst put it some years ago – teachers are able to make 'rationally defensible professional judgements' both while they teach and in their planning and evaluation (Hirst 1979).

But Simon's was nevertheless an uncompromising assessment, and it was open to challenge even in 1981. Research on professional thinking published at about the same time as 'Why no pedagogy?' showed how the decision-making of individual teachers, especially those who had advanced beyond mere 'coping' into the reflective judgement of mature expertise, was more principled, informed and subtle than the Simon characterisation seemed to acknowledge (Berlak and Berlak 1981; Schön 1982; Elbaz 1983; Calderhead 1984; Clark and Peterson 1986). But Simon was concerned less with private theories of teaching and learning than with the theory and discourse that were collective, generalisable and open to public scrutiny.

Simon's claim provoked interest in all sorts of places and 'Why no pedagogy?' has become one of the more frequently cited academic titles of recent years. Interestingly, it has gained this distinction mainly since government and its agencies started issuing pedagogical pronouncements at a level of prescriptive detail that was unthinkable when the first and even the second of Simon's two articles on this theme appeared. For the second 'Why no pedagogy?' article was published in 1994, just two years after the so-called 'three wise men' enquiry on behalf of the UK government into the evidential basis of primary education at Key Stage 2. The document that came out of that initiative began by quoting the then Secretary of State, Kenneth Clarke, who roundly insisted that 'questions about how to teach are not for Government to determine' (Alexander *et al.* 1992: para. 1).

In *Excellence and Enjoyment*, the document with which in 2003 New Labour launched its Primary National Strategy, New Labour Secretary of

State Charles Clarke echoes Conservative Kenneth Clarke's assurance: 'A central message of this document is that teachers have the power to decide how they teach, and ... the Government supports that' (DfES 2003a: para. 2.7). If some people were cynical about the intentions of Clarke K. in 1991 – given that he launched the so-called 'three wise men' enquiry with a pre-emptive strike in the form of a letter to every primary school in England, telling their heads exactly what he expected the enquiry to conclude before a word of its report had been written (DES 1991) – then the contrary evidence about New Labour's approach to pedagogy should make them even more wary about the protestations of Clarke C. in 2003, decisively so since the introduction of the National Literacy and Numeracy Strategies in 1998 and 1999, which are nothing if not pedagogical prescriptions (DfEE 1998a, 1999a), but also in view of other evidence that this chapter considers.

The force of this chapter's title will become apparent as we proceed. Meanwhile, we note that from the moment that New Labour's *Education, Education, Education* project was launched in 1997, government ministers, officials and apologists elevated the quintessentially pragmatic mantra 'what works' to the status of ultimate criterion for judging whether a practice is educationally sound; and the word 'compliance' – not to mention sanctions such as 'special measures' or withdrawal of that accreditation by which compliance is enforced – featured explicitly in the procedural vocabulary of DfES (now DCSF), Ofsted and the Teacher Training Agency (TTA, now TDA).

CONCEPTUALISING PEDAGOGY

Part of the 'Why no pedagogy?' problem is the word 'pedagogy' itself. It is used more frequently than in 1981, but still does not enjoy widespread currency in England. The spectrum of available definitions ranges from the societally broad to the procedurally narrow. Basil Bernstein (1990) saw pedagogy as a 'cultural relay' and located it within his grand theory of social structure and reproduction. However, in England pedagogy is commonly used in a more restricted sense, to equate with the practice of teaching. Symptomatic of this narrower definition is the complaint by Anthea Millett, the previous head of TTA/TDA:

> I am always struck by how difficult teachers find it to talk about *teaching* ... They prefer to talk about *learning*. By contrast, they can talk with great clarity about ... curriculum, assessment ... [and] classroom organisation ... almost anything except teaching itself.
>
> (Millett 1999)

– an agenda that Millett believed should cover 'competence, excellence and failure in teaching methods.' To be fair, I think many of us who have been in this business for a while recognise the condition to which Millett was referring. There certainly was a time when it was common to hear people in primary education say things like 'let's talk about learning, not teaching' or 'child, not curriculum', or 'learner-centred not teacher-centred', and this kind of oppositional pedagogical discourse has been tracked on both sides of the Atlantic (Entwistle 1970; Alexander 1984, 2001a; and Chapter 4 of this collection). It illustrates Simon's concern about the dominance of ideology over principle, and of course sets up dichotomies that are unnecessary and unhelpful, not just when they become part of that 'discourse of derision' which passes for educational debate in some newspapers and among some politicians (Ball 1990b; Wallace 1993), but also within the teaching profession itself. However, Millett's definition compounds rather than resolves the problem, for it simply weights the dichotomy at the other end and excludes matters such as learning, curriculum, assessment and classroom organisation, which are arguably essential not just to a comprehensible pedagogy but also, as it happens, to a meaningful discussion of Millett's own preferred pedagogical agenda of 'competence, excellence and failure in teaching methods'. Tellingly in this era of centralisation and tight political control, her definition also excludes any sense of how pedagogy connects with culture, social structure and human agency, and thus acquires educational *meaning*. Such matters, the definition dangerously implies, are either unimportant or not for teachers to worry about.

In contrast to all this, the continental view of pedagogy, especially in Northern, Central and Eastern Europe, brings together within the one concept the act of teaching and the body of knowledge, argument and evidence in which it is embedded and by which particular classroom practices are justified. Thus, at a typical Russian pedagogical university, pedagogy encompasses: 'general culture' comprising philosophy, ethics, history, economics, literature, art and politics; together with elements relating to children and their learning – psychology, physiology, child development, child law; and as a third group, aspects relating to the subjects to be taught, or *didaktika* and – linking all the elements – *metodika*, or ways of teaching them. The subject element, *didaktika* in Russia, *la didactique* in France, *die Didaktik* in Germany, subdivides variously into, for example, *allgemeine Didaktik* and *Fachdidaktik* (general and specialist or subject didactics) in Germany, *didactiques des disciplines* and *transpositions didactiques*, or *savoir savant* and *savoir enseigné* (scholarly and taught knowledge) in France (Moon 1998; Hamilton 1999; Alexander 2001a: 540–63). These are equivalent to what Lee Shulman (1987) calls 'content' and 'pedagogical content' and TTA/TDA's precursor body, CATE, called 'subject' and 'subject applications'.

Of course, English etymology doesn't help us here. Respectable though on the continent both 'pedagogy' and 'didactics' may be, here we can never completely escape the way 'pedagogy' suggests the pedantry of the pedagogue (and indeed through their shared Greek root the words are related) and 'didactics' elides with the chalk-and-talk intimations of 'didactic'. Thus pedagogy and didactics, to many, suggest just one kind of teaching: traditional direct instruction.

The problem of terminology and discourse is not completely one-sided. What is frequently missing in continental debate about education is the rich discourse surrounding the idea of *curriculum*, which in Britain and the US is more fully developed. That, I submit, is partly because both of those countries inherited traditions of curriculum decentralisation which meant that curriculum matters were always bound to be contested, even more so when their governments sought to curtail that autonomy by introducing a National Curriculum in England from 1988 and state curriculum standards in the USA from about the same time. In contrast, in many continental countries the scope and balance of the school curriculum had long been centrally determined and the remaining questions concerned the character of the subjects of which it was constituted and how they should be taught. There are of course oppositional curriculum discourses there too: that of Pierre Bourdieu in France is a prime example (Bourdieu and Passeron 1970).

The prominence of curriculum in English educational discourse has meant that we have tended to make pedagogy subsidiary to curriculum. My own preferred definition has it the other way round: *pedagogy is the act of teaching together with its attendant discourse of educational theories, values, evidence and justifications. It is what one needs to know, and the skills one needs to command, in order to make and justify the many different kinds of decision of which teaching is constituted.* Curriculum is just one of its domains, albeit a central one.

With this ground-clearing in mind, let us return briefly to Anthea Millett's belief that pedagogy should concern itself with competence, excellence and failure in teaching methods rather than learning, curriculum and assessment. The demarcation is precise and absolutist. It is replicated by DfES/DCSF and its agencies. In tenor and purpose this preferred pedagogy deals with judgement rather than substance and justification; and with teaching rather than the wider sphere of morally purposeful activity, of which teaching is a part, which we call education. Teachers, in this characterisation, are technicians who implement the educational ideas and procedures of others, rather than professionals who think about these matters for themselves.

That is one kind of definition. Here is an alternative: if pedagogy is the discourse that informs and justifies the act of teaching and the learning to which that teaching is directed, then substance, and justification in relation to a view of what it is to be educated, must *precede* judgement. Otherwise it is hard to know by what criteria judgements of competence, success and failure in teaching can be applied.

In the alternative pedagogy, the teacher engages, as a matter of necessity, with three distinct but related domains of ideas and values. These are concerned with:

- *children*: their characteristics, development, motivation, needs and differences;
- *learning*: its nature, facilitation, achievement and assessment;
- *teaching*: its planning, execution and evaluation;
- *curriculum*: the various ways of knowing, doing, creating, investigating and making sense which it is desirable for children to encounter, and how these are most appropriately translated and structured for teaching

– with, that is to say, what is to be taught, to whom, and how. But teaching takes place in an institutional and legal context and responds to formal requirements and expectations. At its most immediate this context comprises:

- *school* as a formal institution, a microculture and a conveyor of pedagogical messages over and above those of the classroom;
- *policy*, national and local, which prescribes or proscribes, enables or inhibits what is taught and how.

There's a third group, for school policies in turn have their larger contexts, and both they and teaching are informed by purposes and values. It may be argued – it is certainly assumed – that in a centralised system of public schooling government policy is purpose enough. But even the pedagogy of compliance is not immune from:

- *community*, the familial and local expectations, attitudes, opportunities and constraints to which schools are subject, and the way these shape learners' outlooks;
- *culture*: the web of values, ideas, institutions and processes that inform, shape and explain a society's views of education, teaching and learning, and which throw up a complex burden of choices and dilemmas for those whose job it is to translate these into a practical pedagogy;
- *self*: what it is to be a person, an individual relating to others and to the wider society, and how through education and other early experiences selfhood is acquired.

Where the first domain *enables* teaching and the second *formalises* and *legitimates* it by reference to policy and infrastructure, the third domain *locates* it – and children themselves – in time, place and the social world, and anchors it firmly to the questions of human identity and social purpose without which teaching makes little sense. Such ideas mark the transition from teaching to education. That is why the omission of culture and ideas in school effectiveness research (see Chapter 1) is so demeaning of what pedagogy actually entails.

Such a list is a start, but obviously not the whole story. So, for example, if we take the domain *teaching* from the first group, it can be conceptually elaborated in several different ways. In the five-country *Culture and Pedagogy* research we needed a framework that was comprehensive yet as close to culture-neutral as possible. We started with the irreducible proposition that 'teaching, in any setting, is the act of using method x to enable pupils to learn y'. From this we constructed a generic model comprising the immediate context or *frame* within which the act of teaching is set, the *act* itself, and its *form*, and then a set of elements within each such category. The core acts of teaching (*task, activity, interaction* and *assessment*) are framed by *space, pupil organisation, time* and *curriculum*, and by *routines, rules and rituals*. They are given form, and are bounded temporally and conceptually, by the *lesson* or teaching session. This model is discussed in Chapter 4.

A framework of this kind can serve both descriptive and prescriptive purposes, and its elements can in turn be elaborated further, as was necessary both within the research in question (Alexander, 2001a: 297–528) and in a developmental programme on classroom talk which the comparative research has prompted since then. In the latter, the action nexus of *task, activity, assessment* and (especially) *interaction* are transformed into a set of principles and indicators of 'dialogic teaching' by way of research on the relationship between spoken language, cognition and learning, and with reference to explicit social values about the kinds of interactive relationship that are implied by the concept of citizenship. This transformation in turn affects the five framing elements and the overall form of lessons. We consider this work in greater detail in Chapter 5 (see also Appendix).

This example underscores a second imperative. It is not enough to delineate the themes of pedagogical discourse: we must also recognise how they inform each other. In the example here, the particular approach signalled by the term 'dialogic teaching' seeks simultaneously to attend to a viable concept of *teaching*, to evidence about the nature and advancement of human *learning*, and to the conditions for *education* in a democracy, in which the values of individualism, community and collectivism stand in a complex and sometimes tense contrapuntal relationship. Dialogic teaching is therefore more properly called 'dialogic pedagogy' in as far as it meets our definition of pedagogy as both the teaching act and its attendant discourse of ideas, values and principles.

No less important, if an intelligent pedagogy dictates attention to domains of ideas and values such as these, and to ways of organising and relating them, it also requires that we are aware that such ideas can be, and are, engaged with in different ways. Simon, as we have seen, commends the continental view of a *science* of teaching grounded in explicit principles relating to what children have in common. Eisner prefers the idea of teaching as an *art* in the sense that it is partly improvisatory, is 'influenced by qualities and contingencies that are unpredicted . . . [and] the ends it achieves are often created in process' (Eisner 1979: 153). Argyris and Schön (1974) show how in understanding professional practice it is essential to distinguish the 'espoused theory . . . to which one gives allegiance' (as in the science of teaching) from the 'theory-in-use' which actually, regardless of what one claims to others, informs one's practice. Taking this further, Brown and McIntyre reveal how the work of experienced teachers is, as a matter of day-to-day reality, grounded to a considerable extent in a *craft* knowledge of ideas, routines and conditions, which they map empirically in respect of pupils, time, content, the material environment and teachers themselves (Brown and McIntyre, 1993). Combining paradigms, Nate Gage and Maurice Galton commend the *science of the art* of teaching in which scientific pedagogic principles are applied 'in a flexible manner, according to the characteristics of a particular group of pupils, taking into account the context in which they are working' (Gage 1978; Galton *et al.* 1999).

There is a slight problem here in that 'science' is used in the continental or Latinate sense by Simon but in its more restricted modern sense by Gage, Galton and many others who apply it to education, that is as knowledge and enquiry concerning the material, physical and – in this case – behavioural universe. That usage prompts, almost inevitably, 'teaching as art' as a riposte, and provokes a 'two cultures' collision that doesn't help our cause at all and would have F.R. Leavis turning in his grave.[1] Indeed, it might be suggested that one of the barriers to the development of a science of teaching on the continental model may have been the very Anglo-Saxon belief that if it does not deal in behavioural laws it is not a science, and therefore not pedagogy: hence, perhaps, the undervaluing of the humanistic contribution to teacher education.

Clearly, pedagogy is a somewhat more complex enterprise than may be recognised by those who reduce effective teaching to 'what works', or 'best practice' lessons downloaded from government websites.

THE 2003 PRIMARY NATIONAL STRATEGY

In the light of all this, what can we say about the pedagogy of the Government's 2003 Primary Strategy? I'd like to pick out three aspects – learning, teaching and curriculum – which relate especially to what I have identified as the necessary core of pedagogical discourse, and in as far as it expatiates on these the Primary Strategy qualifies as a pedagogical statement. Before that, however, we need to consider, in light of the paragraphs above, the tone, character and purposes of the document as a whole.

Tone and intention

First there's the soft sell of that title: *Excellence and Enjoyment*. The default vocabulary for education policy since 1997 highlights 'standards . . . driving up standards . . . underperforming . . . failing . . . intervention . . . hard-hitting . . . the challenge ahead . . . step change . . . tough . . . new . . . tough new . . . world class . . . best practice . . . delivery . . .' and so on (DfEE, 2001). 'Enjoyment' sits unconvincingly with this more familiar ministerial machismo, and in the wake of the unrelenting tide of initiatives, targets and public criticism of schools' performance since 1997, a certain amount of professional scepticism towards the geniality or even hedonism of 'enjoyment' might be understandable.

On the question of the character of the new discourse, apart from the fact that it is frequently ungrammatical and offers bizarre constructions such as 'Every LEA will have a Primary Strategy Manager to provide a one-stop shop support service for primary schools' (DfES 2003a: 6) and 'One common complaint about . . . extra funding was that a lot of it came in ring-fenced pots' (DfES 2003a: para. 8.8), the more serious point is that it privileges some kinds of discourse – specifically the pragmatic and political – at the expense of others. Value-positions are pervasive throughout, but few are argued or justified. The report is positively messianic in its confident prefacing of problematic assertions by 'we believe', 'we want', 'we need', and 'we will'. 'What works' and 'best practice' are by the same token presented as givens. And though the report defines an 'excellent primary school leader' as someone who is 'systematic and rigorous in using evidence to inform the development of teaching' (DfES 2003a: para. 6.2), very little evidence is actually cited in the report itself. Instead, the reiterated appeal to experience and common-sense – 'Every teacher knows . . .' (e.g. DfES 2003a: para. 4.1) – and the wilful amnesia in respect of the accumulated findings of published research on learning and teaching, not to mention the ignoring of findings from the government's own inspections, make it clear that the Strategy is about something other than argument and justification.

So what *is* it about? The Strategy's intentions are more opaque and contradictory than at first sight they seem, especially when the document is set alongside other statements of current education policy. Central to the Strategy's message is the avowed commitment to increasing the autonomy of schools and teachers:

> Teachers have the freedom to decide how to teach – the programmes of study state *what* is to be taught but not *how* it is to be taught . . . the National Literacy and Numeracy Strategies, though they are supported strongly, are not statutory . . . Ofsted will recognise and welcome good practice . . . teachers and schools can decide which aspects of a subject pupils will study in depth . . . how long to spend on each subject . . . QCA guidance suggesting how much time should be allocated to each subject is not statutory . . . Our aim is to encourage all schools to . . . take control of their curriculum, and to be innovative . . .
>
> (DfES 2003a: paras 2.4 and 2.8)

And so on. Legally, the claims about what is and is not statutory are correct, but how many teachers will take this as an invitation to reduce the time spent on literacy and numeracy in order to free time for the rest of the curriculum, knowing as they do how much hangs on the next round of literacy and numeracy targets?

In any event, the messages on this matter are decidedly mixed. The Strategy's DfES press release emphasises that 'testing, targets and performance tables are here to stay' (Downing Street 2003). The 'key aim' agreed by the Ministerial Primary Education Programme Board, which oversaw the development of the Strategy was 'to produce a common approach to teaching and learning across the curriculum . . . identifying the key teaching and learning approaches that the [Literacy and Numeracy] strategies have promoted and provide materials and training to help teachers transfer them more widely' (DfES 2002a). Against the ostensible offer of autonomy, we have the continuing pressure of testing, targets and performance tables and the creeping hegemonisation of the curriculum by the Literacy and Numeracy Strategies, with three-part lessons, interactive whole class teaching and plenaries soon to become a template for the teaching of everything.

The summation of the Strategy's doublespeak on professional autonomy comes in Chapter 8, 'Realising the Vision'. Here, quite apart from the hubris of that word 'vision', there is the problem of its juxtaposition with words redolent of a rather different purpose (my italics):

> We have set out our *vision*, but we want it to be a shared *vision* . . . We intend to spread the *dialogue* more widely . . . This document is just the starting point for that vital *dialogue* which will shape the future of primary education . . . This document begins to offer a *blueprint* for the future . . .
>
> (DfES 2003a: paras 8.14–8.17)

Vision? Dialogue? Blueprint? Elsewhere in the report there is less ambiguous talk of 'the project' (DfES 2003a: para. 8.17). How can it be all of these?

Political culture and the rewriting of educational history

Behind this ambiguity of intent – a desire to be seen to be offering freedom while in reality maintaining control – lies a by no means ambiguous view of recent education history and the condition of the teaching profession. Its exponents and guardians are not so much the Primary Education Programme Board that oversaw the writing of the Primary Strategy, or even the Secretary of State, but the Downing Street Policy Unit.

In autumn 2001 I found myself sharing a platform with Michael Barber, formerly director of the DfES Standards and Effectiveness Unit and at that time head of the Prime Minister's Delivery Unit. The occasion was a conference in Moscow attended by Russian academics and Ministry of Education officials at which I spoke about the *Culture and Pedagogy* research, in which Russia features prominently, and Michael Barber gave a glowing account of New Labour's education project/vision/blueprint. He added:

> Until the mid-1980s what happened in schools and classrooms was left almost entirely to teachers to decide . . . Almost all teachers had goodwill and many sought to develop themselves professionally, but, through no fault of their own, the profession itself was uninformed . . . Under Thatcher, the system moved from *uninformed professional judgement* to *uninformed prescription.*
>
> (Barber 2001: 13–14, his italics)

Note how heavily professional ignorance features in this historical pathology, and how it is presented as an inevitable concomitant of professional autonomy. To be free to decide how to teach is to be uninformed. Those who were teaching before 1988 might care to ponder what those sweeping phrases 'the profession itself was uninformed . . . uninformed professional judgement' say about their competence. Members of the Thatcher/Major governments of 1988–97 might even wish to contest the charge of 'uninformed prescription'. Certainly their advisers on QCA's precursor bodies (the National Curriculum Council (NCC), the School Examinations and Assessment Council (SEAC) and the School Curriculum and Assessment Authority (SCAA)) and Ofsted's HMI predecessors could do so. It sets things up nicely, of course, for the transformation achieved by New Labour and for the Utopia that is now in sight:

> The 1997–2001 Blair government inherited a system of *uninformed prescription* and replaced it with one of *informed prescription* . . . The White Paper signals the next shift: from *informed prescription* to *informed professional judgement* . . . The era of informed professional judgement is only just beginning . . . The era of informed professional judgement could be the most successful so far in our educational history . . . It could

be the era in which our education system becomes not just good but great.

(Barber 2001: 13–14, his italics again)[2]

Note the abrupt tonal gear-change, half way through this extract, from narrative to incipient political rant. In similar vein, Barber's Downing Street colleague Andrew Adonis, at that time the Prime Minister's principal Education Adviser and later a minister in DfES/DCSF, in a paper to the international Policy Network, writes of 'the dire situation in England' as New Labour found it in 1997:

For most teachers, professional development has traditionally been haphazard, off-site, barely relevant, poorly provided, and a chore at best.

(Adonis 2001: 14)

(Studying government material prepared for international rather than home consumption can be very illuminating.) I don't need to labour the point: the Barber–Adonis line is as distorted and partisan an account of recent educational history as one is likely to find, yet *realpolitik* dictates that it's the one that counts. Quite apart from its disparaging view of the competence of teachers and the quality of teacher training before 1997, its sweeping dismissal of the period as one of 'uninformed professional judgement' or at best 'uninformed prescription' simply ignores the vast body of information of which many in the education world were acutely aware.

For the record, this information, during Barber's pre-1988 'era of uninformed professional judgement', included:

- HMI reports on individual schools;
- HMI national surveys on primary and secondary education;
- Her Majesty's Senior Chief Inspector of Schools (HMSCI) annual reports;
- official and independent reports on primary, secondary, further, higher and teacher education, and on English, mathematics, the arts and special needs (Newsom, Plowden, Crowther, Robbins, James, CNAA, UCET, Bullock, Cockcroft, Gulbenkian, Warnock);
- HMI and DES/DfE/DfEE documents on the curriculum;
- local evidence on standards of attainment from LEA annual tests administered in all primary schools;
- local authority curriculum schemes and guidelines, and local authority courses for teachers;
- the results of public examinations in secondary schools;
- national evidence on pupil attainment in English, maths and science at the ages of 7, 11 and 15 from the sampled assessment programmes of the Assessment and Performance Unit begun in 1975;
- reports from Commons Education Select Committees;

- curriculum guidance and other materials from the Schools Council and its successors the School Curriculum Development Committee (SCDC), NCC, SEAC and SCAA;
- courses of initial and in-service teacher training and development;
- information provided by professional and subject associations through their in-house courses, journals and other publications;
- the weekly offerings of the educational press;
- published research and other writing on education, some of it arcane but much of it presented so as to be readily accessible to teachers.

Even on the more limited matter of information about *standards* in primary education with which Barber and Adonis are particularly concerned, the 1991–2 enquiry on primary education was able to interrogate six major domains of published data dealing with standards, most of them annual and cumulative: APU tests, LEA tests, NFER tests and surveys, HMI inspections, National Curriculum assessment, and the programme of IEA international achievement studies of which the PIRLS report on reading literacy marks a later example (Alexander *et al.* 1992: paras 24–50; IEA/ISC 2003). That report cited nearly 100 separate sources of published evidence as well as the extensive pre-Ofsted HMI database and research material in the pipeline (Alexander *et al.* 1992: paras 55–62). Uninformed professional judgement? There was, then as now, a positive glut of information.

This being so, it is clear that in the post-2001 era of 'informed professional judgement' to be 'informed' is to know and acquiesce in what is provided, expected and/or required by government and its agencies, no less and, especially, no more. You may be steeped in educational research and/or the accumulated wisdom of 40 years in the classroom, but unless you defer to all this official material your professional judgements will be 'uninformed'. As Adonis says in his Policy Network paper, writing of university faculties and departments of education:

> We have *imposed* a new national curriculum for initial teacher training, setting out the standards and content of training courses, which all providers *must* follow.
>
> (Adonis 2001: 14, my italics, his verbs)

Not much room for alternative professional judgement there; and little evidence of government relaxing the iron grip of educational centralisation. If you teach, or train teachers, on the basis of other kinds of knowledge you are uninformed. For 'informed professional judgement', then, read 'political compliance'.

Excellence and Enjoyment holds to this view. It shows little awareness of evidence from outside the charmed circle of government and its agencies; and no awareness of what even previous governments and government agencies did before 1997, the year in which, apparently, history and real education began. Political analysts might suggest that rewriting history has become a habitual device of government, especially within adversarial political systems such as ours, and we should therefore not be surprised at its use in a high-stakes policy field such as education (Alexander 1998a). New Labour can also claim, rightly, that their Conservative predecessors were no slouches when it came to mythologising the past, scapegoating professionals and demonising doubters (Alexander 1997a: 183–287; Galton *et al.* 1999: 10–38); and Berliner, Biddle and Nichols have documented, tellingly and in detail, the same process at work in the US from the Reagan era onwards (Berliner and Biddle 1995; Nichols and Berliner 2007). Interestingly, the terms that commentators use to connote this process – 'myth', 'mythologise', and now 'spin' – somehow manage to render it benign and even acceptable. Few are prepared to call claims like those cited above what they really are: lies.

The failure of *Excellence and Enjoyment* in this regard is one of omission. It does not so much rewrite history as ignore it. But in so doing, it tacitly performs its own act of compliance to the Downing Street line: the same line, in fact, that produced the prime ministerial assault on comprehensive education in September 2000 whose mendacity was so scathingly exposed in one of Brian Simon's last articles (Simon, 2000).

Learning

The striking feature of the Strategy's account of learning is its insistence on *individualisation*, or what New Labour called 'personalisation':

> Learning must be focused on individual pupils' needs and abilities . . .
> Every teacher knows that truly effective learning focuses on individual children . . . The new Primary Strategy will actively support more tailoring of teaching to individuals . . . Workforce reform will . . . be critical to helping teachers focus on individual children's needs . . .
> Increasing the focus on individual children will serve every child.
> (DfES 2003a: 39 and paras 4.1–4.5)

In fact, the chapter is not about learning at all, but *social inclusion*, which in itself is a proper and urgent concern, and having trumpeted the importance of individualisation the report then goes on to talk about the needs of specific *groups*: children with special needs; children from minority ethnic backgrounds; the gifted and talented – for which, apparently, in that inimitable Ofsted prose, provision is 'now good or better in almost half of primary schools and satisfactory or better in some 90 per cent of primary schools' (DfES 2003a: para. 4.8).

Interestingly, though, gender is not included in this list, even though David Hopkins, DfES Standards Director, blamed boys for the nation's failure to meet the 80 per cent literacy target in the 2002 KS2 tests, and Schools Minister David Miliband said that schools and society should tackle the 'laddish culture' in order to motivate boys to do well in school (DfES 2002b).

Yet that heavy emphasis on personalisation, and the promise of support for individualised teaching, throws up problematic messages. That children are individuals is self-evident, but how far can this truism be applied in the context of other than one-to-one and small group teaching? The Strategy's authors chose to ignore the classroom research of the 1980s, including major projects from Leicester, London, Exeter and Leeds universities, which showed the limits to fully individualised teaching in classes of 20, 25 and 30 or more children (Galton and Simon 1980; Bennett *et al.* 1984; Mortimore *et al.* 1988; Alexander 1997a). They ignored the subsequent international research, including that reviewed for Ofsted by Reynolds and Farrell (1996), which drew attention to the way teaching in many continental and Asian countries respects individuality yet structures learning tasks on the basis of what children have in common and tries, as far as possible, to bring all the children in a class along together, thus reducing the wide range of attainment and the long attainment 'tail' that has for long been such a prominent feature of English primary classrooms. Most surprisingly, they ignored one of the central contentions of the government's own Literacy and Numeracy Strategies, that treating learning as a *collective* process, notably through interactive whole class teaching, actually benefits individuals.

More fundamentally, the Strategy's account of learning – such as it is, for the document specifies *conditions* for learning but not its character or process – bypasses the shift in learning theory from what Bruner (1996) calls an 'intrapsychic' view, which conceives of the child as a 'lone scientist' to a psycho-cultural account, which emphasises the necessarily social and interactive character of early learning, and argues the case for inter-subjectivity as essential to cultural socialisation. And, hardly surprisingly, there's no mention either of the implications for school learning of recent advances in neuroscience. Had any of this been within the strategists' consciousness they would not have confined their consideration of the importance of talk in learning to one brief and passing mention of National Curriculum English Attainment Target 1, speaking and listening (DfES 2003a: 28).

The section of the report that purportedly deals with learning is also notable for the way it removes any remaining ambiguities about whether the Strategy offers freedom or constraint: 'Learning *must* be focused on individual pupils' needs and abilities' (DfES 2003a: 39). Further:

We have developed a model of intervention for children experiencing difficulties in literacy or mathematics, based on three waves:

Wave One: the effective inclusion of all pupils in a high quality, daily literacy hour and mathematics lesson (Quality First Teaching).

Wave Two: small group, low-cost intervention – for example, booster classes, springboard programmes, or other programmes linked to the National Strategies.

Wave Three: specific targeted intervention for pupils identified as requiring special educational needs support.

(DfES 2003a: para. 4.6)

So prescription it is then, after all: obligatory personalisation, a 'three wave' model of intervention, and – though they are supposed to be non-statutory – the National Literacy Hour and Numeracy Lesson for every child in the land. Almost submerged in the mire of contradiction and confusion here, or overwhelmed by the Three Waves, is one of the biggest contradictions of all: if the 'model of intervention' is for just one group of children – those experiencing learning difficulties – why is it imposed upon all the others?

Insidiously, the report seeks to legitimate or disguise its impoverished reasoning on learning by peppering this section with populist phrases like 'Every teacher knows that truly effective learning and teaching focuses [*sic*] on individual children' and 'Most schools already use assessment for learning' (DfES 2003a: paras 4.1, 4.2). Do they really? Not according to the King's assessment for learning research (Black and Wiliam 1998).

Teaching

Though the Primary Strategy's view of learning unnervingly contradicts the Literacy and Numeracy Strategies while yet endorsing them, in the chapter on *teaching* the two Strategies are more securely in the saddle:

The Literacy and Numeracy Strategies have, according to all those who have evaluated them, been strikingly successful at improving the quality of teaching and raising standards in primary schools. But we need to embed the lessons of the Literacy and Numeracy Strategies more deeply . . . In the best schools, teachers are using their understanding of the principles behind the literacy and numeracy strategies . . . *We want a new approach that will help more schools and teachers to . . . apply the principles of good learning and teaching across the whole curriculum.*

(DfES 2003a: paras 3.2–3.5, my italics)

So at last we come to some *principles*. But would Brian Simon be happy with those that are listed in the report's box headed 'The principles of learning and teaching'? It instructs us that:

Good learning and teaching should

- *Ensure that every child succeeds:* provide an inclusive education within a culture of high expectations.
- *Build on what learners already know:* structure and pace teaching so that students know what is to be learnt, how and why.
- *Make learning vivid and real*: develop understanding through enquiry, creativity, e-learning and group problem-solving.
- *Make learning an enjoyable experience:* stimulate learning through matching teaching techniques and strategies to a range of learning styles.
- *Enrich the learning experience:* build learning skills across the curriculum.
- *Promote assessment for learning:* make children partners in their learning.

(DfES 2003a: 29)

Does this mean anything? Precious little, I submit. We would do better to go back to Comenius in 1657, whose ideas on pedagogical structure and pace are far in advance of those in the Primary Strategy (Keatinge 1896). If that seems obscurantist we could certainly with profit revisit more recent classic pedagogic specifications such as Lawrence Stenhouse's curricular 'principles of procedure' or Jerome Bruner's 'theory of instruction' (Stenhouse 1975; Bruner 1966). In contrast, most of the items above are aspirations obvious to the point of banality: of course we want every child to succeed, to build on what learners know, to make learning vivid, real and enjoyable. How many teachers, though, will read this list, experience a Eureka flash of recognition and thank the Government for a profound and novel insight of lasting practical value? The only item here that has a recognisable empirical basis is the final one, which hints at the important ideas about assessment for learning and its implications for classroom talk that have come from Paul Black and his colleagues in the London King's group (Black and Wiliam 1999; Black *et al.* 2002). Values are central to pedagogy but, as I argued earlier, on their own they cannot define its operational procedures.

Apart from being of dubious provenance, the Strategy's 'principles' also contain more than their fair share of non-sequiturs. What is the connection between building on what learners know, structuring and pacing teaching, and ensuring that students know what is to be learned; or between enjoyment and matching teaching techniques to learning styles? Apart from that, what *is* a 'learning style', and what indeed is a 'learning skill'? Better to define them, for 'learning skills' in particular are liberally scattered across the entire document.

It could be argued that the virtue of so bland a specification is that it makes positive and encouraging noises about the general spirit of pedagogy while leaving teachers free to devise their own more meaningful principles of pedagogic procedure. But if principles have so little purchase on practice, what, really, is their point?

The more contentious the Strategy's claims, the more authoritatively they are expressed. The Strategy's prescription for the future character of primary teaching, quoted above, is predicated on the assertion that (my italics) 'The Literacy and Numeracy Strategies have, *according to all who have evaluated them*, been strikingly successful at improving the quality of teaching and raising standards in primary schools' (DfES 2003a: para. 3.2). That claim, I am afraid, is also open to question. If the Ontario Institute for Studies in Education (OISE, University of Toronto) evaluation commissioned by DfES delivers qualified approval for the Literacy and Numeracy Strategies – 'There is considerable evidence . . . that teaching has improved substantially since the Strategies were first introduced' (Earl *et al.* 2003: 3) – it also warns that 'the intended changes in teaching and learning have not yet been fully realised' (ibid.: 8) and, more critical still for those who would use the Strategies as the template for teaching across the entire primary curriculum, it admits that 'it is difficult to draw conclusions about the effect of the Strategies on pupil learning' (ibid.: 3).

Perhaps, in claiming a ringing research endorsement for the Literacy and Numeracy Strategies DfES wasn't referring to the official NLNS evaluation at all, but to other studies, though it did say 'according to *all* who have evaluated' the strategies, not 'some'. But I'm afraid that this 'all' looks more and more shaky. Quite apart from the ambivalence of the OISE evaluation itself and the methodological questions about that evaluation which Harvey Goldstein (2000) has raised, Margaret Brown's five-year longitudinal study of numeracy teaching and attainment has concluded pretty devastatingly that the Numeracy Strategy 'has had at most a small effect on attainment in most areas of numeracy' (Brown *et al.* 2003a). A similar point is made by Sig Prais, whose no less devastating (though contested) critique of the methodology of the PISA survey of the educational attainment of 15-year-olds shows how that study produced upward bias in English students' mathematical test scores to the extent of compromising their high ranking relative to other countries and, hence, government claims that this ranking shows the beneficial effects of government policy (Prais 2003; Adams 2003; OECD 2005a).

Other studies – by Janet Moyles, Linda Hargreaves, Frank Hardman, David Skidmore and indeed my own – have looked closely at the pupil–teacher interaction on which a large part of the success of the strategies is intended and claimed to rest, and have found that while teaching methods, patterns of classroom organisation and the handling of time, space and resources have changed considerably in literacy and numeracy lessons, practice below the structural surface has changed rather less. Pupil–teacher interaction is still dominated by closed questions, brief answers that teachers do not build upon, phatic praise rather than diagnostic feedback, and an emphasis on recalling information rather than on speculating and problem-solving (Alexander 2001a: 474–90; English *et al.* 2002; Skidmore 2002; Hardman *et al.* 2003; Moyles *et al.* 2003; Smith *et al.* 2004; Alexander 2006b).

These findings confirm those from earlier research, including the CICADA study that compared pupil–teacher discourse before and after the arrival of the National Curriculum, and the ORACLE follow-up project (Alexander *et al.* 1996; Galton *et al.* 1999). Moreover, the Literacy and Numeracy Strategy directors themselves have acknowledged this: the absence of change at those deeper levels of classroom discourse that can impact so powerfully on children's learning is the main reason why in 2002 they and QCA commissioned materials to support 'teaching through dialogue' (later abandoned). It is why QCA belatedly turned its attention to that neglected attainment target En1, Speaking and Listening (QCA 2003; QCA/DfES 2003a, 2003b). And it is why local authorities such as Barking and Dagenham and North Yorkshire launched programmes to transform classroom talk in order, they hoped, to lift tested literacy standards off the 'plateau' on which, in 2001, they had stalled. No mention of any of this, of course, in the Primary Strategy: there, speaking and listening rate just one brief reference, as I have noted.

In fact, against the Strategy's confident claim that every evaluation of NLNS has endorsed its success in transforming teaching and raising standards, it's hard to find even *one* study that actually provides such an endorsement. Perhaps the Primary Strategy's authors had in mind the annual Ofsted Literacy and Numeracy Strategy evaluations. These are certainly very positive, though they are not so much evaluations as checks on compliance with the teaching changes – whole class teaching, three-part lessons, plenaries, the use of big books, writing frames and approved assessment materials, and so on – which the strategies require (Ofsted 2002a, 2002b). Consider, for example, Ofsted's finger-wagging 'not all teachers are using the strategy's assessment materials . . . some do not know about them' (Ofsted 2002b: para. 93). However, such renegades apart, schools are indeed toeing the line:

> The Literacy and Numeracy Strategies were centrally conceived and directed, and our data suggest that schools have generally been inclined to acquiesce to, and approve of, such direction. *Such compliance bodes well for implementing the Strategies.*
>
> (Earl *et al.* 2001: xii, my italics)

But compliance with something believed to be admirable does not guarantee that it is. Would the evaluation report's Canadian authors be so sanguine about professional capitulation to central government prescription in their own country if such prescription were as insecure evidentially as the Primary Strategy? 'Compliance bodes well for implementing the Strategies' might perhaps be offered as an alternative motto to that bulwark of academic freedom and open-minded enquiry, the University of Toronto.

Less waspishly, one might note that a culture of compliance reinforces policies and practices, good or bad, but it cannot *test* them. As if to underline this fatal flaw, the Ofsted evaluation of the first four years of the Literacy Strategy heads its list of 'improvements' produced by the NLS with 'widespread use of the NLS framework for teaching' (Ofsted 2002a: para. 149). So school improvement is measured by the extent to which teachers use the prescribed frameworks, not by whether teaching and learning improve. Compliance is ultimately tautologous.

In similar vein, though it claimed that the Literacy Strategy was firmly based on national and international evidence, DfES took the extraordinary step, *after* the Strategy had been implemented, of commissioning an academic, Roger Beard of Leeds University, to discover what that evidence might be (Beard 1998).

Curriculum

And so to the Strategy's pronouncements on the primary curriculum. In 1984 I suggested that one of the abiding legacies of the elementary education system was that we had not one primary curriculum but two, the 'basics' and the rest. That is to say, a high status, protected and heavily assessed 3Rs 'Curriculum I', which was justified by reference to utilitarian values, and a low priority, unassessed, vulnerable and even dispensable 'Curriculum II' of the arts and humanities, which was justified by high-sounding but ultimately empty notions of a 'rounded' or 'balanced' education (Alexander 1984). The 1988 National Curriculum simply translated the Curriculum I/II divide into the vocabulary and attendant values of 'core' and 'other foundation' subjects, and over the ensuing years successive governments ensured that the whole became more and more difficult to handle by avoiding the radical re-assessment of the Victorian formula of 'basics plus trimmings' that a twenty-first-century curriculum required and simply bolting on more and more – science, ICT, design and technology, citizenship, PSHE, a modern foreign language – all the time insisting that the time for Curriculum I – at least 50 per cent of the week – was sacrosanct, so the ever-expanding range of other subjects were forced to compete, and settle, for less and less.

The depressing logic of this situation is now all too clear. At the start of the 1997 National Curriculum review I argued that we had a chance to tackle this problem and subject the primary curriculum to a principled review based on fundamental questions about the kind of world we now inhabit, the much-changed character of this country's economic and social life, and the consequent needs and rights of children, now and as adults (Alexander 1997b). Instead, the Government insisted that there should be minimal change to the curriculum because nothing must deflect teachers' attention from the 2002 literacy and numeracy targets. In January 1998, the Government underlined that message by removing primary schools' obligation to teach the specified content of the non-core subjects (DfEE 1998b). Subsequently, as Ofsted reports and indeed the OISE NLNS evaluation showed, many schools all but gave up on the original 1988 National Curriculum notion of children's absolute entitlement to a genuinely broad curriculum in which the arts and humanities are treated with no less seriousness – even if with rather less time – than literacy and numeracy (Ofsted 2002a, 2002c, 2003a; Earl *et al.* 2003).

The Primary Strategy does nothing to alleviate the problem. True, it talks of 'children's entitlement to a rich, broad and balanced set of learning experiences' (DfES 2003a: para. 3.1), but by ring-fencing the Literacy and Numeracy Strategies it ensures that the listed Curriculum II initiatives – creativity, the languages strategy, the PE and sport strategy, music – though separately admirable, will in conjunction have a hard time of it. Especially so, since the Primary Strategy proposes at one and the same time to 'widen the scope and range of the curriculum', and to 'reduce the curriculum to make it more manageable' (DfES 2002a). From so elementary a logistical contradiction there can be scant grounds for hope.

The problem manifests itself in logistical terms certainly, but fundamentally it's one of *values*. In a 'strategy' called 'Excellence and Enjoyment' it is made very clear that the 3Rs provide the excellence and the rest delivers the enjoyment: Curriculum I and II yet again. Elsewhere 'standards' are opposed to 'enrichment', even to curriculum itself.

The division is firmly institutionalised, too. In 1997, as a Board member of QCA in deputation to DfEE, I asked the then Minister of State why the Literacy and Numeracy Strategies were run by the Department and the rest of the curriculum by QCA, when the new body had been set up expressly to bring coherence to the hitherto fragmented worlds of curriculum, assessment and qualifications. 'Ah, but Minister' one of her aides smoothly interjected, 'literacy and numeracy aren't curriculum, they're *standards*, and standards are the Department's responsibility, not QCA's.'

Literacy is 'standards, not curriculum': ponder, for a moment, this brutal dismissal of the civilising ideals of universal literacy and of the efforts of the many who have fought for them.

In his Policy Network Paper, Andrew Adonis confirms this revealing perception: 'the raising of literacy and numeracy standards . . . is now a *self-contained* mission in its own right' (Adonis 2001: 9) – and elsewhere in the system the continuing Curriculum I/II gulf, and the sense that all that really matters at the primary stage is literacy and numeracy 'standards', plus perhaps the 'modernising' subjects of science and ICT, is strongly reinforced. Thus TTA requires newly qualified teachers to 'know and understand the curriculum for each of the National Curriculum core subjects, and the frameworks, methods and expectations set out in the National Literacy and Numeracy Strategies', but merely to 'have sufficient understanding of a range of work' (whatever that means) in the rest, including history *or* geography but – bizarrely – not both (DfES/TTA 2002: 7). Ofsted full primary teacher training inspections concentrate on 'English, mathematics and, when at all possible, science' but sample the rest on the basis of what happens to be available, while the short inspections don't even require that (Ofsted 2002d). The 2003 Ofsted school inspection framework is no less casual in its approach to Curriculum II: English, mathematics, science and ICT *must* be inspected, and in depth, but for the rest the requirement is simply, in Ofsted's words 'work seen in other subjects' (Ofsted 2003b: 8).

There's little evidence, then, that the new-found commitment to breadth and balance in the primary curriculum is serious. Were it so, teacher training and inspection requirements would reinforce rather than undermine it, and the entire curriculum enterprise would be co-ordinated by a single agency, rather than be split between QCA and DfES. (If, that is, it is really necessary for the curriculum to be centrally controlled as well as prescribed – but that's another story.)

But all is not lost, for in 2002 Ofsted discovered a link between breadth, balance and standards, and it is chiefly this that has fuelled the change in the government's curriculum rhetoric: this, and the need to be seen to respond positively to the increasing pressure from the arts and sports lobbies. Ofsted found that of the 3,508 primary schools inspected in 2000–1, just 206, or under 6 per cent, achieved both high test scores in English and mathematics *and* consistently excellent teaching and learning across the full range of the National Curriculum. They argued, commendably, that contrary to popular opinion the National Curriculum *is* manageable, and, crucially, that it was the breadth and richness of the curriculum that helped secure the quality of teaching and learning in literacy and numeracy in these schools, and – conversely – that the wider curriculum gave children and teachers a meaningful context in which to apply, reinforce and extend 'the basics' (Ofsted 2002c).

But of course we knew this already. The famous 1978 HMI survey of primary schools, of which – as of so many other key pieces of historical evidence – the Primary Strategists seem unaware, reported that the schools which performed best in the basics invariably did so in the context of a broad curriculum encompassing work in the arts and humanities that was well planned and taught (DES 1978). Then, in 1996, the Conservative government asked Ofsted to examine the relationship between the 1996 KS2 SAT results and curriculum breadth, posing the particular question 'Had schools which did well in the 1996 tests done so at the expense of curriculum breadth and diversity?'

The answer was a resounding 'No', and this time Ofsted showed that the earlier basics–breadth correlation held across *all* primary schools:

> Schools which did well in the tests also provided a broad and balanced curriculum . . . Schools awarded a high grade for curriculum balance and breadth score well in the tests and those awarded lower grades score less well. This trend persists across all schools analysed, regardless of their context.
>
> (Ofsted / DfEE 1997: paras 2 and 7)

The report's publication coincided with the arrival of New Labour, the Literacy and Numeracy Strategies and the attendant targets for 2002: 75 per cent of 11-year-olds to reach Level 4 in mathematics, 80 per cent in English. Like the 1978 HMI primary survey the 1997 Ofsted report confirmed what commonsense dictated: you cannot successfully teach literacy and numeracy in a curriculum vacuum.

However, New Labour were convinced that the rest of the curriculum was a distraction from the targets (and, possibly, a threat to the position of the Secretary of State, who had said that he would resign if the targets were not met). The government ignored the Ofsted report and pushed ahead with its decision to free schools from the obligation to teach the programmes of study of the non-core subjects. Ofsted did not press the point. The report was not publicised. It was an example of burying bad news of which Jo Moore would have been proud.[3] Except that the news was good – or, to be precise, good educationally but bad politically.[4] With that recent history in mind, with the Literacy and Numeracy Strategies firmly in place, and with a continuing commitment to targets, albeit managed differently, who can possibly believe the Primary Strategy's avowed commitment to 'a rich, broad and balanced set of learning experiences?' (DfES, 2003a: para. 3.1).

Do we still need to argue that education is meaningless without the arts and humanities, and without a more generous concept of the teaching of English than basic reading and writing competence alone, or – as persuasively argued by Rowan Williams (2000) – a more coherent approach to moral education? The demeaning reduction of these to 'enjoyment' and 'enrich-ment', and the readiness of the Government to sacrifice them on the altar of 'standards' (as opposed to standards) signals that they remain insecure.

There are two further failures on the Primary Strategy's curriculum front. The first and most obvious is the total absence of real vision about the future of the primary curriculum, a deficiency for which the report's heavy reiteration of the word 'vision' provides no more than a tattered figleaf. Nor does the National Curriculum offer very much more. The published goals of the version that remains in force as this book goes to press (DfEE/QCA 1999: 11–12) are an extraordinary ragbag of values which, if they were deliverable, would secure a nation of men and women at once dynamic, entrepreneurial, athletic, ruthless, successful, rich, multi-skilled, possessed of encyclopaedic knowledge, humane, compassionate, modest, religious, tolerant, cultured, ascetic – and thoroughly confused about their identity. They are what you get if you handle the demands of large numbers of interest groups by adding each one to a lengthening list without attempting to establish whether they are compatible.

The second failure is to come to terms with the managerial implications of a broad and complex curriculum. The Primary Strategy has a chapter entitled 'Workforce reform' that essentially seeks to sell the Government's policy on classroom assistants (DfES 2003a: Ch. 7). The more necessary workforce reform was argued in the 1986 Select Committee report on primary education, which said that the demands of a modern curriculum could not reasonably be met by schools staffed on the basis of one generalist class teacher per class. The Committee secured the agreement of the then Secretary of State, Keith Joseph, for 15,000 extra teachers to inject curriculum flexibility into England's 20,000 primary schools (House of Commons 1986). The agreement was not implemented.

The so-called 'three wise men' report of 1992 took this argument forward, commending a broader repertoire of teaching roles in primary schools ranging from generalists through consultants and semi-specialists to specialists, to enable the full curriculum to be adequately managed and taught, and insisted that to allow schools the necessary staffing flexibility the long-established primary–secondary funding differential must be challenged (Alexander et al. 1992: paras 139–50). That idea didn't get far, partly because it had resource implications that the Commons Education Committee investigated but which the then government passed smartly to the LEAs (House of Commons 1994a, 1994b); partly because many primary teachers – wrongly – saw it as a threat to the class teacher system; and partly because secondary heads, in turn, thought that the money would be taken from them. Then during the 1980s and 1990s there were numerous attempts to find ways of maximising the impact of teachers' specialist subject strengths, within a framework of roles variously called 'curriculum co-ordinator', 'consultant', 'adviser', 'subject leader' and 'curriculum manager'.

The Primary Strategy's chapter 'Leadership in primary schools' talks about leadership in highly generalised terms, focusing on heads and the novelties of 'consultant leaders' and a 'leading practice' programme, but in a way that is utterly divorced from the day-to-day demands of the curriculum. Again, of all the debates about curriculum management of the past 20 years, including major national enquiries, it seems utterly unaware. (For an account of these, see Alexander 1998b: 6–13.)

Meanwhile, it has been hard to escape the conclusion that the erosion of curriculum breadth over the past few years has been a consequence of a persistent refusal by successive governments to grasp the managerial and resource implications of a curriculum that has outgrown the elementary model of 'basics plus trimmings' for which the Victorian class teacher system was just about adequate. The government's 1998 decision to make the non-core subjects effectively optional, and the sad fate of these subjects in many schools once the Literacy and Numeracy Strategies were introduced, suggest that the curriculum has been used as the safety valve, as a way of side-stepping the true 'workforce reform' that primary schools needed. Judged in strictly educational terms, the 1998 decision looks at best ill-informed and at worst – since government was warned of its likely consequences – cynical. The doctrine of 'cheap but efficient', one century on, has resolved the growing mismatch between educational task and professional resources by trimming the education rather than re-assessing the resources. This nettle the Primary Strategy has, in its turn, failed to grasp. Teaching assistants may be useful, but in the context of children's statutory curriculum entitlement they are no substitute for a staffing policy that provides each primary school with a team of professionals who between them have the range and depth of subject knowledge to do full justice to every aspect of the curriculum for every child, and the flexibility to deploy such knowledge as required.

Conclusion

In as far as it offers perspectives on learning, teaching, curriculum, assessment and school management – all of them major themes from my first two domains of pedagogical discourse – and links these to the pursuit of national educational goals, the Primary Strategy manifesto *Excellence and Enjoyment* certainly qualifies as a pedagogical statement. Given its belief that it can harness enjoyable means to achieve excellent ends, it is properly ambitious. Because it comes from Government it must be taken seriously.

Between May and November 2003, and again from January 2004, DfES organised conferences for primary heads, teachers and 'consultant leaders' at which ministers and officials, ostensibly in consultative mode, discussed how the Primary Strategy and its 'vision' were to be taken forward. In rather different mode, the published job specification of the man charged with overseeing this process, the newly appointed Primary Strategy

Director, pinned him not to the Strategy's hope of a curriculum enshrining excellence, enjoyment, breadth and balance, but to the narrower objective of embedding the Literacy and Numeracy Strategies, meeting the national targets for English and Mathematics and ensuring continuity with the KS3 Strategy (DfES 2002c). This task was subcontracted as a commercial operation to the Centre for British Teachers (CfBT) whose job it was, in DfES's words, to 'deliver the Strategy'. In 2006, another commercial firm, Capita, took over.

This more instrumental remit rather undermines the rhetoric of consultation and freedom that is being used to sell the Strategy to teachers, especially when what is to be 'delivered' is so fundamentally deficient. About all but the narrowest range of evidence concerning the impact of recent policies on primary education, *Excellence and Enjoyment* displays amiable ignorance, and such evidence as it does cite – for example that relating to the impact of the National Literacy and Numeracy Strategies – it is not above bending to suit its larger political purposes. As for the wider evidence and debate about children, learning, teaching, curriculum and culture – in which, I have suggested, even a minimal pedagogy should be grounded – a few insouciant platitudes masquerading as 'principles' are as close as we get. These, secondary school colleagues may care to note, have been replicated in a policy for the entire school system, not just primary schools (DfES 2003b).

Excellence and Enjoyment manifests a lamentable detachment from questions of identity and culture (my vital third domain of pedagogical discourse), a studied ignorance about the state of education before 1997, and a crude instrumentalism of purpose that is in no way disguised by the rhetoric of 'enjoyment' and 'enrichment'. The Strategy is ambiguous to the point of dishonesty about the Government's true intentions towards primary education. It fails to observe that most essential condition for the growth of knowledge and understanding and the improvement of the human condition, by which researchers in all disciplines are bound absolutely – *cumulation*; knowing what has gone before, learning from it, evaluating it, building on it. By ignoring this condition, the Primary Strategy not only ensures that much of what it offers is open to challenge; it also perpetuates rather than resolves some of the most deeply seated problems of English primary education, notably in the areas of curriculum and curriculum management. It also subverts its own avowed intentions, for such a stance is deeply at odds with what education should be about.

In all these matters, as in the wider spectrum of public policy in recent years, that 'destruction of the past' which so concerned Eric Hobsbawm in his assessment of contemporary British consciousness (Hobsbawm 1995: 3), seems to be a conscious political act rather than an unfortunate casualty of laudable political ambition. For, as I have illustrated, this 'Strategy' is caught in the Downing Street web of instinctive spin – not just of the policy of the moment but of history itself.

More obviously, *Excellence and Enjoyment* is badly written, poorly argued and deeply patronising in its assumption that teachers will be seduced by Ladybird language, pretty pictures, offers of freedom and enjoyment, and populist appeals to their common sense. There is no case, no argument, some fragments of a strategy, but certainly no vision. Meanwhile, 150 local authorities have dutifully appointed their primary strategy directors. If they value their Ofsted inspection ratings they cannot do otherwise.

And what, a quarter of a century on, of Brian Simon's 'Why no pedagogy?' Pedagogical research has progressed considerably since then, and in the cumulative body of scholarship and evidence about children, learning, teaching and culture that the Primary Strategy has chosen to ignore, not to mention the collective experience of the teachers it claims to respect, I would submit that we have had for some time both an ample basis for a coherent and principled pedagogy and a viable alternative to the pseudo-pedagogy of the Primary Strategy.

Government though, listening only to those who are on its payroll or who speak its language, believes it knows better. Under our now highly centralised and interventionist education system those who have the greatest power to prescribe pedagogy seem to display the poorest under-standing of it, and the discourse becomes mired in the habitual bombast, mendacity and spin of policyspeak. The pedagogy of principle has yet to be rescued from the pedagogy of pragmatism and compliance.

POSTSCRIPT: WHAT PRICE EVIDENCE-BASED POLICY AND PRACTICE?

This chapter started as an open lecture in the Cambridge University Faculty of Education 2003 Research Lecture series and in that form, especially following somewhat sensationalising press coverage (e.g. Ward 2003) it was widely disseminated. It was then revised for publication (Alexander 2004a). Among the resulting responses, three are particularly relevant to the case I have tried to make.

First, my charges about the Strategy's approach to evidence provoked from the DfES Standards and Effectiveness Unit a counter-claim that *Excellence and Enjoyment* was 'based on the latest evaluation and research evidence', and that the National Literacy and Numeracy Strategies 'were based firmly on research evidence ... which is one of the main reasons why ... they have been successful in raising standards and improving the quality of teaching and learning' (Hopkins 2003). Second, however, Margaret Brown's analysis of the evidential basis of the National Numeracy Strategy casts further doubt on the sustainability of such claims (Brown *et al.* 2003b). Third, DfES hastily sought to plug some of the more obvious gaps in the Strategy's prospectus of pedagogical reform, notably in respect of the role and quality of classroom talk. As we have seen, *Excellence and Enjoyment* mentions talk but once, and that very briefly (DfES 2003a: para. 3.3). However – perhaps stung by criticism on this score – DfES later claimed that the improvement of talk was central to the Primary Strategy. It wrote 'speaking and listening' prominently into its Strategy training materials for the autumn and spring terms of 2003–4 (e.g. DfES 2003c; DfES/QCA 2003) and built on this work subsequently (DfES 2004) as did, even more prominently, the Secondary Strategy (DfES 2005). In doing so, it called in some of the emerging work on dialogic teaching, sometimes getting it seriously wrong:

> Thus the *Speaking, Listening, Learning* handbook, adopting the usual DfES practice – though no less reprehensible for that – of lifting chunks of text from elsewhere without acknowledgement, quotes this author's definition of dialogic teaching in its glossary, scatters 'dialogue' and 'dialogic' through the text, but takes the idea no further than that.[5] The accompanying book of classroom activities introduces 'ground rules for dialogue' only in Year 4, term 1 (why not earlier?), then offers nothing more until Year 6, term 3, at which point 'techniques of dialogic talk' are exemplified by reference not to dialogue at all, but to 'formal language and spoken standard English.'[6] DfES and QCA, it would seem, have missed the point pretty spectacularly.
>
> (Alexander 2006a: 18)

This kind of reactive or opportunistic appropriation not only smacks of control freakery but also calls further into question the government's much-vaunted principle of 'evidence-based' policy and practice, which surely implies a process that is much more considered and critical than that. The evidence about the centrality of talk to learning and teaching is so strong and pervasive that it required an almost wilful disdain for research to miss it. Perhaps 'policy-based evidence' is what government is really interested in.

In truth, if DfES seems ambivalent about where it stands on this matter, Downing Street is not. David Hopkins' endorsement of the research connnection, cited above, contrasts with the dismissive claim of Tony Wright, Blairite Chair of the Commons Public Administration Committee that 'the National Literacy Strategy and the National Numeracy Strategy were both undisputed successes which produced extraordinary results without the involvement of academics, and if they had waited for academics to produce this policy it would have taken four years' (quoted in Brown *et al.* 2003b: 655). In the same way that the Barber/Adonis Downing Street line on professional development invalidates the teacher-friendly rhetoric emanating from DfES/DCSF, so the outright rejection of academic research by prime-ministerial appointee Wright undermines the department's avowed respect for evidence. Such developments confirm the continuing hegemony of the culture of pragmatism and compliance.

NOTES

1   The reference is to F.R. Leavis's famous attack on C.P. Snow's musings on the gulf between the sciences and the humanities in modern Britain and the limited value (in Snow's eyes) of the latter. Leavis's ferocity was first unleashed in 1962 at a Richmond lecture in Downing College, Cambridge (reprinted in Leavis 1972), which I attended and vividly remember. See Chapter 7.

2   The final sentence appeared in the 2002/2003 versions of Barber's paper but was not uttered in Moscow. There, in fact, his claims were greeted with considerable scepticism by those whose memories of the language and reality of Soviet power were still vivid. They understood about airbrushing fallen heroes from history. But this was airbrushing history itself.

3   Jo Moore was the ministerial advisor in the Department of Transport who on 11 September 2001 – the infamous 9/11 – emailed her departmental colleagues: 'It's now a very good day to get out anything we want to bury.'

4   For a detailed account of this episode, see my evidence to the 1998 Commons Education Committee enquiry into the work of Ofsted (House of Commons 1999: 144–54).

5   QCA/DfES (2003a).

6   QCA/DfES (2003b: 9 and 11).

Chapter 4

Beyond dichotomous pedagogies

One cold and dank March morning during the late 1990s, I came across this pedagogical manifesto on the wall of a Michigan elementary school classroom:

> Important issues to me –
>
> - Process orientation vs product orientation
> - Teaching students vs teaching programs
> - Teacher as facilitator vs teacher as manager
> - Developing a set of strategies vs mastering a set of skills
> - Celebrating approximation vs celebrating perfection
> - Respecting individual growth vs fostering competition
> - Capitalizing on student's strengths vs emphasising student's weaknesses
> - Promoting independence in learning vs dependence on the teacher.

This was the American mid-west – we were collecting data for the five-nation *Culture and Pedagogy* project at the time – but it could as well have come from an English primary classroom during the 1960s–80s heyday of what in the US was celebrated as 'open education'.

I was reminded of this manifesto when, several years later, I was invited to contribute to an AERA symposium on 'Getting beyond dichotomous notions of inquiry vs didactic instruction'. This somewhat ponderous title signalled a tendency that in Britain and the US remains real, familiar and deeply seated: the reduction of complex educational debates to bipolar slogans cast in a state of permanent and irreconcilable opposition. In fact, the particular pairings above are enjoying a revival in England at present, perhaps encouraged by the apparent weakening of the hold of what is disparagingly called 'the traditional curriculum' as government and its agencies strive 'to promote a world-class curriculum fit for the 21st century' (QCA 2007: 7), whatever that means.

I had tracked some of this during the 1980s (Alexander 1984) at a time when 'the child' was invariably placed at one pole and pretty well everything else, but most notably 'subjects', 'curriculum' and 'society', was securely corralled at the other, and woe betide anyone who dared to suggest that such segregation was undesirable or untenable. I also recalled Israel Scheffler's brilliant deconstruction of the slogans, shibboleths and metaphors that saturate this kind of discourse (Scheffler 1971). The AERA symposium's organisers wondered if comparative international enquiry might at last help to break its iron grip constructively rather than deconstructively; that is, by offering versions of teaching that were framed not as a stark choice between 'child-centred' or 'subject-centred' or 'informal and formal', or between the 'individual' and 'society', or between 'knowledge' and 'skills', or – heaven help us – between 'learning' and 'teaching' (for what is teaching if not bringing about learning?) but in more open and inclusive terms.

The problem concerns more than education and educators. Indeed, such language may be nurtured by politicians and the press long after more discerning educators have abandoned it. In a context where political rhetoric – more than ever since 9/11 – is bounded by the atavism of us and them, the free and the oppressed, the chosen and the damned, to corral educational ideas and practices into the warring camps of 'traditional' and 'progressive' appeals not just to lazy minds but also to more alert calculations about how the world is best represented for the purposes of selling newspapers and winning elections.

That said, in the history of English primary education one of the most revered of all indefensible dichotomies is contained in the 1931 Hadow Report on primary education:

> The curriculum is to be thought of in terms of activity and experience rather than knowledge to be acquired and facts to be stored.
> (Board of Education 1931: para. 75)

Those who habitually defer to this supposed nugget of wisdom would do well to ponder its politics, for as originally drafted it conveyed a very different message:

> The curriculum is to be thought of in terms of activity and experience *and of* knowledge to be acquired and facts to be stored.

The change from the inclusive 'and' to the decidedly exclusive 'rather than' was made in response to lobbying from the Froebel Society, thus providing a credo for several generations of teachers (for this one disputed sentence from Hadow is still approvingly quoted and is probably the only thing about Hadow that most people know) and legitimising an oppositional discourse that is still with us.[1] Indeed, in 2007 it is stronger than ever, except that now 'knowledge' is routinely opposed by something called 'skill', a catch-all that strangely encompasses 'thinking skills', 'personal skills' and 'emotional skills' as well as those attributes that the word 'skill' more usually connotes. I have a thinking skill, therefore I am.

Why, we might ask, do people so resist the idea that education should be about coming to know and understand? Is it genuinely believed that ignorance is a preferable educational goal? Is this just another post-modernist twitch? Or is the problem one of sloppy thinking on the epistemological questions that ought to be fundamental to professional understanding in education?

Sadly, there's prima facie evidence that the latter is the case, for just as Hadow carelessly or mischievously elided knowledge with 'facts to be stored', so there is a general tendency to make knowledge synonymous with 'subjects'. But propositional knowledge isn't the only knowledge; and scientists and others who make knowledge and knowledge-extension their business would find pretty ludicrous both this and the further presumption that facts are there to be unquestioningly 'stored' rather than challenged and tested. Nor are conventional school subjects the only routes whereby students can come to know and understand.

One way of slowing, if not reversing, the downward slide of this debilitating discourse, I have found, is to bat the ball back to the Froebelians' successors and replace the exclusive 'versus' by an all-embracing 'and'. 'Versus' closes debate; 'and' opens it. Courtney Cazden makes the same point in her analysis of the patterns of discourse in 'traditional' and 'nontraditional lessons'. 'Not either/or', she urges, 'but both/and' (Cazden 2001: 56).

However, another frequently observed Michigan elementary school poster – '101 ways to praise a child . . . Wow! . . . Nice job! . . . Way to go . . . You're cute . . .' is less easily tackled, for its entire exclamatory vocabulary blossoms from the belief that praise is the only kind of feedback that children can cope with. The UK equivalent is the robotically genial 'fantastic . . . brilliant . . . good girl/boy . . .', which greets every student response regardless of quality. The belief, of course, manifests the familiar polarisation: in this case, relentless condemnation is deemed the only conceivable alternative to fulsome praise. The idea that feedback can be both critical *and* supportive lies beyond reach, and this in turn sustains the barely productive hegemony of recitation teaching dominated by 'test' rather than 'authentic' questions (Nystrand *et al.* 1997). Dichotomous pedagogies, from the mind-boggling 'child, not curriculum' onwards, can harm the very people whose interests they claim to serve.

By stepping outside such localised ways of thinking and the histories that have made them all but impermeable, cross-cultural comparative enquiry ought to offer a more rounded and coherent basis for reconceptualising curriculum and pedagogy. At the very least, a comparative perspective offers, if not a conceptual solution, then certainly alternative practices that, with any luck, will lodge themselves conspicuously and untidily between the poles of 'process' and 'product' or 'child-centred' and 'subject-centred'.

But we must also note that there are two senses in which comparative enquiry may make matters worse. First, there is the ethnocentric risk of carrying local conceptualisations into the international arena – witness, for example, the opposition of 'ability' and 'effort', as supposedly culture-neutral concepts, in discussions about Asian and American education (Bempechat and Drago-Severson 1999), when in truth in different countries within these regions each of these terms, and indeed other pivotal educational concepts such as 'development' and 'potential', let alone 'achievement', are culturally and linguistically charged in very specific ways (Alexander 2001a: 369–71).

Second, bipolarity is an inevitable hazard when just two countries are being compared. Even a three-country comparison such as Tobin's influential study of pre-schooling in China, Japan and the US (Tobin *et al.* 1989) risks what he later called (Tobin 1999) the 'Goldilocks effect' (this teaching is too formal, this teaching is too informal, but this teaching is just right; this system is too centralised, this one too decentralised . . . and so on). In the *Culture and Pedagogy* research we chose to compare five countries, and so while over such a broad canvas we risked being superficial or just plain wrong, we could at least avoid being ambushed by either pernicious dichotomies or Goldilocks.

But the problem reaches deeper than this. Naive dichotomous representations of complex realities persist in part because there is unfilled conceptual and political space in which they can flourish. People polarise either when it serves their personal or collective interests to deny the possibility of a middle ground, let alone the kind of complexity for which even Goldilocks is inadequate, or when they know no other way. So, if the problem is as real in the US as the AERA symposium organisers appeared to believe, dare we extend Brian Simon's question without risk of causing offence: 'Why no pedagogy in England or America?' And if the implied proposition is admitted, then the reasons must be historical, cultural and political as well as conceptual. I leave others to address the matter of causality: I shall concentrate on the possibilities, drawing on comparative research, for attacking the problem empirically and conceptually.

Pedagogy I have already defined as starting with the discourse that attends the act of teaching. In conscious opposition to the still-prevailing Anglo-American tendency I insist that teaching and pedagogy are not the same. Teaching is a practical and observable act. Pedagogy encompasses that act *together with* the purposes, values, ideas, assumptions, theories and beliefs that inform, shape and seek to justify it.

In acquiring this penumbra pedagogy also connects teaching with the wider culture. Hence the continuum of intellectual preoccupations that it provokes within the research community. At one end are the quasi-scientific minutiae of lesson structure, student grouping, time on task, opportunity to learn, initiation-response-feedback (IRF) exchanges and all that follows from the everyday equating of 'pedagogy' with classroom processes and procedures; at the other end we find the grander questions of culture, structure, agency, policy and control, and the Bernsteinian notion of pedagogy as a 'relay' for the relations of class, caste, gender, religion, region and above all power, coming together tellingly in Freire's title *Pedagogy of the Oppressed* (Freire 1973; Bernstein 1990). Contemporary variants on the latter can be found in the many courses on 'critical pedagogy', 'conflict pedagogy', 'gender pedagogy', 'liberatory pedagogy' and so on, through which American universities seek to sensitise their students to the political function that, in a public system of education, pedagogy inevitably fulfils.

How can one begin to fill the conceptual space that this continuum signals, quite apart from attending to the problem of pedagogical polarities with which we started? Many have been working for years to do the latter, at least. Indeed, to complain about the persistence of the old dichotomies is to run the risk of ignoring the by now considerable literature, both conceptual and empirical, on the art, or craft, or science, or (*pace* Gage 1978) the science-of-the-art of teaching, not to mention the emergence of a literature that explicitly uses the term pedagogy itself, albeit sometimes – as in 'poisonous pedagogy' (Macedo 1999) – pejoratively.

In considering what a comparative perspective might offer to the development of a non-dichotomising pedagogy, I'd like to take three propositions from my own comparative research. First, across cultures one can find a recurrence of many more than two contrasting bedrock views of what teaching is all about, which by surfacing not in their pure form but in different combinations extend the range of pedagogical orientations and possibilities still further. Second, beyond these are primordial values about the relationship of individuals to each other and to society, which have a direct bearing not just on how teachers think but on how they act. Third, the identification of such values, value concordances and dissonances in everyday classroom practice is greatly aided if we have a coherent framework or model for conceptualising teaching itself. In running briefly through each of these suggestions, I can of course only touch on ideas and findings that are developed and explored in detail elsewhere (Alexander 2001a).

In sum then, I'm proposing that one way of breaking free of bipolar models of teaching is to devise frameworks for analysing educational ideas and practices that make such bipolarity as difficult as possible.

CONCEPTUALISING TEACHING

To start with the third proposition above. In *Culture and Pedagogy*, one of the challenges we faced when confronted with a large quantity of qualitative and quantitative data from schools and classrooms in five countries was to find frameworks that encouraged us to make sense of disparate data in ways that showed no obvious bias towards particular cultural contexts. Relatedly, we were interested in seeing how far we could tease out the universal or generic in teaching from the culturally specific – an overweening ambition perhaps, but worth entertaining.

In the literature on culturally located views and models of teaching, generalised 'Asian', 'Pacific Rim', 'Western', 'non-Western' and 'European' 'models' of teaching and learning feature prominently and perhaps over-confidently (Stevenson and Stigler 1992; Reynolds and Farrell 1996; Clarke 2001). If we readily recognise that the geographical and cultural coverage of 'Asian' is simply too broad to have descriptive validity for the analysis of teaching, we should be no less aware of the hegemonic overtones of 'Western'. Does 'Western' encompass South as well as North America? Does it include some European countries while excluding others? With its implied validation of a particular worldview, tellingly captured since 2003 in the Old/New Europe name-calling of the Bush administration, 'Western' may well exacerbate rather than supplant the pedagogy of opposition, fuelling a self-righteous occidentalism every bit as pernicious as Said's orientalism (Said 1979).[2] As for 'non-Western', that is surely a cop-out: is it really believed that education in the rest of the world can be parcelled up in a single category, and a negative one at that?

In preparing for the *Culture and Pedagogy* data analysis, we also reminded ourselves of the many studies of teaching and classroom effectiveness, many of them within an acknowledged or tacit input-process-output paradigm, that seek to represent the whole as the sum of its myriad observable parts (Reynolds *et al.* 1994). For the absence of a genuinely holistic framework was another problem. We are good at dissecting and atomising teaching for the purposes of correlating the variables thereby revealed, but poor at reconstituting it as coherent and recognisable events located in time and space.

Eventually, we built up a framework from two simple and irreducible propositions, the second an extension of the first:

- Teaching, in any setting, is the act of using method x to enable students to learn y.
- Teaching has structure and form; it is situated in, and governed by, space, time and patterns of student organisation; and it is undertaken for a purpose.

Frame	Form	Act
Space		Task
Student organisation		Activity
Time	Lesson	
Curriculum		Interaction
Routine, rules and ritual		Judgement

Figure 4.1 A generic model of teaching
Source: From Alexander 2001a: 325

These translated into a model containing three broad analytical categories – the immediate context or *frame* within the act of teaching is set, the *act* itself, and its *form* – and a set of elements within each such category. The core acts of teaching (*task, activity, interaction* and *judgement*) are framed by *space, student organisation, time* and *curriculum,* and by *routines, rules and rituals.* They are given form, and are bounded temporally and conceptually, by the *lesson* or teaching session (see Figure 4.1).

The next stage was to devise subsidiary analytical frameworks. For reasons of space these cannot be filled out in detail here: they are developed and applied in the full account of this research (especially Alexander 2001a: 267–528). Taken together, they enabled us to apply both quantitative and qualitative techniques to a mixture of fieldnotes, interview transcripts, videotapes and lesson transcripts, and to show how the different elements related to each other (or not). More recently, the framework has been extended further into the key pedagogical domain of that teacher–student and student–student interaction through which both learning and culture are mediated (Alexander 2006b; and Chapter 6 of this volume).

VERSIONS OF TEACHING

If pedagogy combines the act of teaching with its attendant discourses, then the explication of values and ideas will be essential to the process of making sense of observable practice. The *Culture and Pedagogy* research yielded, alongside the expected differences in the goals and orientations of the five education systems, differences no less marked in how schools and teachers were perceived, and how they perceived themselves.

At classroom level – the research offered three 'levels' of data and analysis; national/state, school and classroom – these differences can be grouped most obviously within six constellations of pedagogical values, or versions of teaching:

1   Teaching as *transmission*
2   Teaching as *initiation*
3   Teaching as *negotiation*
4   Teaching as *facilitation*
5   Teaching as *acceleration*
6   Teaching as *technology*.

This, I trust, begins to map an alternative to pedagogical polarities. There are six versions of teaching here, not two.

In a basic transmission model, teachers see their task as passing on information, and it is to information rather than reflective understanding that knowledge tends to be reduced. In India, many of whose primary classrooms until recently illustrated an extreme version of transmission teaching – our initial data preceded the more reciprocal approaches encouraged by the Government of India's DPEP (District Primary Education Programme) and SSA (Sarva Shiksha Abhiyan) reforms – teachers responded with heavily reiterative interactions and lesson structures in order to move their 40 or 60 pupils along, more or less, together. There was little opportunity for fine judgements about the proper balance of different kinds of learning task, since the spread of prior pupil attainment was so wide. Instead, rote served as a kind of cognitive blunderbuss, which, if fired often enough, eventually had some kind of impact on the learning of most pupils, if not all of them. The pre-DPEP/SSA Indian classrooms, though, represented an extreme case but not a unique one. In fact, transmission teaching is ubiquitous, not just as a matter of historical memory and habit, but because there are undoubtedly circumstances in which the transmission of information and skill is a defensible objective, in any context.

Disciplinary initiation elevates knowledge from information to something that confers powers of intellectual precision, agility and discrimination as well as a civilised disposition and outlook; or, in Matthew Arnold's much-quoted and indeed much-abused phrase (from the Preface to his *Culture and Anarchy*), 'a pursuit of our total perfection by means of getting to know . . . the best that has been thought and said in the world'. Disciplinary induction may be associated with expository teaching – as, typically, in our French data – but also with a high degree of structured and sometimes argumentative talk, for the essence of the discipline is that it is a living paradigm for making sense of the world rather than, as in the transmission model, an inert bundle of information. The failure to make this distinction is reflected in the still influential 'knowledge to be acquired/facts to be stored' formulation of Hadow. Yet if disciplinary induction is reduced to the 'recitation' teaching of closed question and recall answer, then Hadow has a point, and induction regresses to mere transmission.

Democratic pedagogy (teaching as negotiation) continues to retain its hold on the thinking of many American and English teachers, though few of the latter may have heard of John Dewey, its progenitor (Dewey 1900, 1916). It also flowered briefly in the Soviet Union during the 1920's period of educational experimentation. Democratic pedagogy rejects the traditional domination–subordination relationship between teacher and taught, makes knowledge reflexive rather than disciplinary, the child an active agent in his or her learning, and the classroom a workshop or laboratory. In all these respects the classroom seeks to enact the ideals of the wider democratic society. Negotiation thus stands in conscious antithesis to both transmission and induction.

Developmental facilitation and its adjunct 'readiness' are key concepts in the Western progressive movement, and they connote the Rousseau-esque principle that children have their own ways of thinking, seeing and feeling, the Piagetian idea that children go through the same stages of development but at different rates, Froebel's use of organic imagery and the metaphor of growth, and the presumed corollary of all these that children must not be 'pushed' and will learn only when they are 'ready'. The teacher's task therefore becomes facilitation rather than direction. In England, this idea reached its apogee in the 1960s and 1970s, following the publication of the Plowden report (CACE 1967), and in the US it remains influential long after the demise of 'open education', where it is usually authenticated by reference to Piaget rather than Rousseau or Froebel.

Acceleration derives from Vygotsky's famous maxim that 'the only good teaching is that which outpaces development' (Vygotsky 1963: 31) and is diametrically opposed to the principle of readiness. When one combines this with the arguments of Vygotsky, Luria and their fellows about the critical role of language in learning, the teaching imperative is clear: the momentum of a lesson must be secured and maintained, it must drive forward, and its engine is what in the *Culture and Pedagogy* project we came to call a proper balance of 'interactive' and 'cognitive' pace (Alexander 2001a: 423–6). Acceleration sits as uncomfortably with developmental readiness/facilitation as democratic pedagogy does with transmission.

Finally, the idea that teaching is first and foremost a technology, guided by principles of structure, economy, conciseness and rapidity, and implemented through standardised procedures and materials, reaches back to a much older central European tradition. These principles were first adumbrated in 1632 by Jan Kamensky (Comenius) in Chapter 19 of his *Great Didactic* (Keatinge 1896: 312–34), and they found their way to Russia and much of eastern and central Europe via Bohemia, Germany and – in Russia's case – German-born Catherine the Great and the imperial court in St Petersburg. In these countries, long before the emergence of modern psychology, there was a prior commitment to economy and pace in teaching, and this fitted as well with the later theories of Vygotsky as, in the contrary tradition, Piaget complemented the earlier ideas of Rousseau.

With this last version I follow Simon in claiming that there is a distinctly continental European pedagogic tradition. In the *Culture and Pedagogy* data, the cultural divide in 'Western' pedagogy seemed to be the narrow stretch of water separating France from England rather than the vastness of the Atlantic Ocean. There was a discernible Anglo-American nexus of pedagogical values and practices centring on developmentalism and democratic pedagogy, just as there was a discernibly continental European one rooted in the Comenian tradition, with Russia at one highly formalised extreme combining Comenian structure, graduation and pace with Vygotskian acceleration, and France – procedurally more eclectic and less ritualised, but firmly grounded in epistemic structure and the cultural primacy of *les disciplines* – at the other. India's pedagogy was both Asian and European, as its history would suggest: an amalgam of Brahmanic, colonialist and post-Independence traditions and values (Kumar 1991).

This, of course, cannot be the whole story. Comparative pedagogical analysis reveals, alongside the obvious national differences, a subtle shading of commonality and variation that reflects the international trade in educational ideas which preceded globalisation by many centuries. It also shows how ideas are domesticated and indeed recreated as they cross national borders, so that, for example, Prussian and American Herbartianism ended up rather different from each other, and different again from Herbart's initial adaptation of the Pestalozzian idea of *Anschauung*. In the same way, more recently, it is interesting to see how Vygotsky's sociocultural perspective has, in Britain, been reconfigured with its cultural and historical elements played down, to generate a pedagogy closer to the dominant individualism.

Further – it goes without saying but it should perhaps be said anyway – the six versions of teaching adumbrated here constitute a continuum of tendencies and not a set of discrete national descriptors.

PRIMORDIAL VALUES

Buttressing these specifically pedagogical positions are three primordial values:

- *individualism*
- *community*
- *collectivism*

which are concerned with that most fundamental human question, the relationship of humans to each other and to the communities and societies they inhabit. These are familiar enough in social and political theory, though less so in accounts of pedagogy.

Within schools and classrooms, a commitment to *individualism* is manifested in intellectual or social differentiation, divergent rather than uniform learning outcomes, and a view of knowledge as personal and unique rather than framed by publicly approved disciplines or subjects. *Community* is reflected in collaborative learning tasks, often in small groups, in 'caring and sharing' rather than competing, and in an emphasis on the affective rather than the cognitive. *Collectivism* is reflected in common knowledge, common ideals, a single curriculum for all, national culture rather than pluralism and multi-culture, and on learning together rather than in isolation or in small groups.

In the *Five Cultures* data, these values were pervasive at national, school and classroom levels. Compare this, for example, with Shweder's contrast of 'holistic, sociocentric' cultures like India, and what he terms 'Western' cultures with their concept of 'the autonomous distinctive individual living in society' (Shweder 1991). Note too the American survey that found that only Britain was within striking distance of American respondents' insistence that freedom is far more important than equality and that personal welfare far outweighs responsibility to society (German respondents voted a balance of both sets of commitments) (Wattenberg 1991). Or even ponder the cultural conditions that make it possible for a head of government to assert, as Britain's Margaret Thatcher infamously did during her period of Reaganite infatuation, that 'there's no such thing as society: there are only individual men and women, and there are families' (Young 1989). Such a sentiment would be inconceivable in the social democracies of continental Europe.

Though there is evidence to support this kind of cultural typology, it is all too easy to demonise one pole and romanticise – or orientalise – the other. Indeed, in the present discussion of dichotomous pedagogies it would be foolish and inconsistent to challenge dichotomies in pedagogy but not in cultural analysis. Further, if the contrast was ever that clear-cut, it is diminished by globalisation, migration and the westernisation of Asian culture.

Yet I think that when it comes to pedagogy the tripartite distinction holds up reasonably well (and anyway we face here the lesser peril of Goldilocks) and it seems by no means accidental that so much discussion of teaching methods should have centred on the relative merits of whole class teaching, group and individual work.

In France this debate can be traced back to arguments at the start of the nineteenth century about the relative merits of *l'enseignement simultané, l'enseignement mutuel* and *l'enseignement individuel* (Reboul-Scherrer 1989).[3] As a post-revolutionary instrument for fostering civic commitment and national identity as well as literacy, *l'enseignement simultané* won. Only now, reflecting decentralisation and the rising tide of individualism, has its hegemony in France begun to be questioned. In contrast, it seems by no means accidental that after years of rejection by England's teachers as authoritarian and indoctrinatory, something called 'interactive whole class teaching' should have found favour as the British government's preferred tool for implementing its National Numeracy and Literacy Strategies.

Individualism, community and collectivism – or child, group and class – are the organisational nodes of pedagogy not just for reasons of practical exigency but because they are the social and indeed political nodes of human relations. However, divorcing teaching as technique from the discourse of pedagogy as we so often do, we may have failed to understand that such core values and value-conflicts pervade social relations inside the classroom no less than outside it; and hence we may have failed to understand why it is that undifferentiated learning, whole class teaching and the principle of bringing the whole class along together 'fit' more successfully in many other cultures than they do in England or the US, and why teachers in these two countries regard this pedagogical formula with such suspicion. For individualism and collectivism arise inside the classroom not as a clinical choice between alternative teaching strategies so much as a value-dilemma that may be fundamental to a society's history and culture.

I should add that as the six versions of teaching and the three primordial values emerged from data collected in England, France, India, Russia and the United States, a comparable study in other countries might well yield additional versions of teaching, and weaken still further the hegemony of Anglo-American pedagogical dichotomies of the kind that prompted a group of AERA members to propose the symposium to which this chapter originally contributed. Indeed, Jin Li's study of American and Chinese beliefs appears to do just that. She contrasts American students' view of knowledge as 'out there', set apart from the learner and available to be willingly or unwillingly acquired, with the Chinese view of knowledge as integral to what it means to be a person. By this view socialisation, education, knowledge and morality are inseparable. And especially pertinent to our starting-point of dichotomous pedagogy, and indeed to the particular dichotomies illustrated earlier, she comments: 'These different construals of knowledge may be one reason why there are so many US concepts referring to mental processes on the one hand and the external body of school subjects on the other' (Li 2003).

DISCUSSION

Let us return to the proposition or hope that the persistence of a dualist teaching discourse can be weakened by the introduction of pluralist frameworks for conceptualising the act of teaching and its informing values, and that comparative study may open the door to these.

The immediate and predictable consequence of this approach is that we confirm that pedagogy, as the purposive amalgam of educational practice, ideas and values, is vastly more complex than those '*x versus y*' slogans can possibly entertain. The range of pedagogical choices available to us becomes broader, more subtle, and ideologically less charged.

That much we knew already. But I'd also suggest that the approach casts doubt on the value and validity of comparativists' current efforts to portray ostensibly monolithic national patterns of teaching. In this matter, though I find Stigler's and Hiebert's idea of culturally rooted 'teaching scripts', which they apply to the TIMSS and TIMSS-R video data, immensely suggestive, I believe that it underplays the dissonances that these contain, certainly in the US (Stigler and Hiebert 1999; Stigler *et al.* 2000; Le Tendre *et al.* 2001). For though our Michigan teachers had recourse to what Stigler and Hiebert call the culturally-evolved 'core beliefs' about knowledge, learning and teaching, their interviews and our classroom observation told a different story. There we found not the coherence of 'teaching scripts . . . consistent with the stable web of beliefs and assumptions that are part of the culture' (Stigler and Hiebert 1999: 87–8), nor the purity of that either/or polarisation with which we started, but contradictory thinking and mixed messages.

The 'teaching scripts' hypothesis prompts other reservations. It ignores the gap between teachers' espoused theory and their theory-in-use (Argyris and Schön 1974), or the public and private languages of teaching, and it reduces the complex relationship between teachers' beliefs and observable practice to a simple linear one when in truth teaching is as much about compromise and the imperfect reconciliation of competing imperatives as the implementation of ideals.

More fundamentally, the 'teaching script' is ahistorical. Educational ideas and practices reflect a long process of accretion and sedimentation, or hybridisation, and the past (and its tensions and contradictions) is always observable within the present.[4] This is another reason why dichotomies are so unsatisfactory, for there is a sense in which education is – if we must use these terms – at the same time both 'traditional' and 'progressive'. Thus, contemporary English primary education displays the simultaneous residues of (i) nineteenth-century mass elementary education (the 'cheap but efficient' class teacher system, the dominance of curriculum 'basics' defined as reading, writing and number), and (ii) the 1960's progressive backlash (small groups, affectivity, the visual environment, resistance to the hegemony of the 'basics'), alongside (iii) the current neo-elementary rubric of the UK government's 'standards' strategies in literacy and numeracy.

Further, the 'teaching script' idea is conceptually and empirically weak, for in terms of our earlier model of teaching it penetrates thus far into teaching but no further: it contents itself, that is to say, with certain aspects of pedagogical 'frame' and 'form' but not with the deeper layers of the teaching 'act', notably the exchange and negotiation of meanings through teacher–student discourse. Once one reaches that layer of teaching the script idea begins to break down. In any case, no script is merely read: it is interpreted, misread and in other ways re-created (always assuming that it is readable in the first place).

For if we take our three primordial values of individualism, community and collectivism, the scenario is not one of singularity. Human consciousness and human relations involve the interplay of all three values. Though one may be dominant, they may in reality all be present and co-exist in uneasy and unresolved tension. In the *Culture and Pedagogy* data nowhere was this tension more evident than in the US, where we found teachers seeking to reconcile – and indeed to foster as equivalent values – individual self-fulfilment with commitment to the greater collective good; self-effacing sharing and caring with fierce competitiveness; environmentalism with consumerism; altruism with self-absorption; childhood innocence with a television-fuelled consciousness of society's dangers and horrors that spilled over into classroom conversations among six-year-olds on child abuse and the relative merits in judicial execution of gas, the bullet, lethal injection and the electric chair. Meanwhile, in the world outside the school, individualism competed with the traditional American commitment to communal consciousness and local decision-making; and patriotism grappled with anti-statism. Such tensions were manifested at every level from formal educational goals to the everyday discourse of teachers and children.

In those classrooms where the ambiguities and unresolved dissonances of American elementary pedagogy were most marked, negotiated pedagogy was compromised by the imperative of transmission, not always admitted and sometimes in disguise. Developmental facilitation and readiness competed with the clock and the sheer impossibility of allowing the degree of divergence of student work patterns and learning outcomes that this belief logically dictates. Physically, classrooms might speak of considerable ambiguity of purpose. With their mix of desks, blackboards, easy chairs, table lamps, carpets and flags it was not clear whether they were places of work, play, rest, relaxation or worship. And though invariably organised for collaborative group work the centre of gravity veered between the group, the class and the individual. The celebration of choice, autonomy and self-discipline sat not always comfortably with the imposed rules and routines that most teachers find essential. Grouping encouraged talk, but the generic learning activities were dominated by individual tasks involving reading and writing. Talk was overwhelmingly conversational in structure, syntax and lexis, and had a casual surface ambience, but was often managed as a kind of recitation teaching and was therefore not conversation at all, and communicative rights veered between the negotiated and the imposed. On the other hand such talk lacked the structure and follow-through of recitation at its most effective. The espoused commitment to 'scaffolded' dialogue (Wood *et al.* 1976; Bruner and Haste 1987) foundered on the rock of the belief that every child must have his or her say, so interactions tended to be brief, random and frequently interrupted. In any case, the purposes of such interactions were often social more than cognitive, about acquiring confidence more than learning to think (like other pairings these, emphatically, are not mutually exclusive) (Alexander 2001a: 490–508).

And so we could go on. In contrast, most of the lessons observed in France and Russia displayed somewhat greater clarity of purpose, procedural coherence and above all consistency in message. Where different values and ideas were simultaneously espoused, they usually managed to reinforce rather than subvert each other. But also, and crucially – as, in both countries, in the treatment of ethnic minorities – value issues and conflicts might be concealed under a blanket of imposed consensus.

I see this situation as not simply a case of 'Why no pedagogy?' For the US is the country of 83,000 governments (McKay 1994), whose constitution requires educational control and decision-making to be devolved to the level of the state and below; and it is the country whose history and political ideology shout plurality and diversity. Perhaps the manifest tensions in both pedagogic discourse and classroom practice revealed by the *Culture and Pedagogy* classroom data are in part the price that American educators must pay for democracy, pluralism and the Tenth Amendment of their constitution, as well as for the much-vaunted celebration of individualism and personal freedom.

Perhaps, too, as Berliner and Biddle (1995) have pointed out, such tensions relate to the massive disparities in finance, policy and provision between states and districts, and the way that teachers' roles, already broader and more diffuse than in many other countries, have somehow to combine instruction with socialisation, community enlightenment and indeed social reform. Within the classroom, it was clear, the aggregation of instructional and social purposes, and the many tensions within and between these, could yield patterns of organisation and teaching that were exceptionally complex and professionally demanding.

Yet by the same pluralist token, nothing is inevitable. Cutting through all this were other teachers who displayed clarity of purpose and coherence of practice of a kind that was no less American. Thus, one teacher neatly manifested a commitment to individualised, collaborative *and* collective pedagogy by getting her six-year-old students to move the furniture –

sometimes several times in a day – between three dispositions: separate tables for individual assignments, combined tables for collaborative group work, and all the tables in a horseshoe for whole class activity (we've already met this teacher, in Chapter 2). These moves, by dint of training and habit, took just 90 unhurried seconds to achieve, and the deeper layers of her teaching – lesson structure, task design, assessment and above all the quality of the classroom talk that she fostered – all displayed the same clarity and coherence. Not surprisingly, our video and transcript discourse analyses showed that she, together with several teachers in France and Russia, came closest to realising the goal on which much psychological and pedagogical research converges: dialogic teaching in pursuit of scaffolded learning.[5]

This teacher explained her approach in both principled and pragmatic terms. Her range of educational goals included fostering children's capacities to work individually, collaboratively and collectively. Though she did not express the matter thus, her ideas and practices convincingly manifested the principle that in teaching – returning to our earlier model – *frame* (in this case classroom and student organisation), *form* (lesson structure and sequence) and *act* (task, activity and mode of interaction) must be precisely aligned both with each other and a lesson's objectives. Thus she achieved what in England was once applauded, before the imposition of government-sanctioned 'best practice', as 'fitness for purpose' (Alexander *et al.* 1992: para. 101 – 'fitness for purpose' has now been politically done to death, too).

But this example raises another and more sensitive issue. For when I described this teacher's work to an American colleague, he immediately and correctly, without further clues, identified the teacher as African American. This, I think should prompt us to consider how far the more acute pedagogical ambiguities and dissonances which our research uncovered in this country are a function of specific kinds of socialisation and consciousness rather than a general condition of American society. The case should also encourage those with an interest in comparative pedagogy to look as closely at – and learn from – differences *within* cultures as between them (Ladson-Billings 1991; Foster 1997).[6]

Once we move beyond the simple nostrums of comparative school effectiveness research, which in its adulation for teaching practices elsewhere largely ignores culture or at best treats it as just another variable to be number-crunched, and indeed – as Berliner and Biddle remind us (1995: 1–2) with respect to the claimed superiority of Japanese education over American – rarely engages either with the downside of what it urges us to emulate, we come to a more qualified conclusion. Yes, there is much that we can learn from education elsewhere, but this example from a Michigan elementary school suggests that the answers may be closer to home than we think.

Whether we compare locally, nationally or internationally, the matter of values must be kept centre-stage. We know that it is a mistake to presume that we can wrench a policy or practice from its context of values and transplant it as it stands; or that we can change teaching without attending to the values underpinning the practice that we seek to transform. If individualism, freedom, choice, community, affectivity, caring, sharing, discovery, negotiation and reflexive knowledge are important, relevant and valid, as many in the US insist, then they can't simply be swept aside in pursuit of something called 'school effectiveness'. The values must be engaged with in the same spirit of seriousness as the observable practice.

We must look no less carefully at the values that inform the practices elsewhere that impress us. Thus, the oral pedagogy of the observed Russian classrooms, with its carefully structured and sequenced lessons, its brisk yet somehow unhurried management of time and pace, and its heavy emphasis on public and dialogic talk in a whole class context, achieves its undoubted efficiency – albeit across a relatively narrow spectrum of objectives – by being part of a package that includes central prescription on curriculum, deference to the authority of the teacher, a belief in knowledge as given rather than negotiable, a commitment to rules and regulation in the domains of knowledge, language and behaviour, a belief in collectivism emblematised in the class and the idea that its members should progress together rather than be encouraged to diverge, and allegiance to the Vygotskian principle of education as accelerated development. Similarly, the drive and precision of the dialogue that many admire in French classrooms is rooted in an unquestioning belief that *les disciplines* are central to a notion of what it is to be educated and indeed civilised, and that it is they, rather than children's 'natural' modes of understanding, that should dictate the structure of lessons and of learning tasks and activities. If it is felt that US teachers could profitably emulate teaching of the kind that one can observe in these two countries, then a lot more than classroom practice will need to change.

Aside from those supposedly quintessential American values such as individualism, community, freedom and choice, two highly influential strands of more specifically *educational* thinking surfaced and re-surfaced in the Michigan teacher interviews and to some extent in the English ones. One, shorthanded earlier as 'teaching as negotiation', was democratic pedagogy (sharing, negotiation, choice, enquiry, reflexive knowledge). The other ('teaching as facilitation') was developmentalism (individualism, readiness, activity, manipulation of materials). The Piagetian legacy seems to be as deeply rooted as the Deweyan one, notwithstanding all the talk of constructivism, partly I suspect because it so comfortably fits the wider ideology.

The case of 'teaching as acceleration' is, in terms of ideological 'fit', rather more complex. True, there is considerable enthusiasm in both the UK and the US for Vygotsky and his legacy, especially in the US, where Vygotskianism underpins the developing discipline of cultural psychology (Wertsch 1985, 1991). It is true, too, that sociocultural and activity theories have become academically popular (Engeström 1996; Daniels 2001), opaque though they sometimes are. Yet, there is no disguising the fact that the principle that education outpaces development is diametrically opposed to the Anglo-American principle of readiness, and that Vygotsky's Marxian goal of taking the child from the 'natural' to the 'cultural' line of development sits at best uncomfortably with the rhetoric of personal knowledge and critical pedagogy, and with antagonism to cultural reproduction.

I find it symptomatic of this underlying cultural tension that when British teachers and teacher educators mention Vygotsky, they usually do so in order to legitimate a localised and somewhat cosy view of learning as a social and preferably sociable process, firmly bounded by the walls of the classroom. The grander themes of society, history and acculturation are nowhere to be seen, for they are outside the walls of Froebel's garden, and it is Froebel's ideas that – to sustain his own metaphor and despite the battering he has received since the early 1990s – seem more deeply rooted in English professional consciousness. Hence, I partly suspect, the seductive but misplaced appeal of *Excellence and Enjoyment*.

I suggested at the beginning of this chapter that in England there is now no shortage of pedagogic research but as yet no coherent pedagogy in Simon's sense of an empirically and ethically grounded theory of teaching. We need, then, to differentiate *descriptive* and *prescriptive* pedagogies.

But cross-cutting these there are *pragmatic* and *political* pedagogies. Indeed in England, now that the UK government has all but completed its takeover of pedagogy – first, under Thatcher, by prescribing a National Curriculum and then, under New Labour, by prescribing teaching methods and ensuring strict professional compliance by policing from the national school inspectorate – this is the prevailing mix; and while academics can and do extend their pedagogical descriptions and analyses, the scope for applying these to the development of grounded pedagogical principles becomes ever more restricted. For the UK government now advances as the sole touchstone for what it calls 'best practice' not those ethical and empirical concerns that ought to lie at the heart of pedagogical discourse in a democracy, but the deceptively simple nostrum 'what works'. The message is clear: government takes care of values; teachers put them into practice.

This, then, is the old theory–practice divide – the ultimate dichotomy – redefined by centralisation. Disingenuously, the UK government also insists that practice should be 'evidence-based' but clearly the evidence, to be acceptable, must fit the policy. 'What works' seamlessly and shamelessly privileges the pragmatic and political in the guise of respecting the empirical. In fact, evidence is the first casualty of this approach, while ethical considerations are nowhere in view. Elsewhere (Alexander 1997a: 267–83) I show that 'good practice' is inherently problematic and requires us to attempt, if not achieve, the reconciliation of conceptual, ethical, empirical, pragmatic and political considerations. The UK government's 2003 Primary Strategy, as adumbrated in *Excellence and Enjoyment* (see Chapter 2) provides a good example of the sleight of hand described here.

In the United States, too, there is no shortage of descriptive pedagogies. Moreover, the effort to devise a grounded prescriptive pedagogy, or a coherent and principled practical theory of teaching, stretches both backwards and forwards from Jerome Bruner's seminal and tellingly entitled *Toward a Theory of Instruction* (Bruner 1966). But we may not be there yet, and one reason may be the complexity of the value questions that, in this almost aggressively plural society, remain unreconciled. Another, of course, is the way the Tenth Amendment prevents even authoritarian federal governments from stepping in and imposing their own solutions, though this is a gap that state governments have been increasingly inclined to plug. It is perhaps symptomatic of the American educational condition that over the years during which I have served on the editorial board of the journal *Teaching and Teacher Education*, most of whose contributors are American, there have been many more articles on teachers' values and beliefs than empirical accounts of learning and teaching, and very few indeed that have sought to reconcile values, beliefs, evidence, learning and teaching within a principled pedagogy.

Perhaps, in that particular country, that is how it has to be. French pedagogy manifests collective beliefs about language, culture, knowledge, identity and civic responsibility largely through collective methods. Russian pedagogy marries four main legacies: the pre-Soviet and Soviet idea of *vospitanie* (personal, social, moral and civic upbringing); ideas from Soviet psychology about human development, learning and the relationship between thought, language and culture; post-Soviet humanist curricular values; and the much older Comenian tradition of highly structured, graduated and predominantly oral teaching. I defined pedagogy earlier as the performance of teaching *together with* the purposes, values, ideas, assumptions, theories and beliefs that inform it. An American pedagogy, we must therefore accept, generates its principles by addressing the values, conflicts and all, that go with the territory, not by wishing they would go away. As those planners of the AERA symposium for which the original version of this chapter was written imply, a dualist, dichotomising pedagogy is no answer, least of all in a country that purports to defend individual voices, no matter how many there be. Nor, clearly, is an imposed monolithic one. A pedagogy that is at the same time pluralist and consensual, individualist and collective, local and national, is of course a much tougher proposition. But out there are teachers who have achieved it.

NOTES

1   The authority for this glimpse into the workings of the Hadow Committee is provided by Brian Simon (1992), who cites his correspondence with a former HM Chief Inspector of Primary Schools, Miss A.L. Murton.

2   This analysis preceded by some years US Defense Secretary Donald Rumsfeld's excoriation of the contrary political allegiances of 'old' and 'new' Europe in the run-up to the 2003 invasion of Iraq. Since that conflict, and the Manachaean rhetoric that fuelled it, the use of geographical–cultural pedagogic descriptors such as 'Western', 'European' or 'Asian' seems even more suspect.

3   'Simultaneous', 'mutual' and 'individual' correspond closely to whole class teaching, collaborative [group] work and one-to-one individual attention, even though at the time the debate about 'l'enseignment mutuel' was more about the application of the Lancasterian monitorial system, of which the Duc de la Rochefoucauld became an enthusiastic supporter after he was forced by the French Revolution to flee to England (Alexander 2001a: 56-7).

4   Anderson-Levitt (2001) uses the idea of hybrid across space, to show how the local is embedded in the transnational. I use it here more to connote a historical process. In fact, as *Culture and Pedagogy* demonstrates by reference to all five of the education systems in that study, the continuities are both temporal and spatial. Anderson-Levitt is also critical of the 'teaching script' idea.

5   See the lesson transcript analyses in *Culture and Pedagogy*, Chapter 16.

6   The practice of this teacher provides a case study in *Culture and Pedagogy* (pp. 508–15).

Chapter 5

Talking, teaching, learning

FIVE PROPOSITIONS

This chapter is about an emerging pedagogy of the spoken word; a pedagogy that exploits the power of talk to engage and shape childen's thinking and learning, and to secure and enhance their understanding. The chapter is framed by five propositions.

- Pedagogy, as this book has insisted throughout, is not a mere matter of teaching technique. It is a purposive cultural intervention in individual human development that is deeply saturated with the values and history of the society and community in which it is located. Pedagogy is the act of teaching together with the ideas, values and collective histories that inform, shape and explain that act.
- Of all the tools for cultural and pedagogical intervention in human development and learning, talk is the most pervasive in its use and powerful in its possibilities. Talk vitally mediates the cognitive and cultural spaces between adult and child, among children themselves, between teacher and learner, between society and the individual, between what the child knows and understands and what he or she has yet to know and understand. Language not only manifests thinking but also structures it, and speech shapes the higher mental processes necessary for so much of the learning that takes place, or ought to take place, in school.
- It follows that one of the principal tasks of the teacher is to create interactive opportunities and encounters that directly and appropriately engineer such mediation.
- Yet though most educators subscribe to this argument in broad terms, and classrooms are places where a great deal of talking goes on, talk that in an effective and sustained way engages children and scaffolds their understanding is much less common than it should be. Teachers rather than learners control what is said, who says it and to whom. Teachers rather than learners do most of the talking. And, as many UK and US researchers have consistently found, one kind

of talk predominates: the so-called 'recitation script' of closed teacher questions, brief recall answers and minimal feedback that requires children to report someone else's thinking rather than to think for themselves, and to be judged on their accuracy or compliance in doing so (Tharp and Gallimore 1988). This script is remarkably resistant to efforts to transform it. 'When recitation starts', notes Martin Nystrand, 'remembering and guessing supplant thinking' (Nystrand *et al.* 1997: 6).

Actually, the tendency is subtler than this. It is true that the so-called 'recitation script' of a closed IRF exchange (initiation-response-feedback) remains dominant; but in many British and American primary/elementary schools, another script is also common: sequences of ostensibly *open* questions that stem from a desire to avoid overt didacticism, are unfocused and unchallenging, and are coupled with habitual and eventually phatic praise rather than meaningful feedback (Alexander 1995: Ch. 4). So we have two deeply seated pedagogical habits to contend with: recitation and pseudo-enquiry.

• There are three consequences of classroom talk which is as one-sided and cognitively undemanding as this: (i) children may not learn as quickly or as effectively as they might; (ii) they may not sufficiently develop the narrative, explanatory and questioning powers necessary to demonstrate to their teachers what they know and understand, or don't know and understand, and to engage in decisions about how and what they should learn; (iii) teachers in these situations may remain ill-informed about learners' current understanding, and therefore lose the diagnostic element that is essential if their teaching is to be other than hit-or-miss. For if children need talk in order to learn about the world, teachers need talk in order to learn about children. The first condition is more generally understood than the second.

THE JOURNEY

The chapter draws again on the *Culture and Pedagogy* research in England, France, India, Russia and the United States, but to these it adds references to work that followed and preceded this: recent work on 'dialogic teaching',[1] and the observational research in UK classrooms that came before *Culture and Pedagogy* and ignited my desire to discover whether the identified features and problems of British pedagogy were universal or whether alternatives were available.

This particular investigative journey started with the 1986–91 study of primary education in the 230 primary schools in the city of Leeds, a large-scale study that was commissioned by Leeds City Council as a formative and summative evaluation of their ambitious programme of systemic and pedagogical reform (Alexander and Willcocks 1991, 1995, 1997a).[2] One part of that evaluation, in effect a project within a project, was a study of teaching in 60 schools. This culminated in a close-grained quantitative and qualitative analysis of teacher–pupil interaction. The methodology combined systematic observation, using simplified variants of the instruments deployed by Galton, Mortimore and their teams in Leicester and London (Galton and Simon 1980; Mortimore *et al.* 1988) together with qualitative analysis of lesson transcripts to enable us to examine those aspects of classroom discourse that pre-coded systematic observation is unable to access.

The data provided confirmation of the earlier findings of Galton and Mortimore in respect of time on task, patterns of classroom organisation and their consequences, and the overall structure of classroom interaction. To these it added a novel analysis of the *generic activities* through which planned learning tasks are pursued, showing how these were dominated by infinitely expandable reading and writing activities that were associated with low levels of pupil engagement and relatively superficial monitoring by the teacher. But the transcript analysis allowed us to go beyond these and identify trends and problems in the *substance* of this interaction, notably the pervasiveness of the pseudo-enquiry and phatic praise referred to above, and the generally low level of cognitive demand associated with what were ostensibly learner-directed methods of teaching (Alexander 1995: 45–219).

In the subsequent CICADA study,[3] we used a modified version of the Sinclair and Coulthard (1975) framework in a computerised analysis of the structure of teacher–student discourse in 60 lessons, working at the level of the discourse act and working from audiotape and transcripts of lessons conducted in 1986, 1990 and 1992. The purpose was to assess the extent of pedagogical change produced by the introduction of the National Curriculum and national testing in 1988. The discourse analysis was set alongside a national survey in which teachers were asked to assess the impact of the reforms on their thinking and practice. The survey confirmed the findings of other studies at the time, namely, a scenario of perceived upheaval in curriculum planning, management, assessment and record-keeping. However, the computerised analysis of the discourse data, using the categories of *discourse, syntax, pedagogy, curriculum, participants* and *lexis*, showed this taking place against a backdrop of continuity at the deeper levels of teaching. Here, independently of the reforms, teacher–pupil discourse tended towards two clear-cut and widely differing clusters. The first involved the teacher in more formative feedback, directing and explaining than the second, which in turn entailed higher levels of explaining, exploring, questioning and eliciting (Alexander *et al.* 1996).

The theme of change and continuity in the context of England's post-1988 and post-1997 educational reforms is a contested one. Governments, naturally enough, claim that everything has changed as a result of the investment of their efforts and our money, and for the better. Researchers are more divided. Webb and Vulliamy believe that their data show that there have been profound changes 'not only in the primary teacher's classroom practices but also in their values concerning desirable practice' (Webb and Vulliamy 2007: 109). Others – the majority – are less convinced. This book's third chapter was critical of the government's claims in its Primary Strategy *Excellence and Enjoyment* manifesto and the government's use of the evidence it cited in support of those claims. Later in this chapter we note research evidence which shows that at deeper levels of pedagogy than those penetrated by Webb and Vulliamy, the discourse default of recitation is alive and well. Indeed, in his most recent study Galton believes that the government's national strategies may actually have consolidated recitation while reducing motivation and impacting only marginally on standards:

> Contrary to the official view, independent evaluations of academic progress suggest that New Labour has been less successful in raising standards than the government and its spokespersons have suggested. Gains, if any, have been limited to the first few years and have been accompanied by a serious deterioration in pupils' attitudes to school in general and to subjects like English, mathematics and science in particular. Motivation appears to have changed in ways that do not encourage pupils to take up new challenges or to express themselves creatively ... Primary classroom practice now seems more akin to stereotyped secondary school lessons, dominated by a fast pace, with restricted questioning and a tendency for teachers to control the discourse such that transmission rather than exploration dominates.
>
> (Galton 2007: 28)

In their survey of a wider range of published research commissioned by the 2006–8 Primary Review, Wyse *et al.* (2008) come to similar conclusions, and later in this chapter we encounter further evidence in support of these somewhat dispiriting findings.

To return to the journey towards dialogic teaching. Planning for the international *Culture and Pedagogy* study started in 1992, the fieldwork was undertaken between 1994 and 1998, writing up was completed in 2000 and the project has had an intermittent follow-up phase during which we have returned to each of the five countries to explore issues of change and continuity.[4] The main study culminated in comparative analysis of classroom discourse from the five countries, and pointed the way towards the possibilities of interaction with a dynamic which at that time was rarely witnessed in British classrooms. The research procedures included interview, non-participant observation, video, photography, and documentary analysis. For the analysis of talk we had observation fieldnotes from 106 observed lessons, 130 hours of videotape, and transcripts of the lessons observed and taped, plus additional data from 60 lessons in England for re-analysis. Much of the non-English material was translated not once but twice, with checks after each translation by native speakers to ensure that they came as close to the original in terms of tone and nuance as translation can ever get. The treatment of translated material in discourse analysis is problematic (Hatim and Mason 1990; Alexander 2001a: 438–41), so as we moved down the Hallidayan hierarchy from lesson to trans-action, exchange, move and act (Halliday 1989), we exercised increasing caution.

The chapter outlines the perspective on classroom talk towards which all this work has led, and presents the idea of 'dialogic teaching' as it currently stands (Alexander 2006a). *Culture and Pedagogy* ended by arguing that of its many possible implications for English education, the pedagogy of the spoken word was perhaps the one that should be pursued with the greatest urgency. This is the challenge that, having set it myself, I could hardly refuse to take up.

CONTEXTUALISING CLASSROOM TALK

The *Culture and Pedagogy* analysis of classroom talk formed one part of a three-level macro-micro study which located the analysis of pedagogy in prior investigation of educational systems, policies and histories, and of schools as organisations and micro-cultures; and at the classroom level, interaction was but one element of teaching that we studied using an ostensibly culture-neutral model encompassing what we defined as teaching's invariants: space; student organisation; time and pace; subject-matter; routines, rules and rituals; learning task; teaching activity; student differentiation for teaching; teacher assessment of learning (see Figure 4.1, page 78).

This contextualising of talk is crucial. Yet though particular descriptive models of teaching such as the one in Figure 4.1 are always open to question, the absence of any attempt at pedagogical framing is a recurrent and serious omission in much research of classroom talk. This lacuna takes two forms.

First, as noted in our discussion in Chapter 3 of the debate about 'interactive whole class teaching', there may be a failure to attend to the *meanings* that are being constructed and exchanged. Instead, the analysis focuses on *structure*, whether this be the IRF/IRE structure that provides the focus for work in the tradition of Sinclair and Coulthard, or – as in the rather different line of observational research which goes back through Galton and his colleagues to Ned Flanders – the frequency of questions, statements and other kinds of utterance (Flanders 1970; Sinclair and Coulthard 1975 and 1992; Galton *et al.* 1980, 1999). Both approaches deconstruct the talk and having done so divest it of meaning, so apart from performing the admittedly helpful task of enabling us to recognise interactive patterns and tendencies, they are unable to elucidate the relationship between talking and learning.[5]

The second omission is of a sense that talk is embedded in the wider structures and dynamics of classroom life. Teachers and students talk as they do within generic constraints of space, time and power, and in response to the complex microculture of the classroom. Their transactions take forms that in part are shaped by the inherited collective consciousness of 'being at school' and in part are created out of each lesson's unique meeting of personalities and circumstances.

If there are echoes here of 1968 and Philip Jackson's three 'facts of [classroom] life with which even the youngest student must learn to deal' – crowds, praise and power – this is as it should be, for these 'facts' are observable constants (Jackson 1968). But only up to a point. In England, the power dimension of classroom life, which for Jackson sufficed to mean the differential between teacher and taught, has acquired a strengthening external aspect because of the real or imagined demands of government policy. Since 1997 this has reached ever more deeply into the remaining recesses of pedagogy in pursuit of the politics of 'standards', 'excellence', 'best practice', 'what works', 'personalisation' and other nostrums that should be questioned but rarely are. Praise (or as Jackson elaborates it, '[the student's] living under the constant condition of having his words and deeds evaluated by others') is now given, withheld or measured by reference to government-defined criteria, and the power differential is no longer merely that between teacher and taught, but between teachers and the official keepers and enforcers of the policies that prescribe their teaching. Further, the sanctions that everywhere attend the unequal distribution of power are no longer limited by the rules and customs of the classroom or school but transmit to students their teachers' consciousness of the national apparatus of targets, levels, league tables and inspections.

This is why the framework in Figure 4.1, or something that attempts the same task, is necessary. But beyond the immediate context of classroom and school is the wider culture, and to this we must now return.

SHIFTING SANDS: THE VOCABULARY OF EDUCATION

Comparative enquiry reminds us that the language of education contains few universals, and educational conversation across cultures is riddled with pitfalls for the unwary. About the nuances of this book's keyword, *pedagogy*, we are by now probably sensitised: pedagogy as practice, as ideas or as both; pedagogy as science, as art, as craft or all three; *la pédagogie* (science of education); *die Pädagogik* (theory and methodology of education).

Press the matter further, though. The English word *education* draws out – *educare* – what is already there, but its non-Latinate Russian equivalent, *obrazovanie*, forms something new. In French, *l'éducation* is closer to the Russian *vospitanie* than it is to the English *education*, which in turn doesn't carry the same overtones of moral and cultural upbringing as either *vospitanie* or *l'éducation*. Thus, to be *bien* or *mal éduqué* is to be well or badly brought up rather than schooled. The English 'instruction' is not the same as *obuchenie*, nor is *la formation* as narrowly instrumental as 'training', even though the dictionaries tell us that these French and Russian terms equate: for the root of *obuchenie* expands to both 'teach' and 'learn', while *la formation* hints at the shaping of the person alongside vocational training. In English, *didactic* expresses disapproval, usually of teaching that is expository and by extension is assumed to be authoritarian; elsewhere, *la didactique* and *die Didaktik* celebrate the place in teaching of the subject and its conceptual imperatives.

Focusing on the learner we find that while in English usage *development* is something that happens naturally and passively to the child, in Russian it may also imply external agency, a process of intervention by others, and the verb is used transitively. *Ability* and *effort*, key terms in the debate about the determinants of children's attainment, are in other languages not the absolutes they are deemed in English. In one culture in our study the most able child was deemed to have the most *potential*; in another the exact opposite applied, because the zone of next development to be crossed was greater.

As to the term *intelligence*, which bears an immense weight of social as well as educational baggage – to the extent it can boost or scar an individual for life – it can signal different capacities in different cultures. As Robert Sternberg's work shows (Sternberg 1997, 2005), drawing on studies undertaken in many different cultures, once one challenges the dominance of theories of general intelligence and considers alternatives such as Gardner's 'multiple intelligences' (Gardner 1983) or Sternberg's own theory of 'successful intelligence', the idea of 'culture fair' tests seems decidedly shaky. Indeed, to an anthropologist striving to understand the almost unfathomable complexity of culture, the 'culture fair' test strikes a frankly ludicrous note – quite apart from the fact, as Berliner and Biddle (1995) also show, that far from being fixed, intelligence is highly susceptible to the effects of schooling.

Perhaps, if we want to be Vygotskian about all this, we might tentatively suggest that in English – or perhaps in the Anglo-Saxon tradition more generally – many of the key terms in the educational lexicon veer towards the 'natural line' of development and are more fatalistic and determinist, whereas in the mainstream European tradition they are more suggestive of the 'cultural line', of human perfectibility, and of external agency in human learning.

These terminological shadings are not academic. Subtly yet profoundly, they may influence how teachers perceive children as learners and their own task as educators. For all, including 'childhood' itself, are cultural constructs, and the power differential of classrooms makes it difficult or impossible for children to resist these constructs' typificatory consequences, especially when classroom interaction is too limited or one-sided to provide the teacher with contrary evidence about what kind of a person each of their students really is.

THE EDUCATIONAL STATUS OF TALK

With these shifting linguistic sands in mind, consider the educational status of talk, for that, too, varies across cultures. On one side of the Straits of Dover is England's traditional and unchanging definition of the educational 'basics' as reading, writing and calculation, but emphatically not speaking. On the other side, French schools celebrate the primacy of the spoken word. Here, literacy: there, language. And while in England literacy is defined as a 'basic skill', in France it reflects a confident and more elevated nexus of linguistic skills, literary knowledge, republican values and civic virtues. The citizen is one who speaks, reasons and argues on the basis of a broad education, not merely someone who reads and writes with tolerable competence and accepts without question the claim that Britain is a democracy.

Further, England has nothing like the tradition of oral pedagogy that is fundamental to public education in many continental European countries. In England the default learning activity is writing, writing and more writing. Yet, as employers and universities frequently complain, all this practice does not make anything approaching perfect. In 2006, a major report from the Confederation of British Industry (CBI) deplored poor standards of spelling, grammar and handwriting among school leavers and the low level of 'functional skill' generally, and found that one in three businesses were obliged to send staff for remedial lessons in the basic literacy and numeracy skills they had failed to acquire in school (CBI 2006).

This problem must be assumed to be rooted in poor teaching of reading and writing per se. But it is also worth asking whether the pedagogical segregation of reading and writing from talk may have contributed to the difficulties that students experience in translating their thoughts into writing, indeed in marshalling their thoughts in the first place. It may also be worth asking how far the perceived decline in the standards of school leavers' written English is related to the loss of oral precision and articulateness, of which the CBI study also complains. Certainly, comparative classroom study shows clear differences not just in the way reading and writing are taught, but in the balance of reading, writing and talking, the different capacities that speaking and writing are held to develop, and the way these relate to each other.

This is a crucially neglected area in British educational research and debate. Instead, what Goody (1993) calls the 'grand dichotomy' (yet another one for the collection) between the oral and the written is sustained, and the opportunities of exploring these as 'overlapping continua' (Heath 1983) are missed. Lexically and syntactically, written and spoken registers take different forms and operate in different time frames. Yet if – as the evidence strongly and consistently shows – talk contributes to learning and understanding, a fortiori it is likely to contribute to learning and understanding *in the domains of reading and writing*.

The historically low status of talk leads to a further problem: an inability to understand what it implies for the work and expertise of the teacher. In dealings over recent years with the QCA and the UK government's national educational strategies, I have found it difficult to secure recognition that dialogic teaching is about *teaching* across the board rather than curriculum more narrowly defined. Instead, 'dialogue' appears as one of a battery of student 'skills' listed under the enhanced framework for 'speaking and listening', which in turn is one of the three components of the subject of English in the National Curriculum. In other words, QCA and the national strategies redefine dialogue as a 'skill' that the student acquires rather than something that students and teachers together do in order to learn. At a stroke, the teacher's agency is excused.

VERSIONS OF HUMAN RELATIONS

The place of talk in teaching is about more than this though, and again we must be alert to values. If the QCA's 'speaking and listening skills' are unacceptably reductionist, then we must also avoid the technicist overtones of 'oral pedagogy'. Talk doesn't just communicate something from person *x* to person *y*; it also reflects and defines human relations.

Our international evidence shows how within both the wider context of education and the more specific domain of teaching, ideas about how people should relate to each other are paramount. Teachers from the five nations in the *Culture and Pedagogy* study articulated, enacted, or steered an uncertain path between three versions of human relations: *individualism*, *community* and *collectivism*.

- *Individualism* puts self above others and personal rights before collective responsibilities. It emphasises unconstrained freedom of action and thought.
- *Community* centres on human interdependence, caring for others, sharing and collaborating.

- *Collectivism* also emphasises human interdependence, but only in so far as it serves the larger needs of society, or the state (the two are not identical), as a whole.

These were discussed more fully in Chapter 4, and we saw there how they map onto that quintessential pedagogical distinction between individualisation, collaborative group work and whole class teaching. I argued also that individual, group and class are the organisational nodes of pedagogy not just for reasons of practical exigency but because they are the social and indeed political nodes of human relations. Such differences profoundly influence the dynamics and communicative relationships of classroom talk. If as a teacher you arrange the tables in a horseshoe or square so that each child can see and interact with all the others as well as with yourself, and you sit with the children rather stand apart from them, you provoke not just a different kind of talk, but also a different relationship from those signalled by having separate desks in rows facing the front, when children can establish eye-contact with the teacher but not each other, and the teacher stands while the children sit.

VERSIONS OF TEACHING

Alongside these three values framing human relations there emerged from our data a second set. Where individualism, community and collectivism start with the relationship of individuals to society and each other, and move from there into the classroom, the six pedagogical values below start with the purposes of education, the nature of knowledge and the relationship of teacher and learner.

- *Teaching as transmission* sees education primarily as a process of instructing children to absorb, replicate and apply basic information and skills.
- *Teaching as initiation* sees education as the means of providing access to, and passing on from one generation to the next, the culture's stock of high-status knowledge, for example in literature, the arts, humanities and the sciences.
- *Teaching as negotiation* reflects the Deweyan idea that teachers and students jointly create knowledge and understanding rather than relate to one another as authoritative source of knowledge and its passive recipient.
- *Teaching as facilitation* guides the teacher by principles that are developmental (and, more specifically, Piagetian) rather than cultural or epistemological. The teacher respects and nurtures individual differences, and waits until children are ready to move on instead of pressing them to do so.

- *Teaching as acceleration*, in contrast, implements the Vygotskian principle that education is planned and guided acculturation rather than facilitated 'natural' development, and indeed that the teacher seeks to outpace development rather than follow it.
- *Teaching as technique*, finally, is relatively neutral in its stance on society, knowledge and the child. Here the important issue is the efficiency of teaching regardless of the context of values, and to that end imperatives such as structure, economic use of time and space, carefully graduated tasks, regular assessment and clear feedback are more pressing than ideas such as democracy, autonomy, development or the disciplines.

Again, each of these is more fully elaborated in Chapter 4.

HYBRIDS AND AMBIGUITIES

Without wishing to oversimplify, I draw on this pair of value frameworks to offer two observations. First, as I hope I showed in Chapter 4, they help us to escape from the universal but debilitating tendency to see pedagogy in terms of simple dichotomies. Second, they offer the alternative, and historically more attuned idea of pedagogical layering, hybridisation and indeed contradiction. Thus, English primary education is best understood not as a pendulum swinging back and forth between 'traditional' and 'progressive' poles (this time the whole of history as dichotomy), but as a complex and unstable amalgam of (i) nineteenth-century mass elementary education (the 'cheap but efficient' class teacher system, and the dominance of curriculum 'basics' defined as reading, writing and number), and (ii) the 1960's progressive backlash (the 'whole child', small groups, affectivity, the visual environment, resistance to the hegemony of the 'basics'), alongside (iii) the current neo-elementary rubric of the UK government's 'standards drive' in literacy and numeracy, veneered by (iv) the would-be modernity of 'skills'. At any one time, reflecting wider cultural trends and preoccupations, one of these will be dominant, but the others are sedimented into our collective consciousness and continue to exert their influence.

The same kind of analysis can be applied to other countries. Indian basic education carries the simultaneous residues of the brahmanical guru–disciple relationship with its ritualised teaching exchanges, Victorian colonial elementary education with its emphasis on the 3Rs and rote learning, and Gandhian post-independence resistance to both of these. Russian pedagogy is not merely Soviet pedagogy cleansed of its ideology but an amalgam of Soviet, Tsarist and central European traditions in which the contrasting legacies of Komensky (Comenius) and Vygotsky are as apparent as those of the Soviet era and pre-Soviet autocracy, all thinly overlaid by recent 'humanising' and 'individualising' government reforms.

The hybrid account of pedagogy means also that the tensions and ambiguities of classroom life can be understood as historically inevitable rather than, somehow, an aberration or the fault of the teacher. Nowhere were these more pronounced than in our American classrooms, where we found teachers trying to reconcile individual self-fulfilment with commitment to the greater collective good; sharing and caring with aggressive win-at-all-costs competitiveness; environmentalism with materialism; and altruism with self-absorption. So, too, negotiated pedagogy was compromised by the imperative of transmission. The imperatives of developmental facilitation and readiness were frustrated by the syllabus and the clock. Though usually organised for collaborative group work the centre of gravity veered more between the class and the individual. These tensions reflected not just a lack of professional consensus about 'best practice' but at a deeper level some of the complexities and unresolved tensions of American culture.

QUESTIONS AND 'QUESTIONS'

The collective ambience of Russian and French classrooms and the dominance of whole-class teaching were buttressed there by the collective and very public nature of teacher–pupil exchanges: children were expected to talk clearly, loudly and expressively, and they learned very early to do so. Further, because both knowledge transmission and cultural initiation were explicit educational goals, the distinctive registers and vocabularies of different subjects were firmly and consistently applied, and language was no less rule-bound than personal conduct.

In contrast, in many of the American classrooms, antipathy towards transmission teaching pushed interaction into an unfailingly questioning mode, whether or not it was appropriate (hence 'pseudo-questioning' as an ostensibly more child-friendly alternative to recitation); while objections to the hegemony of school subjects created a situation where children individually expressed their own mathematical meanings, say, but lacked a common language collectively to make sense of and evaluate them. Indeed, in a climate of sometimes extreme relativism any 'version' of knowledge might be accepted, whether or not it made sense, and all answers might be deemed equally valid. Talk, overall, had a markedly conversational ambience and tone. The teachers themselves defined it thus, usually by reference to negotiated pedagogy and the importance of 'sharing' – the notion of the class as a community – whereas in interview some Russian teachers explicitly distinguished conversation from dialogue and highlighted their role in fostering that dialogue.

Yet was what we recorded really conversation? Like other aspects of the American and English teaching that we observed, such interaction was hedged by ambiguity and dissonance, being conversational in intonation, lexis and syntax but rather less so in content and control. And in England, the ostensibly heuristic device of mainly open questions coupled with the genial paralinguistic features of friendly conversation masked an essentially closed agenda, for only certain answers were accepted and teachers would go on asking or paraphrasing their questions and cueing or even mouthing the required answers until these at last emerged.

A particularly striking instance of this tendency is transcribed and analysed in Alexander 1995 (pp 183–94). Here, a teacher gets children to look at cloth through magnifying lenses in order to report and understand the process of weaving. He does so by asking the question 'What do you see?' and accepting the children's answers but not probing them. Instead he re-states or re-phrases his question and in response to each false trail goes on doing so. The teacher hopes that eventually the children will see what he wishes them to see. They do not, and after twenty minutes or so of the children seeing everything but the required intersection of warp and weft he tells them the answer. It is for this reason that although its form may be different, I see such pseudo-enquiry as closely related to recitation; for 'What do you see?' was, in Nystrand's terms, a 'test' rather than an authentic question, in that its answer was predetermined. However, the context was more confusing for the students than conventional recitation, for the setting, dynamic and task seemed open-ended, whereas in recitation teaching everyone knows the score.

In contrast, in the French classrooms the ambience was more direct and honest: talk might be conversational in tone, but it was never other than firmly directed by the teacher, and the subject-specific referents kept it on its intended epistemic track. There, induction into *les disciplines* remained central.

CONVERSATION AND DIALOGUE

I want to suggest a stipulative distinction, for the classroom context, between 'conversation' and 'dialogue'. This is necessary because most dictionaries treat the two as synonymous. Where the end point of conversation may not be clear at the outset, in classroom dialogue, for the teacher at least, it usually is. Where conversation often consists of a sequence of unchained two-part exchanges as participants talk at or past each other (though it *can* be very different), classroom dialogue explicitly seeks to make attention and engagement mandatory and to chain exchanges into a meaningful sequence.

This, I admit, is an overtly Bakhtinian version of dialogue. Here it is the act of *questioning* that differentiates conversation from dialogue, and the critical issue is what follows from *answers*: 'If an answer does not give rise to a new question from itself, then it falls out of the dialogue' (Bakhtin 1986: 168).

One of the most significant demarcation lines in our international discourse data, then, was between those questions and responses that were chained into meaningful and cognitively demanding sequences, and those that were blocked: whether by the repetitive initiation-response (IR) exchange of rote (as in many of the Indian classrooms); by the ambiguities and vagaries of quasi-conversation (as frequently in the US); by an emphasis on participation at the expense of engagement and thematic continuity (as in England); or by initiation-response-feedback (IRF) sequences in which the initiating move of each exchange was rarely grounded in the response and feedback moves of the exchange that preceded it.

In fact, much of the interaction that we recorded in English primary classrooms was neither conversation nor dialogue. Thus:

- Interactions tended to be brief rather than sustained, and teachers moved from one child to another in rapid succession in order to maximise participation, or from one question to another in the interests of maintaining pace rather than developing sustained and incremental lines of thinking and understanding.
- Teachers asked questions about content, but children's questions were confined to points of procedure.
- Closed questions predominated.
- Children concentrated on identifying 'correct' answers, and teachers glossed over 'wrong' answers rather than used them as stepping stones to understanding.
- There was little speculative talk, or 'thinking aloud'.
- That the questions were – in Nystrand's terms – 'test' rather than 'authentic' (Nystrand *et al.* 1997) was further demonstrated by the fact that teachers gave children time to recall but less commonly gave them time to think.
- The child's answer marked the end of an exchange, and the teacher's feedback closed it.
- Feedback tended to encourage and praise rather than to inform, and in such cases the cognitive potential of exchanges was lost.

VERSIONS OF COMMUNICATIVE COMPETENCE

Though in the real world communicative competence may be defined by reference to the Gricean maxims of *quantity*, *quality*, *relation* and *manner* (Grice 1975), in classrooms the unequal power relationship of teacher and taught may produce a very different set of rules. For students they are dominated by listening, bidding for turns, spotting 'correct' answers, and other coping strategies that anywhere outside a school would seem pretty bizarre.

Since this tendency was identified by Philip Jackson and others nearly 40 years ago (Holt 1964; Jackson 1968), one might suppose that this is the way, everywhere, that classrooms inevitably are. It isn't. Our international data show that these so-called 'rules' of communicative competence, which have come out of mainly British and American classroom research (Edwards and Westgate 1994), are neither universal nor inevitable and that they can be subverted by genuine discussion or by a version of whole class teaching that is rather different from the classic British and American recitation teaching of 'test' questions, minimal 'uptake' and evaluative but otherwise uninformative feedback.

Again, France and Russia provide useful counterpoints. The English tradition emphasises the importance of equal distribution of teacher time and attention among all the pupils, and participation by all of them in oral work, in every lesson. So with only one teacher and 20–30 pupils in a class it is inevitable that competitive bidding and the gamesmanship of 'guess what teacher is thinking', and above all searching for the 'right' answer, become critical to the pupil's getting by. But in many of the Russian lessons we observed, only a proportion of children were expected to contribute orally in a given lesson. Here, instead of eliciting a succession of brief 'now or never' answers from many children, the teacher constructs a sequence of much more sustained exchanges with a smaller number. Because the ambience is collective rather than individualised or collaborative, the child talks to the class as much as to the teacher and is in a sense a representative of that class as much as an individual. This reduces the element of communicative gamesmanship; but also, and crucially, it may be a more powerful learning tool. And because there is time to do more than parrot the expected answer, the talk is more likely to probe children's thinking, and indeed in such settings it is common to see children coming to the blackboard/whiteboard and explaining the way they have worked through a problem while the others listen, look and learn (though of course not always).

Such differences provoke an important question. From what pattern of classroom exchange do children learn more: questioning involving many children, brief answers and little follow up; or questions directed at fewer children that invite longer and more considered answers which in turn lead to further questions? In the first scenario, children bid for turns if they know the answer, or try to avoid being nominated if they do not; in the second, they listen to each other. In the English approach, communicative competence is defined by whether, having been nominated for or having bid for what is probably one's sole oral contribution to the lesson, one provides the answer that the teacher judges to be acceptable or relevant. In the alternative approach, communicative competence is judged by how one performs over the whole transaction rather than whether one gives the single 'right' answer; and by the *manner* of the response – clarity, articulateness, attention to the question – as well as its substance. Closer to Grice, in fact, than to Philip Jackson or John Holt.

PERSPECTIVES ON DIALOGIC TEACHING

I noted earlier that the collective, extended and cumulative kinds of interaction that I recorded outside the UK during the late 1990s were at that time rarely encountered in England, but that things are changing. They are changing partly because of the UK government national strategies' somewhat muddled emulation – in the form of 'interactive whole class teaching' – of other countries' practices (see Chapter 2); and partly because in England, as in the US, there is a growing band of people for whom the notion of 'dialogue' crystallises what the evidence on learning shows is most urgently needed, and what the evidence on teaching shows is most palpably absent. In other words, a movement is gathering momentum.

Lest it be suggested that I base my strictures on a version of British pedagogy that has been seen off by recent reforms, let me register two points. First, long-term follow-up studies such as Maurice Galton's (Galton and Simon 1980; Galton *et al.* 1999) and my own (Alexander *et al.* 1996) have shown that 'deep structure' pedagogical change in the realm of interaction is extremely slow, and that basic interactive habits are highly resilient. Second, this is confirmed in a series of more recent studies of the impact of New Labour's flagship pedagogical reforms, the National Literacy and Numeracy Strategies. Here, the new formalism of highly structured lessons, whole class plenaries and focused group work, coupled with a much greater emphasis on the hitherto neglected National Curriculum attainment target of 'speaking and listening', might appear to provide a recipe for the empowerment of children as talkers and thinkers comparable to that for which the dialogic teaching projects are striving. Yet once one escapes from government rhetoric about the unbridled success of these initiatives – which in any case is challenged by the government's own evaluation (Earl *et al.* 2003) – one encounters this, and it needs to be quoted in full:

> The findings suggest that traditional patterns of whole class interaction have not been dramatically transformed by the Strategies ... In the whole class section of literacy and numeracy lessons, teachers spent the majority of their time either explaining or using highly structured question and answer sequences. Far from encouraging and extending pupil contributions to promote high levels of interaction and cognitive engagement, most of the questions asked were of a low cognitive level designed to funnel pupils' response towards a required answer. Open questions made up 10% of the questioning exchanges and 15% of the

sample did not ask any such questions. Probing by the teacher, where the teacher stayed with the same child to ask further questions to encourage sustained and extended dialogue, occurred in just over 11% of the questioning exchanges. Uptake questions occurred in only 4% of the teaching exchanges and 43% of the teachers did not use any such moves. Only rarely were teachers' questions used to assist pupils to more complete or elaborated ideas. Most of the pupils' exchanges were very short, with answers lasting on average 5 seconds, and were limited to three words or fewer for 70% of the time.

(Smith *et al.* 2004: 408)

This comes from the latest of a sequence of studies of the impact of the UK government's pedagogical reforms from Hardman, Smith and their team. Its findings are in line with those of other studies referred to above and below.

Our stance on these problems, and our view of dialogic teaching, is – in a nutshell – Vygotskian, Brunerian and Bakhtinian (especially Vygotsky 1962; Bruner 1983, 1987 and 1996; Bakhtin 1986), with a heady mix of insights from sociocultural theory, activity theory (especially Daniels 2001) and the research of Douglas Barnes (1969, 1976; Barnes and Todd 1995), Courtney Cazden (2001), Shirley Brice Heath (1983), Gordon Wells (1999), Barbara Rogoff (1990), Ann Brown (especially Palincsar and Brown 1984), David Wood (Wood *et al.* 1976; Wood 1998), Neil Mercer (2000) and many others. This is sobered up somewhat by cautionary evidence on the intractability of recitation and transmission teaching, and the discursive habits with which these are associated, from Martin Nystrand in the United States (Nystrand *et al.* 1997) and, in England, Fay Smith and Frank Hardman in Newcastle (Hardman *et al.* 2003; Smith, Hardman *et al.* 2004), Phil Scott in Leeds (Mortimer and Scott 2003), David Skidmore in Bath (Skidmore *et al.* 2003), Debra Myhill in Exeter (Myhill 2005), Richard Eke in Bristol (Eke and Lee 2004), and my Cambridge colleagues Maurice Galton and Linda Hargreaves (Galton *et al.* 1999; Moyles, Hargreaves *et al.* 2003). In parallel, Sylvia Wolfe has undertaken the difficult but necessary task of testing activity theory's capacity to frame analysis of teacher–student discourse (Wolfe 2006) by linking Engeström's activity system with the model of teaching referred to earlier (Engeström 1996, Alexander 2001a) and using analytical protocols based on those of Linnell (1998).

This somewhat breathless catalogue signals that we have a real movement in the making, in the sense of a coalescence of ideas if not a physical gathering of people. Of course, each of the people named has their own perspective, and the extent of convergence must not be overstated. Further, membership of the dialogic community is in some cases posthumous and overall is highly eclectic. But then, unanimity does not generate dialogue, let alone dialogue about dialogue.

Take Mikhail Bakhtin. He was neither a psychologist nor a classroom researcher. But his lifelong application of dialogism to literature, history, culture, politics and human affairs generally maps convincingly onto pedagogy. And so it should if I am right in my claim that pedagogy and culture are inextricably linked. Further, though apparently Vygotsky and Bakhtin never met, Vygotsky's claim that 'the true direction of the development of thinking is not from the individual to the socialised, but from the social to the individual' is close to Bakhtin's account of social and semiotic influences in the development of thinking, and dialogue provides a potent form of peer or adult intervention in the child's progress across the zone of next or potential development (like Joan Simon (1987) I'm unhappy with the more usual translation 'proximal').

THE NEED FOR PEDAGOGICAL REPERTOIRE

Here then, is the essence, though not the detail, of the approach on which I have been working since collecting and analysing the *Culture and Pedagogy* video and transcript data (see Alexander 2006a for a fuller account).

First, the idea of *repertoire* is paramount. The varied objectives of teaching cannot be achieved through a single approach or technique (and lest it be thought I have a rosy view of Russian pedagogy I would add that it might be as unproductively monolithic as teaching anywhere else, and indeed often is. My main reason for citing Russia is because it provides such a clearly contrasting paradigm to approaches with which we are more familiar). Instead, teachers need a repertoire of approaches from which they select on the basis of fitness for purpose in relation to the learner, the subject-matter and the opportunities and constraints of context.

The idea of repertoire can be extended infinitely, down to the finest nuance of discourse. But to make it manageable, we concentrate in the first instance on three broad aspects of pedagogical interaction: *organisation*, *teaching talk* and *learning talk*.

Repertoire 1: organising interaction

The *organisational* repertoire comprises five broad interactive possibilities reflecting our earlier distinction between individualism, community and collectivism, or child, group and class:

- *whole class teaching* in which the teacher relates to the class as a whole, and individual students relate to the teacher and to each other collectively;
- *collective group work*; that is group work which is led by the teacher and is therefore a scaled-down version of whole class teaching;

- *collaborative group work* in which the teacher sets a task on which children must work together, and then withdraws;
- *one-to-one activity* in which the teacher works with individual children;
- *one-to-one activity* in which children work in pairs.

Thus the organisational possibilities are whole class, group and individual, but group and individual interaction subdivide according to whether they are steered by the teacher or the children themselves. A competent teacher, arguably, needs to able to manage all five kinds of interaction, and select from them as appropriate.

Repertoire 2: teaching talk

The *teaching talk* repertoire comprises the five kinds of talk we observed in use across the five countries in the international study. First, the three most frequently observed:

- *rote*: the drilling of facts, ideas and routines through constant repetition;
- *recitation*: the accumulation of knowledge and understanding through questions designed to test or stimulate recall of what has been previously encountered, or to cue students to work out the answer from clues provided in the question;
- *instruction/exposition*: telling the student what to do, and/or imparting information, and/or explaining facts, principles or procedures.

These provide the familiar and traditional bedrock of teaching by direct instruction. Less frequently, but no less universally, we find some teachers also using:

- *discussion*: the exchange of ideas with a view to sharing information and solving problems;
- *dialogue*: achieving common understanding through structured, cumulative questioning and discussion that guide and prompt, reduce choices, minimise risk and error, and expedite the 'handover' of concepts and principles.

Each of these, even rote, has its place in the teaching of a modern and variegated curriculum, but the last two – discussion and dialogue – are less frequently found than the first three. Yet discussion and dialogue are the forms of talk that are most in line with prevailing thinking on children's learning.

It's important to note that there's no necessary connection between the first and second repertoires. That is to say, whole class teaching doesn't have to be dominated by rote and recitation, and discussion isn't confined

	Rote	Recitation	Exposition	Discussion	Dialogue
Whole class teaching	✓	✓	✓	✓	✓
Collective group work (teacher-led)		✓	✓	✓	✓
Collaborative group work (pupil-led)				✓	✓
One-to-one (teacher led)		✓	✓	✓	✓
One-to-one (pupil pairs)				✓	✓

Figure 5.1 Repertoires combined

to group work. Discussion and dialogue, indeed, are available in all five organisational contexts (see Figure 5.1).

The possibility demonstrated in Figure 5.1 that students can, without teacher intervention, achieve dialogue (which as defined here guides learners cumulatively towards understanding) as well as discussion (which is more exploratory in intent) may elevate some eyebrows. But this is perfectly feasible, given heterogeneous grouping and the different ways and rates in and at which children learn. Vygotsky envisaged the zone of potential development being traversed 'under adult guidance *or in collaboration with more capable peers*' (Vygotsky 1978: 6, my italics).

Indeed, Bell and Lancaster exploited peer tuition 200 years ago in their monitorial systems, though admittedly with rote and memorisation rather than dialogue in mind. The idea has lately been revived in more ambitious form through peer mentoring/tutoring (Hargreaves 2005), and 'learning partners' (Williamson 2006). Hargreaves (2006a) sees co-construction between students as an essential means of realising the initially woolly notion of 'personalised learning' that was put forward by New Labour in 2004 (Miliband 2004).

Repertoire 3: learning talk

The third repertoire is the child's rather than the teacher's. It constitutes not how the teacher talks or organises interaction, but how the children themselves talk, and the forms of oral expression and interaction that they need to experience and eventually master. This *learning talk* repertoire includes the ability to:

- narrate
- explain
- instruct
- ask different kinds of question
- receive, act and build upon answers
- analyse and solve problems
- speculate and imagine
- explore and evaluate ideas
- discuss
- argue, reason and justify
- negotiate

together with four contingent abilities that are vital if children are to gain the full potential of talking with others:

- to listen
- to be receptive to alternative viewpoints
- to think about what they hear
- to give others time to think.

Learning talk repertoires such as this – and others are clearly possible, depending on how one conceives of human development on the one hand and the curriculum on the other – are often missing from discussion of classroom interaction. Because the teacher controls the talk, researchers tend to start and finish there, focusing on teacher questions, statements, instructions and evaluations and how children respond to them, rather than on the kinds of talk that children themselves need to encounter and engage in.

PRINCIPLES OF DIALOGIC TEACHING

So far, we have a view of classroom talk that requires the judicious selection from three repertoires – organisation, teaching talk and learning talk. Now we come to the heart of the matter. I submit that teaching which is dialogic rather than transmissive, and that provides the best chance for children to develop the diverse learning talk repertoire on which different kinds of thinking and understanding are predicated, meets five criteria. Such teaching is:

1 *collective*: teachers and children address learning tasks together, whether as a group or as a class;

2 *reciprocal*: teachers and children listen to each other, share ideas and consider alternative viewpoints;
3 *supportive*: children articulate their ideas freely, without fear of embarrassment over 'wrong' answers; and they help each other to reach common understandings;
4 *cumulative*: teachers and children build on their own and each others' ideas and chain them into coherent lines of thinking and enquiry;
5 *purposeful*: teachers plan and steer classroom talk with specific educational goals in view.

The genealogy of these criteria is complex, and I would need another chapter to elucidate it in full. Suffice it to say that it combines (i) a positive response to what I and others have observed by way of effective classroom interaction in the UK and elsewhere; (ii) an attempt to counter the less satisfactory features of mainstream classroom interaction (which, for example, tends not to exploit the full collective potential of children working in groups and classes, is one-sided rather than reciprocal, is fragmented or circular rather than cumulative, and is often unsupportive or even intimidating to all but the most confident child); (iii) distillation of ideas from others working in this and related fields – thus, for example, the criterion of *reciprocity* draws on the pioneering work of Palincsar and Brown (1984) among others, while *cumulation* reflects not only Bakhtin but also the entire weight of post-Enlightenment understanding of how human knowledge, collectively as well as individually, develops.

In his discussion of this version of dialogic teaching, Skidmore (2006: 508–10) suggests that it, along with the work of Nystrand and Wells, underplays the affective conditions for learning. I do not accept this. The dynamic of dialogic teaching, especially as underscored by the third of its five principles, must be responsive to children's feelings and emotional needs if it is to succeed in yielding cumulation, handover and understanding. Indeed, the dynamic and the cognitive endeavour go hand in hand: 'Teachers and children listen to each other, share ideas and consider alternative viewpoints . . . Children articulate their ideas freely, without fear of embarrassment over "wrong" answers; and they help each other to reach common understandings.' To achieve this demands close attention, by children as well as the teacher, to the development of sensitivity to the feelings of others.

INDICATORS OF DIALOGIC TEACHING

The final element in our framework for dialogic teaching is a set of classroom indicators that help teachers to get the conditions right for talk that meets the five criteria, and to consider how best to structure and manage the different kinds of teaching and learning talk in the various organisational formats that are available – whole class, group, individual. There are some 61 of these indicators and they enlist the various aspects of teaching in the *Culture and Pedagogy* framework discussed earlier – space, time, student organisation, lesson structure, assessment and so on (Figure 4.1) in support of the dialogic pursuit. As noted earlier, too many accounts of classroom interaction have concentrated on talk alone, without perceiving how it is shaped and constrained by these wider aspects of teaching (let alone by culture). Our approach encourages teachers to think, plan and act in a more holistic fashion.

The complete dialogic teaching framework of justifications, principles, repertoires and indicators appears in this book's Appendix. In relation to the distinction made in Chapter 2, I should add that these are indeed *indicators*, not *measures*. They explicate desired and observable behaviours, but do not compute their value. These indicators are offered to support professional reflection and development, not as a checklist for professional accountability.

DIALOGIC TEACHING IN PRACTICE

From 2001–2 I started working closely with two local education authorities, North Yorkshire and the London Borough of Barking and Dagenham, to refine, implement and test these ideas. In North Yorkshire's *Talk for Learning* project and Barking and Dagenham's *Teaching Through Dialogue Initiative*, teachers and local authority inspectors/advisors used different strategies to meet identical ends: fostering the extended repertoires of organisation, teaching talk and learning talk that I have outlined; achieving the shift in the dynamics, structure and content of such talk that is necessary for the dialogic criteria to be met; and re-positioning their approaches to teaching more generally by reference to the five principles.

In both local authorities there was an underlying concern about 'standards' and a belief that these will respond positively to the intensity and inclusiveness of dialogue. Barking and Dagenham had an additional interest. By 2002, they felt that their advocacy of interactive whole class teaching (see Chapter 2) was becoming somewhat tired and formulaic; dialogic teaching could both revitalise professional interest in the place of talk in learning and teaching and move collective thinking and practice forward.

In both local authorities teachers used video to study and evaluate their practice, to record the baselines from which it developed, and to identify aspects of the talk in the classrooms on which they needed to work. There was an unexpected bonus to this. What started as a professional development tool became, in some classrooms, a novel and powerful adjunct to children's learning. Observing the camera observing them, many children asked to see the videotapes and, naturally, having done so they commented on what they saw and heard. Some teachers decided to exploit this interest and started to build video analysis by children into their language teaching. The evaluation studies record teachers' belief that as a result their students showed evidence of growing meta-linguistic awareness. Some of this is itself recorded on camera, and we see young children discussing with increasing sophistication and sensitivity the dynamics and mechanisms of interaction: the use of eye contact, listening, taking turns, handling the dominant individual and supporting the reticent one, engaging with what others say rather than merely voicing their own opinions, and so on (North Yorkshire County Council 2006, sequences 22–24).

The two projects have been evaluated formatively using a combination of observation, interview, video analysis and, as a relatively stable outcome measure in the North Yorkshire project, performance in national Key Stage 2 tests in English and mathematics. The videotapes provided an evaluative baseline for the project as a whole, as well as for each of its participating teachers. At the time of writing neither project is complete, and at this stage we cannot read too much into the albeit encouraging trends in test scores, and for the time being must rely more on the process data.

The Yorkshire year-on-year process data offered evidence of the following changes:

- There is more talking about talk, by children as well as teachers.
- Teachers and children are devising ground rules for the management of discussion.
- Teachers are making their questions more focused yet more genuinely open than hitherto, and are reducing their reliance on questions that cue a specific response.
- There is a discernible shift in questioning strategies away from competitive hands-up bidding to the nominating of particular children, and questions are being formulated more with these children's individual capacities in mind.
- Teachers are giving children more thinking time, and are reducing pressure on them to provide instant responses.
- Children are answering more loudly, clearly and confidently, and at greater length.
- Children are speculating, thinking aloud and helping each other, rather than competing to spot the 'right' answer.
- Teachers are avoiding over-use of the stock response to children's contributions of merely repeating or reformulating them but doing nothing further with them.
- Teachers and children are beginning to build on questions and answers, adopting a questioning strategy of extension (staying with one child or theme) rather than rotation (questioning round the class).

- In discussion, children are listening more carefully and respectfully to each other, and are talking collectively to a common end rather than at or past each other.
- There is greater involvement of less able children who are finding that the changed dynamics of classroom talk provide them with alternative opportunities to show competence and progress, and of those quiet, compliant children 'in the middle' who are often inhibited by unfocused questioning, the competitiveness of bidding and the dominance of some of their peers. The interactive culture in these classrooms is becoming more inclusive.
- The reading and writing of all children, especially the less able, is benefiting from the greater emphasis on talk, thus confirming that the traditional British idea of literacy without oracy makes little sense. Frequently, this gain is most strikingly noted in the context of lessons in which the proportion of time spent on oral and written tasks is changed to allow more discussion and a shorter but more concentrated period of writing. This, incidentally, is more like the continental, episodic lesson trajectory that we observed in the *Culture and Pedagogy* research.

(Alexander 2003, 2004b)

And from the London project:

- Teachers are constructing their questions more carefully. Questions starting with 'What?', 'Who?' and 'How many?' are giving way to those starting with 'Why?' and 'How?'. Teachers, then, are balancing factual recall or test questions with those that probe thinking and encourage analysis and speculation. 'Now, who can tell me . . .?' questions, and competitive hands-up bidding to answer them, are being used more discriminatingly.
- Student–teacher exchanges are becoming longer.
- Student answers are less likely merely to be repeated; more likely to be built upon.
- Teachers are directing and controlling discussion less; prompting and facilitating it more.
- There is a more flexible mix of recitation, exposition and discussion.
- Information and opinion – rather than yet more questions – are being used to take students' thinking forward, so the balance of questioning and exposition is changing.
- Students are showing a growing confidence in oral pedagogy: more are speaking readily, clearly and audibly.
- Students are offering longer responses to teacher questions.
- Student contributions are becoming more diverse. Instead of just factual recall there are now contributions of an expository, explanatory, justificatory or speculative kind.

- There is more student–student talk.
- More students are taking the initiative and commenting or asking their own questions.

(Alexander 2005)

All this is encouraging, and some of it is exemplified on the DVD we made to support the work of the North Yorkshire teachers. This uses 24 sequences from complete lessons, naturalistically filmed without rehearsal or repetition, to illustrate the different kinds of talk in the dialogic repertoire listed earlier, in group and whole class contexts (North Yorkshire County Council 2006). But we also need to be honest about the problems we are encountering in attempting to encourage what, in British classrooms, is in effect a radical transformation of the inherited culture of classroom talk and the attendant assumptions about the relationship of teacher and taught.

First, as with all innovation there is a gap between those teachers who are achieving real change and those whose practice has shifted rather less. That gap is increasing, for success fuels both understanding and conviction.

Second, although children are being given more time to think through their responses to questions, and are more frequently encouraged to provide extended answers, it is rather less common to find the remaining conditions being met: that is, that answers should be responded to in a way that helps the child and/or the class to learn from what has been said. It remains the case that after such extended responses the feedback is often minimal and judgemental ('excellent', 'good girl', 'not quite what I was looking for' or the not-so-ambiguous 'Ye-es . . .') rather than informative. Apart from failing to exploit a critical moment in the dialogic exchange, teachers providing this traditional form of feedback are probably also signalling an equally traditional message to their pupils: that in the end, though there is now more time to think, and space to provide a fuller answer, the answers that count are still those that the teacher expects, and extended thinking time is not so much for thinking from first principles as for deducing even more accurately than hitherto what it is that the teacher wishes to hear. In other words, extended talk and dialogic talk are not the same, and the most frequently observed kind of teacher–pupil talk still remains closer to recitation than to dialogue.

Third, teachers are striving to extend their repertoire of teacher talk, but as yet, rather less attention is being given to the repertoire of *learning talk*, and the systematic building of children's capacities to narrate, explain, instruct, question, respond, build upon responses, analyse, speculate, explore, evaluate, discuss, argue, reason, justify and negotiate, and to judge when each form of talk is most appropriate. This means that the intellectual and social empowerment that dialogic teaching should be able to offer may remain limited even when in other respects talk displays dialogic properties.

Fourth, our efforts to shift from monolithic to repertoire-based models of teaching and classroom interaction have confirmed even more strongly than previously that recitation remains the default teaching mode. It takes little for 'test' questions to reassert their historic dominance, for children's contributions to regress to the monosyllabic or dutiful, and for feedback to become once again phatic or uninformative. Nomination, extended thinking time and longer answers are a step in the right direction but dialogue requires an interactive loop or spiral rather than linearity. A long answer is not enough. It's what happens to the answer that makes it worth uttering, and transforms it from a correct or incorrect response to a cognitive stepping-stone.

Fifth, our evidence shows that one of the criteria – cumulation – is much more difficult to achieve than the others, yet it is perhaps the most important one of all. The first three (collectivity, reciprocity and support) are essentially concerned with the *conduct* and *ethos* of classroom talk. The other two (cumulation and purposefulness) are concerned no less with its *content*. Working with teachers has shown that we can dramatically change the dynamics and ethos of classroom talk by making it more collective, reciprocal and supportive, and by setting out 'rules for speaking and listening' that translate these principles into guidelines that children will understand and identify with. The dynamics and climate of talk then begin to change, often quite quickly.

But what of the content and meaning of talk, as opposed to its dynamics? Cumulation is possibly the toughest of the five principles of dialogic teaching. Collectivity, reciprocity and support require us to rethink classroom organisation and relationships. But cumulation simultaneously makes demands on the teacher's professional skill, subject knowledge, and insight into the capacities and current understanding of each of his/her pupils. Except in a context where teachers take a strictly relativist view of knowledge (such as we encountered in several of the *Culture and Pedagogy* American classrooms), cumulation requires the teacher to match discourse to the learner while respecting the form and modes of enquiry and validation of the subject being taught, seeking then to scaffold understanding between the child's and the culture's ways of making sense. This issue has been forensically explored by Cazden through comparative study of mathematical discourse in classrooms in Singapore and the US (Cazden 2005).

Compounding the challenge, cumulation also tests the teacher's ability to receive and review what has been said and to judge what to offer by way of an individually tailored response that will take learners' thinking forward, all in the space of a few seconds, hundreds of times each day.

So although the five dialogic teaching principles or criteria are intended to be taken as a package – for none of them is dispensable – it is probably helpful to teacher development to divide them into two groups, and this is what we have started working on. If we want to make the transformation of classroom talk achievable for others than the most talented teachers, we might concentrate first on getting the ethos and dynamics right, that is, making talk collective, reciprocal and supportive. In those classrooms where these conditions and qualities are established, we can then attend more closely to the other two principles. Here, we can identify the purposes of the talk and use cumulation to steer it towards those purposes. We can work on listening to and building on answers and getting children to do the same. We can reflect on the feedback we provide. We can re-assess the balance of drawing out (questioning) and putting in (exposition). We can consider how ideas can not merely be *exchanged* in an encouraging and supportive climate but also *built upon*.

There is a final challenge, and it underscores our earlier discussion of the need to relate the analysis of classroom talk to its contexts of pedagogy, policy and culture. Notwithstanding the appropriation of dialogic teaching by QCA and the National Strategies, some of our teachers feel that dialogic teaching's collective classroom ethic, and its emphasis on reciprocity and mutuality in learning, is being increasingly compromised by government policy. In a culture of high-stakes testing, which the UK government insists is here to stay, competition replaces collaboration while coaching for recall against the clock subverts speculation, debate and divergence. Meanwhile, the government's emphasis on personalisation and choice may make the recent British espousal of the idea of classrooms as learning communities somewhat short-lived.

Perhaps, therefore, the bowdlerisation of dialogic teaching by official agencies reflects not so much a failure to understand what dialogic teaching is about as a conscious attempt to force it to fit a framework, and a view of education, with which it is not really compatible. For it is hard to see how learning as dialogue can sit other than very uncomfortably with teaching as compliance.

NOTES

1   Alexander (2006a). The term 'dialogic teaching' is close but not identical to Wells' 'dialogic inquiry' and Lindfors' 'dialogue of enquiry' (Wells 1999; Lindfors 1999). However, Neil Mercer and Phil Scott have recently taken over 'dialogic teaching' for use in an ESRC-funded project on science teaching. As I understand it, this is partly so that they can test the term's robustness and wider applicability, but as their approach is different from mine there's now a risk of confusion.

2   The Primary Needs Independent Evaluation Project (PRINDEP), funded 1986-91 by Leeds City Council and based at the University of Leeds.

3   Changes in Discourse and Pedagogy in the Primary School (CICADA), funded 1990-2 by the Economic and Social Research Council, and based at the University of Leeds.
4   *Culture and Pedagogy* started as the project *Primary Education in Five Cultures*, based first at the University of Leeds, then at the University of Warwick. Both it and its Cambridge-based follow-up were funded by the Leverhulme Trust.
5   Lest it be thought that by saying this I have invalidated two of my own research studies, I should mention that in the Leeds research we combined systematic observation with transcript analysis, while in the CICADA project our interest was limited to discourse structure. *Culture and Pedagogy* attempted something much more ambitious, by way of the semantic and cultural framing of discourse, than either of these projects.

Chapter 6

Pedagogy for a runaway world

THE DIALOGIC IMPERATIVE

The proposition that education requires dialogue is self-evident: education is inherently contestable, especially during a time of rapid change. However, in this essay I want to show that two quite distinct kinds of dialogue are needed: one about the proper purposes of public education during the first half of the twenty-first century; the other as an essential element of the pedagogy through which these purposes are pursued and from which education's character and force chiefly derive. That is to say, we need dialogue both *about* and *within* education.

Since few people doubt that there is a connection of some kind between education, social development and economic performance, the case for dialogue about public education is in the first instance pragmatic. If 'a connection of some kind' sounds unduly cautious, that is because we also know – and discussed in Chapter 2 – that cause and effect in this area are notoriously difficult to demonstrate and that many other factors intervene (Levin and Kelly 1997; Robinson 1999), notably policy, demography, pedagogy and culture.

Take China: since 1979 it has quadrupled its GDP, and by 2010, according to the OECD, China will be the world's biggest exporter (OECD 2005a). This economic achievement, clearly, is remarkable. Yet China's no less remarkable educational achievement, of raising literacy levels from a low base in 1949 to over 90 per cent,[1] took place during the 30 years before the economic reforms of the 1980s, and during much of that time the country's economy was stagnant or growing very slowly (Drèze and Sen 2002). Now high literacy levels are certainly a major plank in the platform on which economic success is built, but it could be argued that it was the dramatic change in national economic policy that really made the difference. On the other hand, without that earlier educational investment the economy might not have taken off so spectacularly.

If the relationship between education and economic performance is complex, the social outcomes of public education are even harder to predict: all the more reason, therefore, for us to engage in informed and reflective dialogue, rather than naive futurology, about the purposes such education should serve and the form it should take.

The case for pedagogical dialogue is to a degree pragmatic too, for both commonsense and research tell us that teaching is more likely to be effective if it actively engages students' attention and interest, and is reciprocal rather than merely transmissive. But if we seek to know exactly why a dialogic pedagogy works better than a monologic one, then the case we uncover is more than pragmatic, for it touches on the nature of brain and mind, on the relationship between language and thought, and on the complex interweaving of the cognitive, social and cultural in human development and learning.

Squaring the circle, we can recognise the necessary link between dialogue about the future of education and dialogue as a guiding principle of effective teaching and learning. Looking at our world as it stands at the start of the twenty first century, we can hardly argue that we as adults and professionals should debate its future, but that our children – who as the next generation of adults will inherit our problems and failures as well as our successes – should not be able to do likewise. The imperative of dialogue is therefore absolute, and it is to education that we should look for the development in our future citizens and decision-makers of the capacities and skills of which true dialogue is constituted.

Such dialogue, as we use the term here and in the previous chapter, is more purposeful and disciplined than mere conversation, and it is more complex than what some people reductively call 'communication skills'. Nor do I mean by 'dialogue' what happens when politicians of implacably opposing views meet but fail even to communicate, let alone agree, yet afterwards issue a press release saying they have had a 'constructive dialogue'. That misuse of 'dialogue' fools nobody.

Dialogue requires willingness and skill to engage with minds, ideas and ways of thinking other than our own; it involves the ability to question, listen, reflect, reason, explain, speculate and explore ideas; to analyse problems, frame hypotheses and develop solutions; to discuss, argue, examine evidence, defend, probe and assess arguments; and to see through the rhetorical games that people play in order to disguise their real intentions or deny access to the truth. Dialogue about education is a prerequisite for social and economic progress. Dialogue within the classroom lays the foundations not just of successful learning, but also of social cohesion, active citizenship and the good society.[2]

EDUCATION, GLOBAL FUTURES AND NATIONAL NEED: TWO KINDS OF INTERNATIONALISM

For centuries people have looked to public education to meet national needs and solve national problems. Governments have established public education systems in order to focus and sustain national identity, to consolidate revolutionary ideals, and to strengthen the partisan interests of political parties, social classes or cultural elites. Education was once expected to meet the manpower needs of industrialisation and empire; now it is called upon to prepare for the post-industrial 'knowledge economy'. In some countries education has been required to mould individuals into compliant subjects; in others it has attempted to develop active and questioning citizens. It has been enlisted to nurture democracies and republics, but also to legitimate oligarchies and monarchies and prop up dictatorships.

Thus, education may empower and liberate, or it may disempower and confuse. It may be genuinely universal in aspiration, or it may use the claim of universality to disguise and reinforce the sectional interests of wealth, class, race, gender or religion. Equally, education may be used to counter these same sectional interests, seeking to overcome racial inequality, segregation and discrimination, demolish class barriers, reduce gender disparity, and promote the just and liberal society.

There are few causes, in fact, to which education has not been enlisted. But where schools once transmitted values that were clear and unquestioned, now, at a time of increasing secularism and international migration, when the borders of states and cultures no longer neatly match (if they ever did), the same schools are expected to respond coherently to ethnic and cultural diversity, moral relativism, the loss of individual and collective identity, and the growth of grass-roots activism in response to disenchantment with the decision-making structures of supposedly democratic regimes (Castells 1997).

National education systems, inevitably, are primarily concerned with what are perceived as national needs. It is much less common to find education being used to address international challenges – other, of course, than those that are thought to bear directly on the national interest. Yet the educational corollary of globalisation is surely that unless national educational systems go more comprehensively international, then they will become less and less relevant to the national needs they claim to address.

There are two broad senses in which the architects of a national education system can think internationally. They can view the world as an essentially competitive arena of trade and influence and use education in order to maximise national advantage – economic, scientific, technological, ideological, military – over other countries. Alternatively, they can apply a more genuinely international outlook (international rather than contra-national), acknowledging that global interdependence carries moral obligations from which no country is immune; and that education can serve to unite rather than divide.

In the first category I place the kind of internationalism adopted by many of the world's advanced economies in response to globalisation. Consider, for example, these two goals from the 1994 Educate America Act of the first Clinton administration (somewhat over-optimistic, as it turned out):

> By the year 2000, United States students will be first in the world in mathematics and science achievement . . . By the year 2000, every adult American will possess the knowledge and skills necessary to compete in a world economy.
>
> (US Congress 1994: Section 102)

In such a climate the school curriculum concentrates on those subjects that are deemed to offer the greatest economic leverage, and students' attainments in these are not merely assessed, as they should be, but they are also translated into local, national and international league tables of educational performance, and the reports on each successive round of testing, from FIMSS, SIMSS, TIMSS, TIMSS-R, PISA, PISA+ and PIRLS, and the analysis provided by IEA, OECD and others, are anxiously awaited and eagerly studied.

This, I think, is also the force of all the talk in Anglophone countries of 'world class schools', a 'world class curriculum', 'world class skills' and 'world class tests' (e.g. Reynolds *et al.* 2002; US Department of Education 2007; QCA 2007; DfES 2007b). If 'world class' here means anything (and it is now such a cliché that it may not) it means 'world beating'. Thus, on the United States Department of Education website, 'putting a world class education at the fingertips of all children' is clearly linked to President Bush's 2007 American Competitiveness Initiative (ACI) that aims to 'keep America the most innovative and competitive economy in the world'. The goal becomes all the more urgent in the face of the growth of the economies of India and China and the inevitability that China's economy will shortly become the world's largest.

Nuanced somewhat differently, the UK government has modified its 2004 five-year educational strategy to promote an international outlook alongside global competitiveness (DfES 2007b). Yet there is a certain ambiguity in the DfES documents about the balance of interest in global awareness and competitiveness, given that the starting point for both is the 2006 Leitch Report on 'world class skills' which addresses the question of how to keep a small country with a large population and limited natural resources economically competitive: ' "Economically valuable skills" is our mantra' says the report's author, Sandy Leitch (HM Treasury 2006: 7).

Hong Kong students have done exceptionally well in the international tests, especially the 2003 PISA tests taken by 15-year-olds.[3] They were ranked sixth out of the 43 participating countries in reading literacy, third overall in science, and first overall in mathematics (OECD 2005b; Ho 2005). Judged by this particular measure, and assuming that the measure itself is valid, Hong Kong's education system must rate as one of the world's most successful. However, OECD's analysis of the results also suggests that for many students and teachers these successes come at a price: students' achievement is high but their self-confidence and sense of belonging seem to be low, as does teachers' participation in decision-making (Ho 2005).

PISA 2003 was followed by debates and post-mortems about methodology, as well as what each participating country might learn from its results (CUHK 2005; Micklewright and Schnepf 2006; Whetton *et al.* 2007). Meanwhile, I trust it will be understood that I am in no way diminishing any country's educational achievements in these tests when I suggest that another kind of internationalism may be no less necessary for tomorrow's world. In this second sense, policy makers and educationists look to what is in the collective interest of humanity as well as to what is in the interest of individual nations.

When or if they do so, they find a situation that is very different from the levels of comfort and security and the high literacy, high life expectancy and low infant mortality that are associated with high GDP. They discover that the combined income of the world's poorest 416 million people is less than that of the mere 500 individuals who are the world's richest; that while the global economy delivers unprecedented wealth, health and life expectancy to some, every year nearly 11 million children do not live to see their fifth birthday, and every ten days the number of children who die because of malnutrition, poor sanitation and preventable disease matches the number of victims – 300,000 – of the 2004 tsunami (UN 2005a).

And while in rich countries the sense of global insecurity is linked to terrorism and the spread of nuclear weapons, in many developing countries violence is low-grade, local, direct, widespread and habitual, and the poor are its most frequent victims (UN 2005a: 1–14). For the rich, violence may be no more than an occasionally nagging unease that their carapace of comfort could be thinner than they would like; for the poor it is as likely to be the way things ineluctably are.

Further, for all that Western leaders talk about spreading the benefits of globalisation to developing countries, or translating corporate billions into aid, it's clear that economic globalisation and global economic inequality feed each other. Even consumers in affluent countries such as Britain are beginning to be aware of the exploitation of cheap labour that underpins Western corporate profit – sometimes, as in the case of Chinese cockle-pickers, Romanian hotel cleaners or Ukrainian seasonal agricultural workers, the evidence is uncomfortably close to home. Surveying the prospects for the twenty-first century from the understandably pessimistic vantage-point of a historian of the twentieth century, Hobsbawm makes three confident claims about the impact of globalisation:

First, the currently fashionable free-market globalisation has brought about a dramatic growth in economic and social inequalities both within states and internationally . . . This surge of inequality . . . is at the root of the major social and political tensions of the new century . . . Second, the impact of this globalisation is felt most by those who benefit from it least. Hence the growing polarisation of views about it, between those who are potentially sheltered from its negative effects – the entrepreneurs who can 'out-source' their costs to countries of cheap labour, the high-tech professionals and graduates of higher education who can get work in any high-income market economy – and those who are not . . . Third, while the actual scale of globalisation remains modest, except perhaps in a number of smallish states, mainly in Europe, its political and cultural impact is disproportionately large.

(Hobsbawm 2007: 3–4)

This, then, is the alternative international reality, the one that provides the focus for the eight United Nations Millennium Development Goals (MDGs) for 2015, in which education plays a pivotal part (UN 2005b).[4]

As if this were not enough, there hangs over poor and rich alike the spectre of climate change – still denied by those who remain wedded to the most self-serving and short-sighted definitions of national or commercial interest, but acknowledged by most reputable scientists as possibly the greatest threat humanity as a whole has ever faced.

By now we know the scenario well enough: the profligate use of fossil fuels; spiralling carbon dioxide emissions; global warming; the destruction of the forests, wetlands and other ecosystems that mitigate these processes; rising sea levels, and the already evident increase in extreme droughts, storms, floods, and forest fires, and the failure of the crops and water supplies on which human life depends, all exacerbated by rapid and probably unsustainable population growth. Each year climate change becomes more of a present than a future threat, because global warming has a feedback loop that accelerates the process exponentially towards the point of no return. (UN IPCC 2001, 2005, 2007; Stern 2007). Some, looking at the melting of the polar and Greenland ice sheets, or at the raised sea temperatures that increased the ferocity of Hurricane Katrina, believe we have already reached that point (Lovelock 2006; Schellnhuber et al. 2006).

Nor is the problem merely a physical one. Long before an eventual environmental collapse, the world's political, social and economic systems would break down under the strain of increasingly desperate competition for the dwindling resources of living space, energy, arable land and fresh water. If, in August 2007, problems as local as the US housing market were able to cause stock markets to tumble worldwide, then imagine the global economic consequences if a modest rise in sea levels were to inundate

America's eastern seaboard – naturally flooding London, Amsterdam and several other world capitals at the same time, not to mention most of Bangladesh.

Even if apocalyptic scenarios like this can be averted, there is no shortage of critics of the onward march of globalisation, the Disneyfication of culture, the McDonaldising of cuisine, and the imposition of Western free-market capitalism in the name of freedom and democracy, if necessary by force. With political and religious opinion worldwide now alarmingly polarised, Western bookshops are generously stocked with titles such as *Globalisation and its Discontents*, *The Delusions of Global Capitalism*, *Lawless World*, *The West and the Rest*. Some – *The New Rulers of the World*, *Stupid White Men*, *Why Do People Hate America?* – point the finger and name their villains. Others – *Lost Icons*, *The Moral State We're In* – quietly despair at the way people and nations behave. (Stiglitz 2002; Gray 1998; Sands 2005; Scruton 2002; Pilger 2002; Moore 2001; Sardar and Davies 2002; Williams 2000; Neuberger 2005).

I cite these disturbing visions and critical voices not out of inverted millenarianism – and to some they will look like just the kinds of nightmares through which the comfortably-off use fear as a proxy for action and thereby assuage their liberal consciences ('We may have two homes and three cars but we *do* care, and anyway we recycle our wine bottles . . .') – but in order to add a further proposition to those with which we started: that the necessary dialogue about the purposes and content of national education systems can follow very different trajectories, depending on the view that one takes about the condition of the wider world and the place of one's own country within it.

If we presume that the most important goal of a national education system is to expand indefinitely a conventionally configured economy that depends on non-renewable or ecologically harmful resources, then it's clear what we must do: give priority to the knowledge and skill deemed likely to produce the best economic returns and relegate the attendant moral questions to the margins of the curriculum, meanwhile dispelling any doubts about the wisdom of this strategy by saturating the media with images that celebrate consumerism over environmentalism and individual gratification over equity and the collective good.

But if we contemplate the increasing fragility, inequality and instability of our world as a whole, and believe that these are not only unacceptable in themselves but are also, as a matter of fact, contrary to the national interest – because like first-class passengers in an aircraft crash, in a global catastrophe no country remains immune – then education will need to espouse very different priorities: moral no less than economic, holistic rather than fragmented, and collective rather than individualistic.

In the first instance, therefore, we should honestly and unflinchingly lay out for inspection competing future scenarios such as those I have exemplified (and there are others), assess their reliability, and decide which of them represent visions to which education can help us aspire, and which of them are nightmares that education should play its part in helping us to avoid.

Yet we should also be realistic about the chances of success if we concentrate on education alone. We know, most palpably perhaps in the context of development economics, that 'improvements in rural roads, better access to water and sanitation and child health programmes . . . all have a positive impact on education achievements' (DfID 2005: 13). We know also how closely the demographies of illiteracy, poverty, gender inequality, ill-health and low life expectancy coincide; how by attending to one of these the others may be affected to a degree; but how attending to all of them simultaneously may yield transformations that are rapid, dramatic and – especially – lasting. That, indeed, is the thinking behind the UN's Millennium Development Goals.

By the same token, in the matter of moving from runaway consumption to sustainability in the very different context of high per capita GDP, education will achieve little if it espouses values that are negated by a country's economic and environmental policies. Nor, except by setting a worthy example – and certainly the world stands sorely in need of that – can one country do very much on its own, unless of course that country just happens to be the world's richest or largest, in which case its potential impact on the world's future, for better or worse, is enormous.

In this vein, as James Lovelock (2006) suggested, what really matters is not whether people in the small countries of Western Europe recycle plastic bottles, erect wind turbines or fit solar panels to their houses (though such practices and their attendant attitudes should certainly not be discouraged), but how the governments and peoples of those four countries whose sheer scale dwarfs all others choose to respond to the growing crisis.

Thus, will the US – still the world's most powerful nation and its biggest per capita polluter – be prepared drastically and urgently to rethink those habits, values, beliefs and policies that have encouraged its inhabitants to believe that the planet exists to be 'subdued'[5] rather than respected and protected? How will Russia, the world's largest country in terms of area, choose to treat its vast reserves of oil, gas, coal and virgin forest? Will China and India, the world's two largest countries by population, use their new-found economic muscle to achieve the Western levels of personal wealth, material consumption and energy use to which their peoples are being encouraged to aspire, or will they choose the less popular path of sustainability?

On present form, the answers to these questions are far from encouraging. China is meeting fast-growing energy demands by building large numbers of new and mainly coal-fired power stations, which in turn reduce economic growth since, according to the World Bank, pollution is now costing China up to 5.8 per cent of GDP per year (World Bank 2007). As always, its impact is greatest on the poor (ibid.: xv). It is even being seriously argued by some that countries like Britain should not compromise their economies by cutting carbon emissions since such cuts will be wiped out by the increases from China and India. The Stern Report on the economics of climate change gave that argument short shrift (Stern 2007).

Having said all this, I would stress that this is no naive diatribe against globalisation, corporatism or economic growth. It's true that in the context of the Bush presidency's oil-drenched Manichaeanism it makes useful journalistic copy to portray Shell, Microsoft, Wal-Mart, Monsanto, Nike, Coca-Cola, Starbucks, McDonalds, Tesco *et al.* as the authentic 'axis of evil', and to postulate 'consumerism *versus* citizenship'[6] as the true 'clash of civilisations'. But though there are grounds for deep unease about the activities of some of the multinationals, matters, as always, are not that simple. The question concerns not the fact of globalisation – which historically is hardly a new phenomenon anyway (Landes 1998) – but its form and consequences. Similarly, the issue is not economic growth as such, but the way it is achieved and the uses to which it is put. This is a moral issue first, an economic one second. As Jean Drèze and Amartya Sen warn:

> It must be remembered that not all countries with high growth rates have succeeded in translating an expanded command over material resources into a corresponding transformation of living conditions for broad sections of the population. In fact, the development experience of some fast-growing countries during the past few decades has resembled one of 'unaimed opulence', combining high rates of economic growth with the persistence of widespread poverty, illiteracy, ill health, child labour, criminal violence and related social failures.
>
> (Drèze and Sen 2002: 72)

Here they refer particularly to Brazil (where one highway to 'unaimed opulence' happens to be the destruction of that vital ecosystem, the Amazon rainforest) though they also pursue their analysis in the context of south and south-east Asia. But Drèze and Sen also point out, citing as positive examples China during the pre-reform period and the Indian state of Kerala, that quality of life for the majority can be vastly improved, given political will and an efficient infrastructure, even during periods of relatively slow economic growth.

Incidentally, it has been suggested that the American neo-conservative/ Christian fundamentalist alliance looks to the book of *Genesis* to justify its unapologetically exploitative view of the world's natural resources.

However, while *Genesis* certainly commands its literalist readers to 'have dominion over' all other life, it also charges them to 'replenish' the earth, not merely to 'subdue' it.

As I say, it's a moral question; a religious one too, seemingly.

THE UNIVERSALITY OF DIALOGUE

Let us turn now to the parallel theme of dialogue as an educative process. All teaching is interactive, whether the interaction is between teacher and student, student and student, student and text or student and computer. This is interaction in its most basic sense, and hence the basic tautology of 'interactive whole class teaching.' But dialogue, as I have noted, stands in opposition to that one-sided and cognitively undemanding interaction that has been exposed, consistently and dispiritingly, by classroom research. In this version, the teacher asks questions to which he or she knows the answers; the students dutifully spot or guess those answers. The teacher transmits the information; the students write it down. What the teacher says, even if it is mere unsubstantiated opinion, carries authority; what the student says carries authority only if the teacher allows it to do so. Either way, the teacher's view of the world remains paramount. These processes much less frequently work in reverse, and classroom interaction has a now famous asymmetry: students are in the majority, but teachers do most of the talking; much is made of learning through discovery and enquiry, but actually it is teachers who ask most of the questions. At its worst, classroom talk does the opposite of what one might reasonably expect it to do: it disempowers the student. (UK and US research on this matter is synthesised in Edwards and Westgate 1994 and Alexander 2006b.)

In contrast, dialogue presumes a greater degree of reciprocity in classroom talk and relationships – teachers ask questions, but so do students; such questions are framed on the assumption that there are alternative answers, some of them unanticipated, not just answers that are known in advance; ideas are exchanged rather than merely transmitted; it is accepted that students sometimes know things that the teacher does not; and that the teacher wants to hear about them.

This is dialogue as a kind of talk that presupposes if not absolute equality, then at least that each participant is genuinely interested in what the other is saying and thinking. But the essence of dialogue is not so much its observable dynamics, important though these are, as that it marks an exchange of ideas. Beyond the dialogue of *voices*, then, is a dialogue of *minds*.

The Russian philosopher Bakhtin has provided a pre-eminent vocabulary for exploring the nature and possibilities of dialogue. Like his compatriot Vygotsky, Bakhtin was interested in the relationship between the individual and society present and past, between the developing mind and the thinking embodied in the wider culture, between our inner and outer worlds. But Bakhtin applied the dialogic idea to many facets of human existence, showing, for example, how in the greatest works of literature a dialogue is set up between reader and author as the reader gains access to the author's thinking and allows it to interrogate his or her own; but also that such writing contains many voices, and that through their characters authors set up other dialogues on which readers may eavesdrop and on which they in turn can reflect (Bakhtin 1981, 1986; Holquist 2002).

Dialogue, in the sense that Bakhtin uses it, is thus multiple rather than singular, and endless rather than finite. Bakhtin writes:

> There is neither a first nor a last word. The contexts of dialogue are without limit. They extend into the deepest past and the most distant future.[7]

Such an idea might make particular sense in China, this most ancient of continuous civilisations, where despite the seismic changes of the past 100 years, the abiding potency of the Confucian Analects can telescope the centuries in an instant and connect present with distant past and offer a cautionary window on the future. Even more to the point in the particular context of educational dialogue:

> He who by reanimating the Old can gain knowledge of the New is fit to be a teacher.[8]

Provided, that is, that the dialogue of Old and New is allowed to take place. In this matter we would do well to heed the warning of historian Eric Hobsbawm, speaking of a growing tendency in Britain:

> The destruction of the past, or rather of the social mechanisms that link one's contemporary experience to that of earlier generations, is one of the most characteristic and eerie phenomena of the late twentieth century. Most young men and women grow up in a sort of permanent present, lacking any organic relation to the public past of the times they live in.
>
> (Hobsbawm 1995: 3)

If young people lack that 'organic relation' to the past, they will probably also lack the capacity to project forward and contemplate the consequences of their actions for the next generation. Hobsbawm writes of today's youth in Britain and America. But youth becomes middle aged, middle-aged people become politicians, and politicians exercise power only in the direction that their imagination and ambition allow. And for politicians – as the example of New Labour so powerfully illustrates (see Chapter 3) – the 'destruction of the past' reflects not only the carelessness of youth or the negligence of schools but a deliberate and calculated act aimed at manipulating public consciousness in the pursuit of power.

We have also known, ever since Bronfenbrenner's pioneering comparative studies of the 1960s, that peer segregation of adolescents from adults, and a decline in intergenerational respect and indeed contact, are increasingly marked features of American and British society (Bronfenbrenner 1974). In Britain this seems to be associated in the young not just with an extreme emphasis on living for the present and for oneself alone, but also with growing disaffection and violence. It will be instructive to see how far such trends will be mirrored in China and India, and to what extent, for example, the traditional Chinese values of holism, familial harmony and mutual responsibility will offset the countervailing values of generational segregation and individualism that seem to be an ineluctable part of the globalisation package.

Ecological catastrophe and the concomitant social collapse, if or when they happen, will be a consequence not just of capitalistic greed, but more fundamentally of a simple failure of the collective imagination, a failure to relate cause and consequence, to make connections, to enter into the necessary dialogues between past, present and future, between the hard-won experience of one generation and the casual aspirations of the next, between humankind and the natural world, and between the expectation of infinite material gratification and the fact of finite resource.

All this 'the world well knows yet none knows well'.[9] And to such a condition of knowing without understanding or connecting, dare I suggest, dialogue offers a promising antidote.

DIALOGUE, LEARNING AND TEACHING

I argued that dialogue in education entails a meeting of minds and ideas as well as of voices; and it is therefore mediated through text, Internet and computer screen as well as through face-to-face interaction. Yet there are sound reasons why in the particular context of educating the young we should pay special attention to the last of these, to the dialogue of the spoken word.

We have long known that, for the young child, language and the development of thinking go hand in hand. Halliday (1993) argues: 'When children learn language, they are not simply engaging in one type of learning among many; rather, they are learning the foundations of learning itself.' To that proposition we now add two others.

First, drawing on insights initiated by Vygotsky and Bruner and consolidated by later cognitive and cultural psychologists, we have replaced the view of the developing child as a 'lone scientist', who learns by interacting with materials (derived from Piaget, though not necessarily with total justice), by one of learning as necessarily a *social* process. In this, significant others – parents, teachers, peers – provide the mediation or intervention that scaffolds and takes forward the child's understanding (Bruner and Haste 1987; Wood 1998; Wells 1999).

Second, neuroscience shows us that between birth and adolescence, brain metabolism is 150 per cent of its adult level, and synaptogenesis causes the brain's volume to quadruple. In this process, language, and especially spoken language, plays a vital part. Although synaptogenesis can occur at any period of life (and neuroscience thus provides biological confirmation of the value of lifelong learning) it is nevertheless the case that the periods from birth to three years, and from then to adolescence, are critical for subsequent development, for during this phase of life the brain in effect restructures itself (Johnson 2004; Howard-Jones 2007). I repeat: language, and especially talk, help to drive that process.

Unfortunately, research shows us that the interaction which children experience in classrooms is not necessarily the kind that will maximise cognitive engagement and growth (Galton *et al.* 1980, 1999; Nystrand *et al.* 1997, Alexander 1995, 2001a), and in my own work I have charted the recurrent use of three kinds of teaching talk: *rote*, or the drilling of facts, ideas and routines through constant repetition; *recitation*, or the accumulation of knowledge and understanding through questions designed to test or stimulate recall of what has previously been encountered, or to cue students to work out answers from clues provided in the question; and *expository instruction*, or imparting information and/or explaining facts, principles or procedures (Alexander, 2001a: 526–7; see also Chapter 5 in this volume).

Drilling, questioning and telling are used in some form worldwide, and they certainly have their place. But they remain one-sided. American researchers from the 1960s onwards have documented the dominance of recitation. This endlessly and remorselessly repeats the initiation–response-evaluation sequence that centres on what Nystrand calls 'test' questions to which there is only one possible answer, which the teacher knows and the student must correctly remember, work out or guess. These test questions are contrasted with 'authentic' questions that encourage students to think for themselves and which, on the basis of his large pre-test–post-test study, Nystrand showed were much more likely to lead to successful learning and genuine understanding (Nystrand *et al.* 1997; Cazden 2001).

The tendency is no less common in Britain. Thus, from Smith *et al.*'s studies of the impact of the UK government's National Literacy and Numeracy Strategies on classroom discourse we find the classic indicators of low-grader recitation alive and well. This evidence, from one study among several with similar findings, is quoted in full on pp. 107–8, and a depressing picture it makes.

Yet all may not be lost. Albeit considerably less common than rote, recitation and exposition, classroom research uncovers two other forms of pedagogical interaction that have greater power to provoke cognitive engagement and understanding: *discussion,* or open exchanges between teacher and student, or student and student, with a view to sharing information, exploring ideas or solving problems; and *dialogue,* or using authentic questioning, discussion and exposition to guide and prompt, minimise risk and error, and expedite the 'uptake' of ideas between teacher, student and student, and the 'handover' of concepts and principles (Alexander, 2001a: 527).

Teaching consisting mainly of the rote of antiphonal chanting is a feature of the large classes and limited resources one sees in many of the world's poorer countries – anything from 50 to 100 children packed into a room or outdoor space with no equipment other than slates and a blackboard. (It occurs elsewhere too, with less obvious justification.) Recitation remains prominent in British and American classrooms (Alexander 2001a; Nystrand *et al.* 1997; Galton 2007) and comparative research suggests that both recitation and exposition are firmly embedded in traditional Chinese pedagogy (Hull 1985; Potts 2003). Yet the more dialogic forms of talk can also be found, and they have been observed and studied in continental Europe, Scandinavia, Japan and Singapore (Broadfoot *et al.* 2000; Stigler *et al.* 2000; Alexander 2001a; Ofsted 2003a; Cazden 2005). Here, perhaps the critical difference is that questioning is more likely to be authentic and therefore to lead to discussion, and exchanges between teachers and students tend to last longer. This allows a fuller and more critical exploration of ideas and, crucially, enables the teacher to uncover the true nature of the student's thinking, including any conceptual difficulties, and to work on these.

The dialogic teaching approach that is described in Chapter 5 builds on psychological and pedagogical evidence of the kind to which we referred earlier. It is a pedagogy that comprises a three-part *repertoire* which is informed by five *dialogic principles.* The notion of repertoire is based on the self-evident truth that the variable contexts, conditions and objectives of education require a range of teaching procedures, and that a single, supposedly multi-purpose teaching strategy such as direct instruction through whole class teaching is a wholly inadequate basis for engaging with a modern curriculum. As Desforges reminds us:

> Direct instruction is best used for knowledge transmission, for showing, telling, modelling and demonstrating. It is never, on its own, sufficient to ensure deeper understanding, problem solving or creativity.
>
> (Desforges 1995: 129)

Similar limits apply to other strategies, including group work. Each has its most appropriate context and purpose.

The first part of the dialogic repertoire requires the teacher to understand and foster the various kinds of *learning talk* that as learners and future citizens students need: the ability to narrate, explain, question, answer, analyse, speculate, imagine, explore, evaluate, discuss, argue, justify and negotiate; and the dispositions with which these are necessarily associated: the preparedness to listen, to be receptive to new ideas, to think, and to give others time to do so.

The next part of the repertoire entails the teacher's mastery and appropriate use of the five kinds of *teaching talk* already referred to – rote, recitation, exposition, discussion, dialogue – giving particular attention to the skills of clear exposition, authentic and extended questioning, and the handling of discussion. That is to say, the comprehensively trained and adaptable teacher does not abandon the first three methods, for they all have their uses, but shifts the interactive centre of gravity towards the last two.

The third part of the repertoire comprises the five *interactive strategies* that classroom settings typically allow: whole class teaching, group work led by the teacher, group work on set collaborative tasks led by the students themselves, one-to-one discussion between students (what in Britain is call 'paired' talk) and one-to-one discussion between student and teacher.

Together, the teacher's repertoires of teaching talk and interactive strategy provide a more promising vehicle for developing and extending the students' repertoire of learning talk, thereby empowering them both cognitively and socially, than when classroom talk is restricted to the recitation sequence of closed 'test' question, predictable answer and minimal feedback, endlessly repeated. This sequence, though it involves more than one person, is in fact monologic rather than dialogic, because there is no true exchange of meanings, and the teacher controls its content and direction, thus inhibiting the autonomous thinking on which the student's development of talk for learning and understanding depends. As Nystrand concludes from his process–product study of interaction in American classrooms:

> What ultimately counts is the extent to which instruction requires students to think, not just to report someone else's thinking.
>
> (Nystrand *et al*: 1997: 72)

The tripartite dialogic *repertoire* – learning talk, teaching talk and interactive strategy – is guided, informed and tested by five dialogic *principles* or *criteria*. Interaction is likely to be genuinely dialogic, whichever way it is organised, if it is: *collective* (teachers and students address learning tasks together, whether as a group or as a class); *reciprocal* (teachers and students listen to each other, share ideas and consider alternative viewpoints); *supportive (*students articulate their ideas freely, without fear of embarrassment over 'wrong' answers, and they help each other to reach common understandings); *cumulative* (teachers and students build on their own and each others' ideas and chain them into coherent lines of thinking and enquiry); and *purposeful* (teachers plan and steer classroom talk with specific educational goals in view) (Alexander 2006b: 38).

In a British and American context, shifting towards a more collective and less individualistic learning culture may demand considerably more than it does in Asian classrooms, where the collective principle is more firmly established. But – and an example of the dangers of international cherry-picking of the kind we discussed in Chapter 2 – interaction that is collective without being reciprocal remains monologic and therefore suitable only for transmission teaching, while a classroom culture that is collective yet intimidating rather than supportive will be one in which learning is frustrated because students will be unwilling to reveal the misunderstandings that are a vital ingredient of cognitive scaffolding. Indeed, collectivity without reciprocity and affective or discursive support is precisely the condition of some of the Asian patterns of teaching that British teachers were urged to emulate in the mid 1990s.

Meanwhile, if exchanges consist of a sequence of disconnected questions and answers, with little extension or development, then students learn to repeat what is expected of them rather than think for themselves. Together, these tendencies make assessment for learning, that essential ingredient of successful teaching, virtually impossible (Black *et al.* 2003).

While the principle of purposefulness is self-evidently essential to all educational interaction, and while the principles of collectivity, reciprocity and support establish the climate and relationships in which successful learning through dialogue are most likely to take place, the acid test of dialogic teaching and learning is the fourth principle, cumulation. Not surprisingly, formative evaluations of current dialogic teaching development projects in British classrooms show that although cumulation is the most vital condition of dialogic teaching it is also the most difficult to achieve (Alexander 2006b). Thus it is that I tend to repeat, almost as a mantra of dialogism, Bakhtin's assertion that:

> If an answer does not give rise to a new question from itself, it falls out of the dialogue.
>
> (Bakhtin 1986: 168)

Classroom researchers and teacher trainers have long argued the need for teachers to sharpen their techniques of *questioning,* and indeed American and British schools currently make questioning central to quasi-dialogic strategies such as thinking skills (Adey and Shayer 1994; McGuiness 1999) and philosophy for children (Lipman *et al.* 1980; Fisher

1998). But the most refined and searching questioning technique is pointless if the teacher does nothing with the answer that the student provides other than pronounce it correct or incorrect, or – equivocating to avoid even that elementary judgement – 'interesting'.

Of course, the skill of framing questions has an educational value in itself, especially if it is the student rather than the teacher who is encouraged to do the questioning, as in philosophy for children programmes (Lipman *et al.* 1980). Asking questions rather than merely accepting what one is told, as I have argued here, is an essential part of the student's developing repertoire of learning talk, and questioning is a necessary ingredient of both intellectual enquiry and the nation's political health. Yet in our British dialogic teaching projects it is on *answers* – what they are, what they tell us about the student's present understanding, and what, vitally, we might do with them in order to move that understanding forward – that we are increasingly needing to concentrate. For what students in classrooms say is an exceptionally precious learning resource. Every time a teacher receives an answer but does nothing with it, which in some classrooms happens dozens of times each day, that resource is squandered.

It is for others to apply these ideas to the condition and future of pedagogy in Hong Kong schools. But there are some obvious starting points, of which I offer two. First, various studies report that Chinese teaching is relatively teacher-centred, textbook-dominated and monologic, that expository teacher talk predominates, and that teacher authority is not open to question (Hayhoe 1984; Hull 1985; Sharpe and Ning 1998; Parmenter *et al.* 2000; Potts 2003). I myself have observed Hong Kong classrooms that illustrate an extreme variant of this, and where unremitting recitation is amplified – on the teacher's side at least – by microphones and loudspeakers, and to call this 'karaoke pedagogy' might not seem unjust or unduly flippant. If this is so, how far does it compromise the pursuit of those educational objectives for which more reciprocal and reflective forms of interaction are necessary, both within the three subjects tested by PISA and across the wider curriculum? Is monologic teaching appropriate for, say, personal, social and humanities education, for moral and civic education, for creative thinking and for independent learning, all of which feature in the Hong Kong school curriculum?

A second starting point might be the PISA finding that success for Hong Kong students in the international league tables may be achieved at the cost of students' self-confidence and sense of engagement (Ho 2005). This, too, might dictate a more reciprocal, supportive and collective or inclusive pedagogy, for dialogue by its nature engages, and participation in dialogue increases self-confidence (Nystrand *et al.* 1997; Alexander 2006b). At the same time, it would be as well to note the methodological difficulties in comparing so elusive a condition as self-confidence across countries and cultures. One might also suggest that in a culture where humility is traditionally deemed a virtue, students will be more inclined to be pessimistic about themselves than in those cultures (such as the US) where schools explicitly work to boost student self-belief in a climate that is already redolent of a sense of national superiority. Then again, we might simply ask what the insistent orientation in Hong Kong towards success in public examinations does to the adolescent psyche. These are complex matters, though none of these caveats undermines the evidence showing that participatory dialogue engages and motivates.

THE DIALOGIC CURRICULUM

Let us take stock. I have argued that we need dialogue both *about* and *in* education; that is, both educational and pedagogic dialogue. I have talked about the need for the educational dialogue to be strongly informed by an international perspective, and the very different complexion this can have, depending on whether you confine education's task to pursuing the competitive opportunities of globalisation or attend more holistically to the social uses of economic advancement and the condition of the entire family of nations and the planet they inhabit.

Drawing on Mikhail Bakhtin, I have outlined a notion of dialogue that is more pervasive than talk alone, that encompasses the interaction of minds and ideas as well as words, that transcends the boundaries of time, space and culture, that entails imagination, empathy and the making of connections, and that may even be one of the keys to our survival as a species. I have applied this idea to teaching, justifying it by reference to psychological, neurological and pedagogical research; and setting out an approach that is grounded in a three-part repertoire of organisation, teaching talk and learning talk, and which is informed by the principles of collectivity, reciprocity, support, cumulation and purposefulness.

In the last part of this essay I want to return from pedagogical dialogue to the educational dialogue with which we started, and to consider, by reference to some examples published or in use, what a dialogic curriculum for the twenty-first century might look like.

There are a number of starting points, of which we might consider these five:

1 Realms of knowledge/ways of knowing
2 Generic skills
3 Forms of intelligence
4 Ways of learning
5 Hybrids.

Some might wish to read into these options two dichotomies, one old and the other more recent (see Chapter 4). In 'ways of knowing' and 'ways of learning' we may find the familiar opposition of 'subject-centred' and 'child-centred' education; and in 'realms of knowledge' and 'generic skills' we may detect a more recent concern: the contrast of past certainty with future uncertainty, or the problem of how far today's knowledge is relevant for tomorrow's world.

As always, I would prefer these dichotomies to be resisted. Take the first of them. Feeding the subject-centred / student-centred opposition are two questionable assumptions. First, that to be concerned with the knowledge, understanding and skills that a child needs in order to become culturally socialised and competent is somehow to be acting against the child's interests. Second, that the development of the child can be conceived independently of the culture in which that child grows up, and which indeed has evolved the very concept of childhood that is adduced to defend the notion of child-centredness. Twenty years ago I was arguing against these dichotomies on philosophical grounds (Alexander 1984). Now we operate with a more subtle awareness of the interactions of what Vygotsky called the 'natural' and 'cultural' lines in human development, and this makes the opposition of child and subject, or child and society, even less tenable.

To these objections we may add a cultural argument of special pertinence in Hong Kong. In her studies of American and Chinese students Jin Li contrasts American students' view of knowledge as 'out there', set apart from the learner and available to be willingly or unwillingly acquired, with the Chinese view that knowledge is integral to what it means to be a person, and that socialisation, education, knowledge and morality are inseparable (Li 2003). Opposing child and subject is a very Anglo-American preoccupation, and indeed the oppositional tendency owes much to the thinking of a leading American philosopher, John Dewey (Dewey 1990). That should make us even more cautious about proposing it as a universal educational truth.

As for the second dichotomy – between ostensibly outmoded knowledge and future-oriented skills – I consider that shortly. Meanwhile, I suggest that we view the various curriculum starting points as complementary rather than mutually exclusive.

Realms of knowledge

If we devise a curriculum starting with realms of knowledge we are on familiar territory, for this is the way that schooling has mostly been conceived up to this point in human history, and international curriculum comparisons show that there is remarkable consistency across space as well as time in the school subjects that are included and given priority in national curricula (Benavot et al. 1991).[10]

Some, as I have hinted, now argue that this approach is no longer appropriate, because knowledge so rapidly becomes obsolete that a knowledge-based curriculum risks becoming irrelevant. There are a number of reasons why we should question this claim.

Most fundamentally, the question of the relevance of particular kinds of knowledge depends on how that knowledge is conceived, packaged and taught. If knowledge is perceived as mere *information*, and if the teacher's task is to transmit that information to students who are expected to accept it unquestioningly, then it is certainly likely that during a time of rapid change some of it will become redundant, especially when so much more information is available to students on the Internet than any school textbook is likely to contain.

But if one views the various domains of knowledge not as bodies of information but as *distinct ways of knowing, understanding, enquiring and making sense*, which include processes of enquiry, modes of explanation and criteria for verification that are generic to all content in the domain, then far from being redundant, knowledge thus defined provides the tools for tackling future problems and needs as well as offering a window of unparalleled richness on past and present. Knowledge in this sense also provides the student with essential tools for testing the truth and value of all that information that pours from Internet, television, radio and newspapers, and the teacher's task becomes one of *initiation* rather than mere *transmission*. This is the view that was developed during the 1960s by Phenix (1964) in the US and Hirst (1965) in the UK, before it fell foul of the neo-Marxist sociologists of knowledge who argued that such initiation was merely a mechanism of social control (Young 1971; Apple 1995), a device for securing capitalist hegemony (Bowles and Gintis 1976) or a means of enforcing the power of the 'ideological state apparatus' (Althusser 1972).

Despite these assaults, ways of knowing – sometimes softened to 'areas of learning and experience' (HMI 1985) or 'areas of learning and development' (QCA 2000)[11] – remain a popular and probably permanent formulation. In Britain, replacing the words 'subject' or 'knowledge' by 'development' sends more palatable signals to those who prefer to see education as about facilitating children's 'natural' development rather than transmitting or initiating children into 'adult' versions of knowledge. This partly cosmetic preference has a complex ideological pedigree, and is rooted in very British notions of child-centredness (Alexander 1984).

To a degree, the bad press for a knowledge-based curriculum reflects a simple misapprehension about the nature of knowledge itself, and the highly partisan bodies of information with which mere transmission pedagogy and its totalitarian variant, indoctrination, are associated. But all curricula are *selections* from knowledge and culture (Lawton 1989), so no curriculum can be politically or culturally neutral.

Hence, in a politically polarised society such as the US, Donald Macedo's scathing analysis of the textbook *What Every American Needs to Know* in which he counters each of the textbook's statements in a parallel column headed 'What every American needs to know but is prevented from knowing' (Macedo 1999). And hence Howard Zinn's alternative history of the US, told from the 'bottom up' as a tale not of 'political leaders, heroes and saviours of the nation' but of their casualties and opponents; and of those 'hidden episodes of the past' rather than those more familiar set pieces of warfare and conquest sealed against re-assessment by deference and compliance (Zinn 2003).

Macedo's is a denunciation not of knowledge as such but of its political appropriation and educational abuse through a pedagogy from which dialogue and critique are absent and which therefore verges on indoctrination. Yet clearly, in a processual sense mathematics, the sciences, the arts and the humanities will be no less relevant and useful in the twenty-first century than they were in the twentieth. For they develop rather than stand still, proceeding on the basis of cumulation, verification and/or falsification. Even Matthew Arnold's 'high culture' view of education, as initiation into 'the best that has been known and said in the world' (Arnold 1869), quaintly traditional and elitist though it is seen by some, does not need to submit either to relativist sneers or to postmodernist nihilism. For by its sheer intellectual and imaginative power, and by its fierce integrity, the best of past thinking always tells us something new about ourselves and our world. Knowledge may be cumulative, but certain knowledge transformations and acts of artistic creation are so fundamental that they never lose their power and should be visited afresh by each generation.

> So long as men can breathe or eyes can see,
> So long lives this, and this gives life to thee.[12]

From lesser poets than Shakespeare – again – such a bid for immortality from a mere fourteen slender lines of text would have been a gamble indeed, but the fact that we read and are moved by Shakespeare's *Sonnets* four hundred years after his death both justifies his poetic conceit and proves our general point. The past, as Confucius reminded us earlier, is a profoundly illuminating teacher.

That said, we must accept that another reason why the knowledge-based curriculum has had a bad press is because historically it has been associated with transmissive, monologic teaching by rote, recitation or exposition, which too often destroys what it is supposed to arouse: the excitement of knowing and understanding. It is schooling that has reduced knowledge to 'subjects' and teaching to mere telling.

With that reductionist lesson in mind, we might acknowledge the alternative, transformatory possibilities of these same realms of knowledge. We know that scientific knowledge is always on the move, that the arts are constantly pushing at the boundaries of form and expression, and that for every conventional history there is a non-establishment or anti-establishment alternative. But what of that traditional core of all curricula: literacy? What counted as literacy for the pen-pushing Victorian clerks of the British Empire can hardly serve also as a literacy for the global information age. Yet there are still those who confine the literacy debate to slogans about the 3Rs and endlessly recycled arguments about phonics. As Luke and Carrington argue, we now need a pluralist vocabulary of 'literacies' that can accommodate in a convincing and coherent way text both print and virtual, literature both canonical and popular, and narratives both local and international (Luke and Carrington 2002); and that manages to be 'fusionist' (Millard 2003) without being merely confused.

Generic skills

Those who see knowledge as inherently obsolescent, or who criticise the inert or elitist complexion of school subjects, tend to prefer a curriculum grounded in *generic skills*. They believe that skills are the antidote to subjects because they combine contemporary relevance with hands-on experience. For example, in Britain the Royal Society for the Encouragement of Arts, Manufactures and Commerce (RSA) has reworked the entire curriculum in terms of five areas of 'competence': for learning, citizenship, relating to people, managing situations, and managing information (Bayliss 1999). Similarly, the British government has identified three broad domains of 'skill': vocational skills that are specific to particular work settings; job-specific skills distinctive to particular positions within a given occupation; and generic skills, transferable across different work and life settings (DfEE 1998c).

Clearly, the first two groups – vocational and job-specific skills – may provoke the same objection on the grounds of built-in obsolescence as knowledge-as-information. For this reason many advocates of this approach prefer to transfer them to the category of training/retraining in the more specific domain of vocational education, and place greatest emphasis during general schooling on the lifelong learning potential of the third group, generic skills. Here is a typical list:

- managing one's own learning
- problem-solving
- thinking
- research, enquiry and investigation
- invention, enterprise and entrepreneurship
- communication

- social and interpersonal skills
- teamwork
- leadership.

(Hargreaves 2004a)

Lists like this are usually justified on the grounds that unlike knowledge-based specifications they do not date; and that they provide the wherewithal for learning throughout life rather than during childhood, adolescence and early adulthood, or the first quarter of a typical lifespan, only. David Hargreaves has strengthened the case for generic skills in lifelong learning by arguing that the traditional teacher–student relationship should be replaced by the more mature relationship of learner and mentor, and that projects rather than lessons should provide the context in which the skills are acquired (Hargreaves 2004a). His view of lifelong learning appears to be implicitly dialogic.

However, if generic skills are *all* that a curriculum offers then we have a problem. Even when one hives off the explicitly vocational skills, most such models tend to be more strongly influenced by the needs of the workplace than by other contexts for life after school. They are therefore open to the same objections on the grounds of cultural bias as are realms of knowledge. And though the generic-skills approach claims to address the needs of lifelong learning, it actually sells such learning short, for it elevates being able to do something over knowing, understanding, reflecting, speculating, analysing and evaluating, which arguably are no less essential to the fulfilled, successful and useful life. Indeed, without these capacities the exercise of skill becomes, in a very real sense, meaningless. Further, though I've noted the risk of cultural bias, the more fundamental problem is that in a generic-skills approach questions of culture and identity are simply ignored.

For reasons of this kind, I submit that though generic skills are certainly a necessary component of a future-oriented curriculum, on their own they do not constitute an education, still less equip the individual with the tools of learning for life.

There is a further point to make here. With one possible exception, the skills listed by Hargreaves meet the *Oxford English Dictionary* definition of skill as 'Ability to do something (esp. manual or physical) well; proficiency, expertness, dexterity; an ability to do something, acquired through practice or learning.' Hargreaves' list is therefore a helpful one to work from. However, in recent years the term has become rapidly and startlingly debased, especially with the arrival of 'thinking skills', 'life skills' and 'emotional skills' (and its inevitable adjunct 'emotional literacy'), each of which begs all kinds of question. What exactly is an 'emotional skill?' Is 'thinking skill' a tautology, in that without thought the notion of skill becomes meaningless? (The juxtaposition of 'problem-solving' and 'thinking' underscores just this point, for what is problem-solving if not a particular way of thinking?)

What seems to be happening here is that the growing instrumentalism of public education policy in the face of globalisation has produced a sense that skills, and skills alone, will deliver economic salvation – even, paradoxically, in a 'knowledge-based economy' (for where is the knowledge if students are only taught skills?).

We met this belief earlier in the present chapter, and the Leitch Report puts it as succinctly as: ' "Economically valuable skills" is our mantra' (HM Treasury 2006: 7). That being so, national agencies not only undertake the necessary and entirely credible task of identifying the skills that a future workforce will need, but feel obliged to re-designate everything else a skill too, just to be on the safe side. That way, the problem of obsolescent knowledge is at a stroke resolved, because knowledge itself disappears, and everything remains 'relevant' because it acquires the timelessness of relativism. And that way, too, educating the artistic imagination and developing artistic capacities are re-designated 'fostering creative skills', and their context of application is 'the creative industries'. At worst, there's a kind of skill-fascism at work here, and the ready capitulation to it of those in the arts world is its humiliating measure. In such a climate, few dare claim that the arts can serve purposes other, or larger, than the pursuit of economic growth. If they do so, they are accused of being cultural elitists.

But sweeping up all manner of human attributes and educational goals into the single basket of 'skills' eliminates distinctions that are vital developmentally, epistemologically and pedagogically: between knowing, understanding and doing; between different kinds of knowledge and understanding; and between doing and feeling. Above all, this particular exercise in reductionism downgrades knowledge to mere 'information', to be downloaded from Wikipedia as needed in support of the skill, but no longer to be questioned or subjected to the kinds of tests that differentiate knowledge from belief or opinion, or science from New Age fantasy.

Skills are vital. We cannot survive without them. But educators should use the term rather more discriminatingly, otherwise we shall carelessly lose not only knowledge and understanding, but also skill itself.

Forms of intelligence

A rather different curriculum starting point is provided by considering the nature and capacities of the human mind itself, rather than what one group of human minds sitting in committee believes that other human minds should know or do.

The old idea that underlying all cognitive capacities is a general or g factor, and that this can be reliably tested to produce an intelligence quotient or IQ, has begun to give way to two claims. First that intelligence thus measured is not fixed, but is environmentally-responsive (Berliner and Biddle 1995); second, that intelligence is multiple rather than singular. Hence there are those who argue that whatever employment people may undertake, whatever kind of life they may lead, whatever kind of world they may inhabit, education – since these things cannot be predicted – should concentrate on nurturing the different kinds of intelligence.

The most celebrated theorist in this vein is Howard Gardner (1999), who posits eight 'multiple' intelligences together with a possible ninth:

- linguistic
- logico-mathematical
- spatial
- musical
- bodily-kinaesthetic
- interpersonal (relating to other people)
- intrapersonal (understanding oneself)
- naturalist (understanding the observable world)
- existential (understanding one's existence and place in the universe).

Gardner claims empirical evidence to support his model – he asserts, that is to say, that the brain does indeed operate in these distinct ways and domains.

However, it will also be observed that the model is not that far removed from a typical generic approach to a knowledge-based curriculum such as those of Phenix or Hirst. But then, we must ask, which came first, a human mind that has linguistic, mathematical and musical intelligences, or a curriculum which contains the language, mathematics and music that such intelligences have created? It would be stranger still if the culturally evolved forms of knowledge and understanding and the posited multiple intelligences bore no relation to each other. If that happened, we might conclude that either Howard Gardner, or several centuries of education, had got it entirely wrong. The fact that there *is* overlap between the two models, from utterly different starting points, actually strengthens the argument for a curriculum grounded in the different ways of knowing and understanding through which humans have made sense of their world.

Midway between theories of general and multiple intelligence is Robert Sternberg's (1985) 'triarchic' theory, which – to oversimplify, admittedly – conceives of three kinds of general ability: *analytical, creative* and *practical*. Unlike Gardner's multiple intelligences that are separate and distinct, Sternberg's three components are generic. They are all drawn upon, though in different ways, in a wide range of life situations – educational, occupational, social and so on. On the other hand, individuals may not excel equally in all three.

The curricular argument from this model would be that education should seek, in its foundation stages, to nurture all three components, because all three will be needed throughout life. Later on, however, the curriculum might provide opportunities to students to apply that aspect of their intelligence in which they are strongest. For, Sternberg argues:

> The theory does not define an intelligent child as someone who necessarily excels in all aspects of intelligence. Rather, intelligent children know their own strengths and weaknesses and find ways to capitalise on their strengths and either to compensate for or to correct their weaknesses.
>
> (Sternberg 2004: 609)

Versions of learning

So we come full circle, back to the view of learning on which my case for dialogic teaching was partly constructed. Jerome Bruner suggests that over centuries and across cultures four common 'folk pedagogies' have come to dominate our thinking about education. In these, children and students are seen as standing in various relationships to learning and knowledge:

- children as imitators: learning from modelling (which in its vocational or professional form becomes apprenticeship);
- children as recipients: learning by didactic exposure to propositional knowledge, or learning by telling; with knowledge viewed as independent of the knower;
- children as thinkers: learning by intersubjective interchange and collaboration; with knowledge seen as co-constructed;
- children as knowledgeable: learning by exploring the relationship between what is known personally and what is known canonically (i.e. from the culturally-evolved realms of knowledge with which we started).

(Adapted from Bruner 1996: 53–62)

Bruner does not argue that any of these is redundant, even though imitation and being told things ('didactic exposure') are the essence of a traditional curriculum. This would suggest that it is possible to conceive of the curriculum in terms of *ways of learning* as well as *ways of knowing* and to argue that all four ways of learning described by Bruner have their place.

However, Bruner does argue that intersubjective learning ('children as thinkers') and learning by exploring the relationship between subjective and objective knowledge ('children as knowledgeable'), or between Popper's Worlds Two and Three (Popper 1972), build metacognitive awareness. Sternberg, too, in his definition of the intelligent person as the one who understands his or her cognitive capacities and builds on strengths while compensating for or remediating weaknesses, also takes a strongly metacognitive line. And both the third and fourth model are strongly dialogic: in one there is a dialogue of minds and voices in the here and now; in the other, the dialogue is between minds present and past.

This, as I say, squares the circle, for the kinds of interaction between teacher and student that characterise dialogic teaching presuppose dialogue at these other levels too: between 'I' and 'me', between self and the outside world, between subjective and culturally given knowledge, between different ways of knowing and understanding, and between past, present and future. The framework can also accommodate the relationship between learner and *mentor*, which Hargreaves (2004a) proposes as a more appropriate model for older students than the traditional one of teacher and taught, tacitly rooted as the latter one is in Bruner's 'learning by didactic exposure'.

Naturally, Bruner does more than merely identify four 'folk pedagogies'. Since the 1960s he has been famously preoccupied with the need for educators to find ways to bridge Vygotsky's 'natural' and 'cultural' lines of human development, and to scaffold the learner's thinking from the known to the yet-to-be-known. The first of these tasks used to be conceived as reconciling the logical and the psychological, or the immutable imperatives of curriculum subjects and child development (Hamlyn 1970). Now, increasingly influenced as we are by perspectives from anthropology, history and cultural as well as cognitive psychology, not to mention post-modernism and Edward Said's dire warnings against cultural imperialism (Said 1994), we see both tasks as saturated by culture, and problematically so.

Latterly, in a way that resonates to a degree with theories of diverse intelligence such as those of Gardner and Sternberg, but with a more explicit cultural take, Bruner has suggested that 'there appear to be two broad ways that humans organise and manage their experience . . . These are conventionally known as *logical-scientific* and *narrative* thinking' but that schools have treated the 'arts of narrative – song, drama, fiction, theatre – as more "decoration" than necessity'. Yet, Bruner urges:

> The importance of narrative for the cohesion of a culture is as great, very likely, as it is in structuring an individual life . . . Narrative skill does not come naturally . . . it has to be taught . . . A system of education must help those growing up in a culture find an identity within that culture. Without it they stumble after meaning. It is only in the narrative mode that one can construct an identity and find a place in one's culture.
>
> (Bruner 1996: 39–42)

Note that for Bruner the cultural narrative comes from the arts rather than programmes of civic or nationalistic education. In terms of this paper's central theme, the arts are quintessentially multi-vocal and dialogic, but in many countries civic education is a single voice whose tone brooks no argument and whose message none may question.

Hybrids

Finally, there is the hybrid approach to curriculum. As we see when weapons get into the wrong hands or when people with leadership and communication skills but limited understanding and imagination gain political power, a skill exercised without knowledge is meaningless, pointless and sometimes downright dangerous.

Sensibly understanding this, or perhaps simply hedging their bets on the relative importance for our future world of realms of knowledge and generic skills, many curriculum planners opt for a combination. Thus France has both 'les disciplines' and 'les domaines et compétances transversaux' – disciplinary knowledge and cross-curricular domains and competences (Ministère de l'Éducation Nationale 2002). England had the ten subjects of the National Curriculum and the cross-curricular 'key skills' of communication, application of number, ICT, working with others, improving one's learning and performance, and problem solving (DfEE 1999b); an earlier British model had nine 'areas of learning and experience' (aesthetic and creative, human and social, linguistic and literary, mathematical, moral, physical, scientific, spiritual, technological) and four 'elements of learning' (knowledge, concepts, skills and attitudes) (HMI 1985).

Ted Wragg has added a further axis by proposing a three-dimensional 'cubic curriculum' of ten subjects (English, maths, science and so on), eight 'cross-curricular issues' (aesethetic, citizenship, linguistic, etc.) and six 'teaching/learning styles' (tell, discover, imitate, practise, etc) (Wragg 1997). His model, as one would expect from someone who spent much of his professional life studying – and celebrating – teaching, grasps the all-important point that you cannot conceive of a curriculum without attending to the *how* as well as the *what* of learning, to process as well as content. The cubic curriculum comes in two versions: in the first, which is designed for basic school education, the 'subjects' axis consists of conventional domains of knowledge; in the second, which is vocational in orientation, these are replaced by various work domains (retail, business, construction, etc.) and whereas the 'learning styles' axis remains constant, the 'cross-curricular issues' axis is also modified. In fact, 'cross curricular issues' is a weak label: 'generic skills' is clearer.

Following the 1999–2000 Curriculum Development Council (CDC) review of the school curriculum the government of the Hong Kong Special

Administrative Region produced its own hybrid curriculum. This starts with eight *Key Learning Areas* (KLAs), which despite their names are essentially realms of knowledge.[13] These are cross-cut by nine *generic skills*.[14] Then there is a third dimension of 74 *values and attitudes*, divided into 'personal' and 'social' and each of these further subdivided into 'core' and 'sustaining'. But there are also the four *key tasks*,[15] five *essential learning experiences*,[16] and finally seven *learning goals*[17] (Education and Manpower Bureau 2005).

I have to say that this is one of the more complex of the hybrid specifications that I have seen, because although it starts as the familiar two-dimensional grid (key learning areas – or subjects – and generic skills) it actually has six dimensions. This degree of complexity raises the stakes when it comes to implementation, and makes it possible that some elements, in some schools, will be delivered more as rhetoric than practice, for it is hard to pursue so many objectives simultaneously. The proposals have not been without controversy, particularly where the politicisation (or 'depoliticisation' or even 're-depoliticisation') of civic education and primary school general studies are concerned (Morris 1988; Cheung and Leung 1998; Murphy 2004).

CONCLUSION: MOVING FORWARD

These are typical starting points for a twenty-first-century curriculum. Although I ended with the Hong Kong curriculum framework, this was by way of example only, and my concern here has been to identify issues with which we might *all* be concerned, wherever we live and work, when we think about the future of education in a world characterised not just by the opportunities of the global marketplace, but also by the less palatable global realities of poverty, inequality and the denial of human rights, and when we dare to contemplate the ultimate endgames of nuclear war, environmental collapse and social disintegration. Education, surely, can and must be used to address these challenges before they overwhelm us. Or is that asking too much of even the best that education can offer? I earnestly hope not.

Meanwhile, it seems pretty self-evident that each of the starting points for curriculum design that I have identified has something to offer, and for this reason a hybrid model of some kind is probably inevitable. However, whereas knowledge/skills hybrids are common enough, those that attend to forms of human intelligence and ways of learning are much rarer than they should be. Further, many curricula still deal with realms of knowledge in the reductionist and intellectually impoverished way that has given knowledge-based education in any form a bad name. These deficiencies of omission and commission need to be remedied.

That leaves open one vital question. What should be the balance and priorities among the various ways of knowing and learning, skills and forms of intelligence? Should it be the familiar mixture or something more radical?

That, of course, depends on whether we wish children to acquire Bruner's vital 'narrative' of cultural identity through dialogue or to have a monologic identity imposed upon them. It also depends on what kind of future we predict or wish for our children. I offered what were deliberately stark and opposing scenarios: the dream of infinite economic expansion and the nightmare of ecological catastrophe; enclaves of super-rich minorities in a world in which the majority live well below the poverty line; the pursuit of self-gratification and material gain subverting the struggle for equality, justice and the collective good; the geopolitical lottery of lives, which for some are long, healthy and fulfilled while for millions of others they are cut short by malnutrition, disease or war, or survived but with their true potential never realised.

I did this not to imply that these are the only futures or choices available, for they are not, but to signal that national education debates need international perspectives, and that these must reach considerably deeper into the condition and prospects of our world than the usual bland rhetoric about the global economy and the information society; to signal, too, that the ultimate questions in education are moral rather than pragmatic; and that they are now very, very urgent. This, then, is where the dialogue about education should start.

And if, having made our choice about the future direction of education, we wish to create a curriculum that is worth more than the paper on which it is printed and that truly comes alive in the classroom, we must add a pedagogy that directly engages children's thinking and leads it forward. I have placed the spoken word central to that endeavour. Hence my argument that good teaching is collective, reciprocal, supportive and cumulative as well as purposeful, and that dialogue *within* and *about* education are sides of the same essential coin.

POSTSCRIPT

When, in October 2005, the original version of this chapter was delivered to a Hong Kong audience, it was suggested that to refer so directly and uncompromisingly to climate change and global inequality in a public lecture about pedagogy and educational policy was somewhat risky. Climate change was already much talked about, but rarely as an educational issue. Political and corporate America were still insisting that the science proved nothing, and the British subservience to Washington that passes for a 'special relationship' had silenced many of those in the major political parties who believed otherwise. Meanwhile, 'education for sustainable development' was relegated to the outmost fringes of the English National Curriculum, which meant that in most schools it was ignored. To raise the issue thus, it was suggested, was just too controversial for comfort. As if on cue, one member of the Hong Kong audience asked if the author was 'some kind of socialist'.

By 2007 a great deal had changed. United States President George W. Bush's open contempt for the 2006 Kyoto Protocol on climate change had morphed into a subtler or perhaps more insidious attempt to reconcile his insistence that American business imperatives must at all costs be protected with public acknowledgement that global warming was a problem. Al Gore, his erstwhile Presidential opponent, had achieved massive success and a Nobel Prize with his campaigning film about global warming: *An Inconvenient Truth*. British politicians were falling over each other in their race to demonstrate their green credentials, and international report after report argued the growing urgency of the crisis. Climate change and global warming had captured the centre ground; though, as we noted earlier in this chapter by reference to the Leitch report and government documents, there remained a sense that government remained more interested in saying than doing what was needed. Indeed it continued to press simultaneously for carbon reductions and the doubling of the capacity of Heathrow and Stansted Airports.

So too in education. When the independent review of primary education in England (the Primary Review) was launched in October 2006, it placed matters such as those explored in the first part of this chapter squarely on the agenda, alongside a raft of other possible issues that an internationally oriented curriculum might consider addressing. As in Hong Kong, this prompted someone to ask what climate change had to do with education. Yet as the Review team toured the English regions as part of the enquiry's 'community soundings' strand, they found – unprompted – not just heightened global awareness but a pervasive pessimism about the prospects for children and the world in which they are growing up. On the basis of no fewer than 87 witness sessions with teachers, children, heads, parents, school governors and a wide variety of community representatives, the Review reported:

> In spite of our careful attempts to elicit and record difference, what is striking about the Community Soundings is the extent of consensus which they reveal, especially in the key areas of educational purpose, curriculum and assessment, the condition of childhood and society, and the world in which today's children are growing up. This tendency to consensus on the big issues transcends both constituency and location.
>
> What is no less striking is the pessimistic and critical tenor of much that we heard on such matters. Thus, we were frequently told children are under intense and perhaps excessive pressure from the policy-driven demands of their schools and the commercially-driven values of the wider society; that family life and community are breaking down;

that there is a pervasive loss of respect and empathy both within and between generations; that life outside the school gates is increasingly insecure and dangerous; that the wider world is changing, rapidly and in ways which it is not always easy to comprehend though on balance they give cause for alarm, especially in respect of climate change and environmental sustainability; that the primary school curriculum is too narrow and rigid; that the curriculum and children's educational careers are being compromised by the national tests, especially the Key Stage 2 SATs; that while some government initiatives, notably *Every Child Matters*, are to be warmly welcomed, others may constrain and disempower rather than enable; and that the task facing teachers and other professionals who work with children is, for these and other reasons, much more difficult now than it was a generation ago.

(Alexander and Hargreaves 2007: 1)

The passage is quoted in full to show that witnesses were worried about far more than climate change, and that their concerns included others we have discussed in this chapter. Yet this particular anxiety contributed to their sense of unease and apprehension.

However, there was a positive element too:

Pessimism turned to hope when witnesses felt they had the power to act. Thus, the children who were most confident that climate change need not overwhelm them were those whose schools had decided to replace unfocussed fear by factual information and practical strategies for energy reduction and sustainability. Similarly, the teachers who were least worried by national initiatives were those who responded to them with robust and knowledgeable criticism rather than resentful compliance, and asserted their professional right to go their own way. There is an important lesson from such empowerment for governments with centralising tendencies, as well as for primary schools themselves ... Of course, not even the most enterprising school can reverse some of the social trends which worried many of our witnesses. That being so, these Community Soundings have implications for social and economic policy more generally, and for public attitudes and values, not merely for government and the schools.

(Alexander and Hargreaves 2007: 44)

This takes us back to the dialogic imperative, for dialogue as proposed in this and earlier chapters is also about empowerment: empowerment of the learner and the citizen; empowerment of the mind through knowledge, understanding and the capacity for enquiry and critique; empowerment by translating these into practical courses of action; empowerment of the teacher no less than the learner, for a compliant teacher is unlikely to produce a liberated student. But these witnesses' voices also run counter to the view, fashionable in millennial Westminster, that knowledge has had its day and skills will suffice for tomorrow's world.

NOTES

1   It is only fair to point out, *pace* Drèze, Sen, the United Nations and other sources, that the official figures on literacy in China are not universally accepted as reliable. See also p. 19.
2   A large claim, admittedly, though the wide-ranging 2005 EPPI review of evidence on citizenship education confirms that dialogic pedagogy is essential to the development both of true understanding of what citizenship in a democracy entails and of the capacities needed in order to translate that understanding into effective democratic action (Deakin Crick *et al.* 2005).
3   UK readers are reminded that this chapter started as a presentation given to a Hong Kong audience. Given that Hong Kong is part of China, the world's most populous country and the century's fast-approaching economic giant, it is entirely appropriate to retain the reference here and elsewhere in a chapter that is concerned with the international dimension of national education systems.
4   (1) Eradicate extreme hunger and poverty. (2) Achieve universal primary education. (3) Promote gender equality and empower women. (4) Reduce child mortality. (5) Improve maternal health. (6) Combat HIV/AIDS, malaria and other diseases. (7) Ensure environmental sustainability. (8) Develop a global partnership for sustainable development.
5   *Genesis*, Chapter 1.
6   The phrase is Naomi Klein's (2000), though her analysis is more subtle than the one implied here.
7   From Bakhtin's *Estetika*, in Holquist (2002) p 39.
8   Confucius, *Analects* II, 11, in Arthur Waley's 1938 translation (2000).
9   Shakespeare, Sonnet 129.
10 The 2000 National Curriculum for lower secondary schools in England was a characteristic formulation of this kind: English, mathematics, science, design and technology, ICT, history, geography, modern foreign languages, art and design, music, physical education, citizenship.
11 For example, the Foundation Stage curriculum for children aged 3–5 in England: personal with social and emotional development, communication, language and literacy, mathematical development, knowledge and under-standing of the world, physical development, creative development.
12 Shakespeare, Sonnet 18.
13 KLAs: Chinese, English, mathematics, personal with social and humanities education, science, technology, arts, physical education.
14 Generic skills: collaboration, communication, creativity, critical thinking, IT, numeracy, problem-solving, self-management, study.
15 Key tasks: moral and civic education, reading to learn, project learning, using IT.
16 Essential learning experiences: moral and civic education, intellectual development, community service, physical and aesthetic development, career-related experience.
17 Learning goals: familial, societal and national sense of responsibility, national identity, independent reading, language skills in Chinese including Putonghua, creative thinking and independent learning skills, breadth of knowledge in the 8 KLAs, healthy lifestyle.

Chapter 7

Words and music

EXCEPTIONAL TEACHERS

Many of us – sadly, not all of us – are fortunate to encounter teachers who seem to be exceptional. What they do exceeds competence and expertise – the conventional gradation of professionals who have passed the novice stage[1] – for these can be taken for granted and such individuals offer something deeper and more enduring. This essay is about one such exceptional teacher.

I have met and observed a number of teachers whose work in my view justifies the epithet 'exceptional'; not a large number, but sufficient to make it clear that excellence can take many forms and may be highly idiosyncratic. Some demonstrate an apparently effortless expertise against the odds, in circumstances that would leave the rest of us floundering. There are many such teachers working in British and American cities, and as the world outside their schools becomes more divided, anomic and violent, so their task becomes harder and the immensity of their talent becomes more evident. Others exhibit a range, completeness and adaptability of pedagogical command, allied to an energy that ordinary mortals can manage, at best, for only a few minutes but which somehow exceptional teachers sustain indefinitely.

One such might be the elementary school teacher in Flint, Michigan whom we met in Chapters 2 and 4. Her mastery of a wide array of pedagogical options was total, yet it was so understated that without transcript analysis and repeated viewing of her videotaped lessons we might not have registered the extent of her achievement, and the seamlessness with which she moved from one action or decision to the next. Yet, as anyone who knows Flint – a ghost town of high unemployment and severe social problems following the departure of General Motors – will attest, the circumstances in which she was teaching were unusually challenging.

Another would certainly be the head of a primary school in the state of Haryana in India who appears in *Culture and Pedagogy*. Her school was under-resourced to a degree that British or American teachers would find inconceivable. The surrounding community was poor, parental illiteracy was running at well over 50 per cent, and for largely economic reasons – migrant labour and families' needs for help in the fields or with siblings – there had been an acute problem of prolonged and unpredictable pupil absence. Yet she achieved and maintained high pupil attendance, the school yard was a paradise of dappled shade, whitewashed stone and plants in mighty earthenware pots, a perfect forum for the many school events that took place there, and the children were both engaging and wholly engaged in their learning. Meanwhile, her fellow-teachers worked with her to keep things that way, making visits to the children's homes a routine after-hours commitment. This teacher's excellence lay in a special combination of secure expertise, inspiration, leadership and – that overused word – dedication.

Or we might nominate, saving their modesty, one or other of the small group of primary teachers in London and North Yorkshire who have incorporated dialogic teaching into their professional repertoire and have transformed both their own practice and the experience of their pupils, in each case translating the principles outlined on pages 112–13 into something highly individual. There is little resemblance between the way their pupils talk – confidently and articulately, yet also, when appropriate, speculatively and tentatively – and what one hears in so many other classrooms; the same goes for the mature and considerate ways that teachers and pupils relate to each other, for this is an essential aspect of the approach adopted. One might add that what also marks out these teachers is their self-awareness, for they know that once one surpasses the 'competent' stage teaching becomes infinitely improvable. As a teacher from a much earlier project commented in the context of a programme of videotaping and interviews that was intended to explore the thinking and dilemmas that go with professional maturity, the job gets more rather than less difficult, because a teacher who is free from the pressure of merely 'coping' realises the ever-receding immensity of doing full justice to the needs and learning of every one of a class of 25 or 30 children (Alexander 1988).

This essay celebrates such people as a very special group but does not describe any of those just mentioned. These are teachers whom I have observed and talked with, and whose work in many instances I have studied in depth with the help of videotape, formal interviews and lesson transcripts. But the admiration for these teachers, which grew from what started as dispassionate analysis, remains that of the outsider. I do not actually know what it feels like to be taught by them. Hence Douglas Brown.

I realised when I was taught by Douglas between the ages of 11 and 18 that he was exceptional, but, as Jung reminds us, we need to outgrow and even disown our strongest early influences in order to discover our autonomous selves. I did reject Douglas's influence, and decisively, soon after leaving the school where he taught. But as I look back on a career in education I understand just how much I owe to him – helped by those of my contemporaries who came together in 2005 to pay tribute on the fortieth anniversary of his tragically early death at the age of 43. It is thus fitting that the final essay in this sequence should be about not teaching in general but one teacher, for teaching is a complex amalgam of the person and the professional, and it may well be impossible to be a teacher of the kind that stretches minds and fires imaginations unless one is also a rather special person.

Douglas Brown (1921–65) does not obviously fit the pedagogical mould indicated by our earlier discussion of dialogic teaching. Talk was hugely important to him, and I have met few talkers as fluent or as undemonstratively eloquent, but in today's classrooms he would be counted somewhat monologic. Yet, not once in my recollection did he take the easy route of recitation teaching, the ritualised default mode of class-room interaction, for he saw learning as enquiry and advocacy rather than simple transmission, and in that spirit his questions were utterly authentic. In any case, he had no need of the safety net that recitation affords for those teachers whose limited knowledge of what they teach confines them to the security of test or recall questions, beyond which they stray at their peril. Instead, his forte was a kind of two-layered exposition: telling and explaining, but also and especially, *showing*. That is to say, letting the words and music that were his passion themselves do the work, having sensitised us to their power and inducted us in ways that this power might be unlocked. Dialogue in its more restricted oral sense came later, in less formal settings, when he discussed our progress individually.

Douglas Brown, though, was a dialogic teacher in a more profound and no less Bakhtinian sense. For him the dialogues that mattered in the teaching of English language and literature were between language and the ideas that language conveys, whether such dialogues manifest harmony, counterpoint, tension or conflict: between the creative urge and the constraints of form; between reader and text; within a text between character and character, idea and idea; within a character between competing internal voices; and out again into the wider dialogues between literature, music, culture, politics and history. For Douglas the teacher, as for great yet equally self-effacing performing artists such as Alfred Brendel, his task was to set up as direct as possible a dialogue between author and reader, or composer and listener, a dialogue that the teacher/performer mediates with consummate skill and empathy but without vanity.

The remainder of this essay falls into two parts. The first is by way of background. It places Douglas Brown in the context of 1950s/1960s English secondary education. This is necessary because we are talking here about a country and an education system that in the intervening 50 years have changed almost beyond recognition. The second part is more personal, and the chapter's change of tone and style reflects this. It offers one ex-student's response to a man who I hope readers will accept – if I can sufficiently persuade them – stands on one of the pinnacles of this complex and essential activity we call teaching. I say 'one of', for exceptional teaching comes in many forms and exceptional teachers mediate their talents through very different personalities.

The school

Douglas Brown taught English at the Perse School, a direct grant grammar school for boys situated in Cambridge and enjoying close historical ties to that city's 800-year-old university. Under the direct grant scheme, which went back to 1919 and was consolidated by the 1944 Education Act, those endowed secondary schools that were not able or did not wish to be fully independent reserved at least a quarter of their places for non fee-paying children from local authority primary schools in return for freedom from LEA control and a grant from the Ministry of Education, precursor to today's Department for Children, Schools and Families. By 1964 the direct grant amounted to 75 per cent of their income. Entry to the Perse by this minority route was on the basis of the 11-plus examination, so the school was able to take the cream of local talent – in as far as this test delivered on this dubious notion, which of course was hotly disputed. This system both alleviated the financial problems of many independent schools and provided a sop to those who believed that as strongholds of privilege such schools had no place in a country ostensibly committed to equality of educational opportunity. The debate had been heated before the 1939–45 war, but the strongly hierarchical system inherited from the nineteenth century not only survived the 1944 Education Act but was confirmed by it in an extended league table of state-maintained establishments. This included technical and secondary modern as well as grammar schools.

In terms of the 1950s/1960s criterion of Oxbridge entry, the Perse retained its position near the top of the hierarchy, though not at the very top. Its then headmaster, Stanley Stubbs, insisted on calling the Perse a public school, which it was not. In reality its status was at best ambivalent. With the widespread introduction of non-selective comprehensive schools following the Labour government's Circular 10/65, the position of direct grant schools became increasingly anomalous, and the scheme was withdrawn ten years later (it reappeared in a different guise in the Conservatives' 1981 Education Act as the means-tested Assisted Places Scheme). Now, of course, the Perse is fully independent.

Douglas Brown had little time for public-school posturing and by the early 1960s he was an active member of the campaign for non-selective comprehensive education. He contributed to *New Left Review* and worked closely with Brian Jackson, a former university student of his who was an untiring advocate of reform. Jackson, Brian Simon and others amassed influential and damaging evidence on the then near-universal practice of streaming in primary schools, the device by which the system spotted its future 11-plus stars as early as age 7 and trained them for the big event, often leaving the rest to fall by the wayside – meanwhile, as it happens, confirming what R.H. Tawney (1923) had called the 'hereditary curse of English education ... its organisation along lines of social class'. This evidence led directly to the Plowden Committee's 1967 decision to recommend the abolition of streaming in primary schools.

The Mummery

Douglas taught, pupil age-wise, at the bottom and top of the school. For the first two years English lessons took place mainly in the Mummery, a small makeshift theatre that had been started by Henry Caldwell Cook, author of the once-influential *The Play Way* (Cook 1917). Douglas had been one of Cook's pupils. He went on to read English at Cambridge University, finishing with a double starred first and the Charles Oldham Shakespeare Prize, a feat seldom equalled. After war service in India and Burma as a conscientious objector serving in the Friends' Ambulance Unit, he decided against an academic career, returned to his old school and revived the Mummery, which by then had fallen into disuse.

Caldwell Cook had been a true original. In building on his work Douglas was not tapping a solid educational tradition so much as continuing to blaze an unusual and highly distinctive trail. The Mummery's position somewhat apart from wider trends and debates in the teaching of English is confirmed when one notes how negligibly it resonates with the growth of educational drama in secondary schools from the 1970s onwards, and how instead it seems to have been associated – not wholly appropriately – with the progressives' advocacy of 'play' in the nursery and primary years. One authority even places Cook confidently in the tradition of Pestalozzi, Froebel and Montessori. Nevertheless, Mummery 'play' was dramatic rather than ludic, planned and staged rather than spontaneous. And whereas mainstream secondary school drama, like progressive primary teaching, worked from and with pupils' everyday experiences, Mummery teaching was unapologetically grounded in Shakespeare and a dramatic line stretching back to ancient Greece. Douglas Brown made, for Mummery use, his own translations of the *Antigone* and *Philoctetes* of Sophocles (Brown 1969a, 1969b).

In any case, the Mummery stood for more than drama. Mime and dance also featured and – the critical link with Douglas's work with older pupils and indeed undergraduates – his teaching there above all sought to foster an acute and responsive engagement with language, spoken as well as written. In combination all this constituted a spectrum of professional skill that only an exceptional teacher might emulate.

Literature, culture and the Cambridge connection

It is impossible to ignore the significance for the Perse of its Cambridge location and connections. Founded in 1615 as a free school by a fellow of Gonville and Caius College, the Perse enjoyed close connections with the university at several levels, and W.H.D. Rouse, a previous headmaster, had simultaneously held school and university appointments (as did Douglas Brown). Indeed, for Perse pupils during the acutely snobbish 1950s other universities might as well not have existed. But while Douglas was Cambridge through and through – Perse, St Catharine's, Perse – he had not a trace of that Cambridge arrogance or affectation that one still far too frequently encounters. So too his inspirational but vituperative mentor F.R. Leavis: Perse again, Emmanuel, Downing. For both of them, war service had intervened (for Leavis it was the 1914–18 war), decisively and traumatically enlarging their perspective on the human condition, on their moral responsibilities as teachers and scholars and, no doubt, on Cambridge itself.

Almost single-handedly, Leavis had brought about a revolution in how English as a university subject was perceived and taught. Almost: at Cambridge a shift away from the literary dilettantism of gentrified dons on the one hand and a heavily Germanic approach to Old Norse and Old English philology on the other had already begun, steered by the likes of Hector Chadwick, A.C. Haddon and I.A. Richards, whose *Practical Criticism* showed the very different possibilities of close engagement with English poetry (Richards 1929). The English Association had been founded in 1907 to place the study of English language and literature at the heart of cultural renewal. In 1921 (the year of Douglas's birth) the Newbolt Committee revived the spirit of Matthew Arnold in its report *The Teaching of English in England* (Board of Education 1921), and insisted that English should be accorded status at least equal to that of other university subjects. Leavis himself placed the study of literature, and especially of that extended, psychologically acute exploration of human dealings represented by the English novel at its best, at the heart of his quest for a new moral community.

Douglas was thoroughly schooled in this still-emerging tradition, though not uncritically so. His sixth-form teaching had none of the intemperate edge of Leavis's: he concentrated on the tale not the teller, and though as a member of the English Faculty he was close to Leavis's colleagues, he stood well apart from the vendettas that Leavis and his wife Queenie pursued with such legendary zest.

For one teacher so seamlessly to combine the *Play Way* with the intense seriousness and close-grained linguistic scrutiny of Leavis's literary and cultural engagement is nothing short of remarkable: one teacher, two utterly different pedagogies. What was also exceptional about Douglas in this context was that he wasn't only a schoolteacher: simultaneously he was supervising undergraduates at two Cambridge colleges and by 1960 he was lecturing on Conrad for the university's Faculty of English. Few have achieved that double career, though Rouse had set a precedent by combining his Perse headship with the university's chair of Sanskrit.

This was not all. Douglas was also a fine and hugely knowledgeable musician. By the time he was offered the first chair in English at the newly founded York University in 1964 he was ready to take forward the combined study of literature and music, working with that university's first professor of music, Wilfred Mellers. Cambridge and Leavis again, almost inevitably: Mellers had been at Downing (and remains an honorary fellow there, having recently celebrated his ninetieth birthday) and was a regular contributor to Leavis's *Scrutiny*. Douglas also knew Cambridge's great musicologist John Stevens, whose studies in mediaeval and Renaissance song demonstrated the productive potential of this kind of interdisciplinarity.

In the end, in relation to the study of English as a university subject one has a sense of immense promise fulfilled in his teaching but only provisionally in his research and publication. In 1961, Douglas took everyone by surprise by leaving the Perse and moving to a lectureship in English at Reading University. He was rapidly promoted to the English chair at York University but died before taking it up. He had produced and revised a book on Thomas Hardy (Brown 1962), had edited an edition of George Herbert's poems (Brown 1960) and an anthology of modern prose, and had written a number of articles. Though my fellow-contributors to the 2005 Douglas Brown anniversary tribute (Loades 2005) noted his growing politicisation through the late 1950s and into the 1960s, we cannot know how this would have influenced his mature academic work. His 1962 Hardy revision registers more powerfully than the 1954 edition the contemporary resonance of Jude Fawley's devastating, class-based exclusion from Oxford University in *Jude the Obscure* ('. . . judging from your description of yourself as a working-man, I venture to suggest that you will have a much better chance of success in life by remaining in your own sphere and sticking to your trade than by adopting any other course. That, therefore, is what I advise you to do.'). We know that in 1957 Douglas was hugely excited by Richard Hoggart's reflections, in *The Uses of Literacy*, on pre-war working-class culture in Leeds (Hoggart 1957), and that he commended Raymond Williams' no less visionary *Culture and Society* (Williams 1958) when it appeared a year later. These offered rather different takes on culture to Leavis's, and they linked to the sociology that

Douglas was also reading at this time but which as a discipline was not yet countenanced in Cambridge. Had he lived, Douglas – dare one suggest – might have become a major figure in the then embryonic field of cultural studies.

English in schools: Cambridge and London

Douglas followed and intervened in the wider national debate about the teaching and assessment of English in secondary schools, contributing several articles to *The Use of English*. This journal, for teachers of English in schools, was founded by Denys Thompson, grammar school head-master and co-author with F.R. Leavis of the textbook *Culture and Environment* (Leavis and Thompson 1933). Christopher Parry, Douglas's pupil and successor, was a later editor. Douglas became an examiner for the Cambridge local examination board and offered trenchant criticism of the heavily edited 'editions' of the classics that some schools used, and of the O level English language paper.

He did so at a critical time in the development of secondary school English. Historians of the subject have recorded the way that Leavis's influence spread into schools through his many students who became English teachers, and fostered a discernible 'Cambridge' tradition. Central to this, inevitably, was the study of literature as a moral pursuit and as an antidote to the perceived degeneracy of contemporary mass culture.

Such teachers, no less inevitably, tended to end up in public, direct grant or maintained grammar schools rather than in secondary moderns or the then small number of comprehensives. Neither their clientele nor their pedagogy encouraged much in the way of engagement with the lives and experiences of the majority of the school population.

Opposing the Cambridge tradition, and acquiring a sharper and more confident edge from the 1960s onwards, was 'London' secondary English. This focused on vernacular language rather than canonic literature, on mass rather than elite culture, on the present rather than the past, on social relevance rather than heritage, and was grittily urban rather than nostalgically rural.

Not that Douglas represented the 'Cambridge' stereotype implied here. He was too voracious a thinker and reader, and just too intelligent and politically radical, to be blind to the stern challenges that changes in English society and education posed to teachers of English language and literature. But again, though we know that he attended meetings of the London Association for the Teaching of English (LATE), which was absorbed into the National Association for the Teaching of English (NATE) in 1963, we cannot know how he would have handled the increasingly polarised debates about English teaching that characterised the 1960s, 1970s and 1980s.

Anyway, in some respects he was ahead of the game. Douglas's approach to children's writing, via the 'explorations' that punctuated his Mummery work within the first two years, anticipated the explosion of school creative writing by more than a decade. Yet his was a more exacting process than much of what passed for creative writing during the 1960s and 1970s. The appeal to felt experience demanded a fierce honesty. Each sense in turn must be interrogated. He would have had no truck with those later teachers who saw correct spelling and grammar as tiresome obstacles to self-expression. Douglas insisted that true self-expression demanded precision in the choice and use of language, that writing was a discipline, and that words and phrases should be weighed for their expressive integrity. This was utterly consistent with his approach to literature in the sixth form, informed as it invariably was by Leavis's 'This is so, isn't it?', 'Yes, but . . .'.

Adult education

Douglas Brown bridged educational worlds other than school and university. Like Richard Hoggart and Raymond Williams, whose work he commended to his Perse pupils, and those grand figures of the left, Eric Hobsbawm and E.P. Thompson, he was also deeply involved in adult education. Perversely, perhaps, in terms of what in other respects they had come to represent socially, both Oxford and Cambridge had strong extra-mural departments. Now, of course, we prefer 'lifelong learning' even to 'adult education' let alone 'extra-mural' – a term that bridges but first signals the divide between those who have had access to higher education and those who have not. Condemned by his social origins to remain outside the walls of Biblioll College, Hardy's and Douglas's Jude would have taken the full sense of 'extra-mural' and in Douglas's day *extra muribus* it still was. He was a member of the university's Extra-Mural Board, a keen supporter of the Village College movement that had started in Cambridgeshire during the 1930s under Henry Morris, and of the Workers' Educational Association (WEA) founded much earlier, in 1903, which during the post-war years had a considerable membership. As early as 1952 we find Douglas contributing to a WEA journal.

His chief venue was Madingley Hall (now Cambridge University's Institute of Continuing Education). There, winter and summer from the mid-1950s onwards, he ran intensive week-long courses on English literature – Dickens, Yeats, Hardy, Conrad – and a tremendous following and impact they had too, by all accounts.

I have identified here five educational contexts of Douglas's teaching, or five communities of discourse in which, as a teacher of English, he engaged. 'As a teacher of English' is the necessary proviso: music, religion and politics were no less significant to him. What was exceptional about

Douglas the teacher, apart from his massive intelligence, his self-sacrificing intensity, rigour and conscientiousness, and his utter and infectious belief in the power of English well-studied to make individual and collective life more meaningful and morally engaged, was his *range*. That is to say, the range of his interests and the range of educational contexts in which he worked: English and music; drama with the youngest pupils, quasi-undergraduate study with the oldest; school and university; university and adult education; elite and mass education.

A tantalising and perhaps provocative hint of how things might have turned out comes from Douglas's own account (to David Grugeon) of his interview for the chair of English at York University. In the year of Labour's comprehensive school Circular 10/65, Douglas was asked by Eric (later Lord) James – ex-headmaster of Manchester Grammar School and York's first vice-chancellor – where he hoped to be in five years' time. 'Heading an English department in a university' replied Douglas, 'or in a comprehensive school.' But that was then, long before New Labour dismissed most of Old Labour's proud creations as 'bog standard' or worse. As for targets, naming and shaming, league tables, strategies, initiatives, step changes and the rest, he would have counted the thinking as impoverished and dishonest as the language. And yet – as with his gentle subversion of the Perse's aping of 'public school customs and costumes', as he called them – he would somehow have retained his independence and flair. Until, that is, the inspectors called – only to retreat baffled that he managed utterly to defy their checklist of 'best practice' while yet surpassing it.

WORDS AND MUSIC

Some encounters with Douglas Brown were common to all who passed through the Perse. Others were confined to a smaller number. About Douglas's Mummery teaching in the first two years I say little, for I remain uncertain how to assess his updating of Caldwell Cook's *Play Way* and the apparatus of mediaeval guilds and Elizabethan theatre in which this part of his work was set. The dank Pendene House cellars, the wheezing gas fire, the musty costumes in the Tiring House, the colour-coded 78s from which Masters of Music made their more or less suitable selections, and of course the gamut of productions from *Julius Caesar* to Douglas's own translation of the *Philoctetes of Sophocles* – all this reminds us of how atmospherically charged were the Mummery sessions, as well as how strikingly different from the more standard fare that one received in the structurally less precarious main school building. (Had current health and safety legislation been in force, the Mummery would have been instantly closed down.)

So too his approach to writing, with its appeal to felt experience and to descriptive honesty and precision in committing that experience to paper.

Every word counted – the commanding yet hushed intensity of his reading aloud demonstrated this without further injunction – and every lesson was an event. Nothing was routine, and if we worked hard we knew that he worked harder still: no other teacher provided feedback on written work as comprehensive as his.

Then there was his spellbinding and liberating use of the spoken word. Donald Davie, academic and poet, had been Douglas's fellow under-graduate at Cambridge and remained one of his closest friends. In his autobiography *These the Companions* Davie writes of Douglas:

> For it was when he spoke rapidly in his quiet voice, that everyone was astonished. I have never, before or since, encountered such a gift for articulation, and in the strictest sense; for his vocabulary was wide, fastidious and choice, but what was remarkable was the marshalling of that vocabulary in spoken syntax, the leaping and springing clauses that unwound luxuriantly, crossed over, and yet drew unerringly home. It was daunting, and finding it in a fellow-student I was daunted indeed.
>
> (Davie 1982)

I don't think that as Douglas's pupils we were daunted, for being so much younger we didn't dream of comparing ourselves with him. But we were certainly riveted by that quiet voice that compelled you to listen without his needing to command that you should do so, by his ability to make words do whatever he wanted, and by the power and discipline of the thinking that was thereby intimated. Yet, unlike lesser teachers Douglas spoke thus not to impress or control, but to initiate, provoke and inspire.

These things, as I say, are familiar to all who attended the Perse during the Douglas Brown years, and merely summoning their outward features points up the distinctiveness of his teaching, and perhaps a hint of its quality. A much smaller number of us later encountered Douglas the musician, or were steered by him towards the December entry for Cambridge English, a process that started in the lower sixth and ran alongside the A level course, taking over completely once that exam was out of the way. There I find myself on firmer ground.

Timetabled music at the 1950s Perse was abysmal, for it fell outside the then headmaster's canon of proper academic, physical and military pursuits (a judgement in which, as a matter of fact, he showed some ignorance of the public-school values he sought to emulate). So there were raucous renderings from the *New National Song Book* during the first two years and, until the arrival of a proper teacher of class and specialist music at the end of the decade, little else save for what those staff appointed to teach subjects other than music offered by way of compensation in their own time and sometimes at their own expense. That included fine pianism from Cecil Crouch, who taught art but in fact had attended the Royal

College of Music as well as the Slade and was part of a musical dynasty that thrives still, and the less polished but more flamboyant talent of chemist F.C. Brown. Together with Douglas they set up the Perse Friends of Music and under its auspices ran an ambitious programme of professional concerts. Then there were the entrepreneurial efforts of pupils themselves: a group of us set up the Pendene Ensemble – memorial to a crumbling building on the Perse's old Gonville Place site in the centre of town; and of course Douglas's musical evenings.

These last were attended with particular relief by those of us who had the misfortune to be boarders in a mostly day school and were therefore denied the range of out-of-school activities that genuine boarding schools offer. Saturday evenings offered a walk to Douglas's house, music from his extensive and fast-expanding record collection, talk about music and much else, and refreshment. After the Spartan culture of the senior boarding house it was all so – well – civilised. We could and did ask to hear particular pieces (and his library was such that every request could be met) but generally the evening's programme was devised by Douglas and was at the same time engaging and didactic.

The range of music we thus encountered was vast. Douglas himself possessed a Broadwood grand and a square piano and played both of them well, so keyboard music featured prominently. For me, he once singled out a starkly percussive performance by Geza Anda of Beethoven's Waldstein sonata, which I was at that time struggling to learn with Cecil Crouch and which he knew would challenge Crouch's preference for a more conventional reading. (Douglas himself had been my piano teacher for my two years, after which Crouch took over.) He inducted us into the growing debate about authentic ornamentation, instrumentation and performance, which at that time was confined to baroque music but in which, headed by Thurston Dart, Cambridge musicians were already prominent; and he illustrated its concerns by comparing the Bach playing of, say, George Malcolm, Dinu Lipatti and Glenn Gould. He covered the Viennese orchestral repertoire from Mozart to Mahler and Bruckner. He explored with us twentieth-century music, especially Bartok and Stravinsky but also the less accessible Webern and Berg. I remember him playing a record of Stravinsky's neoclassical piano sonata, giving me the score and challenging me to master it. It was much more difficult than it sounded. He ventured much further back, to mediaeval and Renaissance music, picking out the best of the relatively small number of recordings that were then available. He registered, and recorded off air, new music as it appeared.

What I think we took for granted about all this was Douglas's extraordinary generosity, as well as his compendious musical knowledge and deep insight. The Saturday evenings just happened. They were fixed, inevitable and as much part of school life as those daily assemblies with their hearty hymns and interminable announcements about playing field prowess attained or hoped for, though infinitely more educative. With professional workload agreements half a century away nothing was more natural than that an already dedicated teacher should give up part of his weekends to remedy deficiencies in the school's provision. But then for Douglas spare time seemed an alien or frivolous concept. We had already inferred that from grapevine intelligence about his parallel careers as director of studies in English at St Catharine's College and extra-mural lecturer at Madingley Hall ('Not much to look at but what a *voice!*' gasped a female family friend after one of his sessions), not to mention his allegiances to the Labour Party and St Bene't's Church.

So too in his work with the small group preparing to seek entry to Cambridge University to read English. Clearly, some of this was timetabled and salaried but much more was not. Our group, which must have been his last, sat the scholarship exams in December 1960. There were, I think, six of us. For each he marked out a distinctive programme of reading and writing, though for all of us Shakespeare and Leavis's 'great tradition' of the English novel – Austen, Eliot, Dickens, James, Conrad, Lawrence – were obligatory. But he also encouraged us to read non-English writers in the original (if we could) or in translation, hence our introduction to Stendhal, Ibsen, Chekhov and Tolstoy. The important thing was to read and keep reading. Nothing so mundane as coaching for expected exam questions: this was no less than a second education in itself. The books kept coming and coming.

So, combining his undemanding generosity with pre-emptive insight he appeared one morning with a complete set of George Eliot that he had bought from David's secondhand bookshop, thrust the pile of books upon me and told me to start with *Adam Bede* and not to stop until I had finished *Daniel Deronda*. Challenging essay titles followed, and essays generated no less challenging evaluations, and as a result of this total immersion *Middlemarch* became and remained – with *Anna Karenina* – the novel to which I most frequently and admiringly return.

I'm far from alone in my addiction to *Middlemarch*, so the admiration may seem a bit obvious or even hackneyed, but Douglas alerted us to the extraordinary psychological depth of George Eliot's portrayals of the central characters and their dealings with each other, and it's that aspect which impels me to read the book again and again; for there are no limits to what such art can offer. The conversations between characters and between writer and reader in literature of this stature are, as Bakhtin proposed in his account of Dostoevsky, truly unending. And as one grows older they become more and more enthralling – a test that most of the thousands of novels published each year decisively fail, because even if their prose is not as downright clichéd as that of *The Da Vinci Code*, psychological authenticity is what they most conspicuously lack. When one is young, Edward Casaubon is a ludicrous, heartless and tyrannical pedant who undeservedly lands himself a beautiful and devoted young wife. But when in later life one re-reads of Casaubon's embittered and lonely final months as he faces his approaching end and recognises the futility of his years of arid and misdirected scholarship, the portrait becomes profoundly tragic.

Douglas's written evaluations of our work were models from which all teachers could learn. Full, generous, perceptive, but where necessary hard-hitting though never destructively so, they really did honour Bakhtin's maxim by provoking new questions from our answers. Their italicised typescript, conversational prose, speculative asides and open questions underlined his insistence that such evaluations were contributions to a dialogue rather than final judgements – or, as we now also say, they were 'assessments for learning', and against that or any yardstick they were models worthy of emulation.

The explorations could take unusual turns (and using that word reminds me that 'explorations' was Douglas's own name for the writing we did with him in the first two years at the Perse, a decade or so before the vogue for creative writing). One such was when he added to my George Eliot collection a version of *Daniel Deronda* in which all the Deronda passages were blacked out so that I could test Leavis's proposition that there were two novels here rather than one and that the better one should have been called *Gwendolen Harleth* (Leavis 1960). Some of my contemporaries were shocked at this act of vandalism, but it certainly made the point. And of course the Eliot set – with an unmarked copy of *Daniel Deronda* – was mine to keep.

Douglas demanded the closest possible attention to language. Also to beginnings: my battered Harrison edition of *Othello* from 1959 retains pencilled annotations for Act I, Scene I far more extensive than the text itself. They alert one to the way the verse signals the villainy about to be unleashed and before that to the historically shocking racial and cultural juxtaposition of 'Moor' and 'Venice' in the play's subtitle, for Douglas was no less effective in relating text to context. Here, as with *Macbeth* and especially *King Lear*, he brilliantly linked the fates of verse, psyche and social order: the bombast, the incomplete lines, the wrenching caesuras.

For this treatment to work, editorial fidelity was essential. Not for Douglas the interventions of the editor we called 'Virginity' Verity because of his prudish cuts to the Miranda/Caliban episodes in our A level text of *The Tempest*. I have managed to retain, inside my ex-Perse Harrison edition of Shakespeare's *Sonnets*, Douglas's three versions of Sonnet 129, 'Th' expense of spirit in a waste of shame': from the 1609 Quarto; from what he calls 'a characteristic modern edition', which not only tidies up the spelling but also manages to halt the poem's disturbing momentum with a Victorian cold shower of intrusive punctuation; and his own 'proposed text for study', which is closer to the Quarto again and allows the verse to speak for itself.

So too with prose. 'The cow is there' in the opening of Forster's *The Longest Journey* evoked discussion of both Berkeleianism and – a trifle uncomfortably I suspect for some of us grammar school sixth formers who thought we knew it all – callow pretentiousness. Douglas's celebrated treatment of 'It is a truth universally acknowledged . . .' at the opening of *Pride and Prejudice* didn't just make the standard A level point about Jane Austen's irony; it also forced us to watch for much more delicate shades in her moral positioning later on, there and – especially – in *Emma*. In this, Douglas of course didn't follow the tendency to write off some of Austen's supporting characters as the one-dimensional comics or villains of countless televised Jane Austen costume dramas. Mr Bennett's patience may have been sorely tried by his wife's inanities, but his entertaining put-downs betrayed cruelty as well as resignation.

One day, by way of helping us to work out for ourselves the difference between art and artifice, Douglas gave us without comment or attribution four poems on the theme of loss: Wordsworth's 'A slumber did my spirit steal', Tennyson's 'Break, break break', 'They told me Heraclitus' by William Johnson Cory (a piece of doggerel not as risible as McGonagle but whose pain was no less bogus) and one that he himself had written for the purpose but of course didn't admit to. Extreme contrasts – Wordsworth and Cory, for example – made the art/artifice distinction easy enough, but for novices like us less unequal comparisons provided a much more exacting exercise. Douglas had judged precisely where to pitch his own poem between tolerable and good.

I said that Douglas marked out both a shared course and individual pathways for all members of the Cambridge December scholarship group. Sometimes the latter converged and allowed useful discussion – as when two of us worked on different Pope poems – but at other times they were more tightly tailored and we went our own ways, converging on the set pieces of the Great Tradition and Shakespeare. The canonical teaching of English literature has long since been reviled as narrow and elitist or has given way to cultural 'relevance' and relativism, and a shift of some kind was certainly needed. But Douglas's position on this was not the same as that of Leavis. He shared Leavis's belief in the central place in a proper study of English literature of the work of certain major authors, but beyond this his politics as well as his appetite for advancing the boundaries of his and our understanding made him very eclectic. In performance, too: we would attend safe Shakespearean productions at the Cambridge's Arts Theatre, but Douglas also encouraged us to see, say, the film version of *Julius Caesar*, starring Gielgud, James Mason and – yes – Marlon Brando; or to catch up with the latest Bergman or Fellini.

One staging post on my own journey, given my struggles against the institutional odds as a would-be musician, was the dialogue (again) between words and music. Characteristically, Douglas set this up in both familiar and less obvious ways. So I studied vocal settings, and, naturally, Douglas lent the necessary recordings and scores so that I could explore what composers did with words when they turned them into song.

Of these, I particularly recall my first encounter with Britten's stunning settings of Donne's *Holy Sonnets*, performed by Peter Pears and Britten himself and culminating in the sustained, defiant, double-forte F sharp of 'Death thou shalt die'. This contrasted with an account closer to Donne's time, by Purcell's one-time teacher Pelham Humfrey, of the 'Hymn to God the Father', with its repeated punning on done/Donne. On Douglas's 78 rpm recording it was achingly sung by counter-tenor Alfred Deller, and I played it so many times that I almost wore it out. The less obvious line of enquiry was in the area of musical and literary form. So, for example, while I was working on T.S. Eliot's *Four Quartets* Douglas pointed me towards the Bartok string quartets and late Beethoven and I began, but only began, to tease out the relationship of form, tension and the crystallisation of feeling.

[The importance of *form* remains a pedagogical as well as a musical, literary or dramatic preoccupation. It is the act of submitting to but then exploiting and testing the disciplines and boundaries of form, to and beyond their apparent limits, which unites some of the greatest composers, writers and painters. So too with teachers and the elements of pedagogic form: lesson structure, time, space, organisation, subject-matter, task, activity, interaction, assessment. Indeed, in making sense of observational, videotape and transcript data from classrooms in England, France, India, Russia and the United States I have found the vocabularies of musical composition and performance to be powerfully suggestive of lesson planning which specifies everything in detail to that which encourages extemporisation on a theme (content) or ground (structure); teaching in action which ranges from the formally-slavish to the improvisatory; time conceived as the security of pulse and rhythm combined with the judicious tempo of cognitive pace rather than the hectic scramble through prescribed content of what Ofsted and the UK government's national strategies call 'pacy' teaching; the weaving and recurrence of discernible leitmotifs as a device to consolidate understanding; the contrast between the rigidity of the three/four part lesson structure as prescribed by the National Strategies, the formlessness of some of the 1970s/1980s teaching to which these prescriptions have claimed to provide the necessary antidote, and the more episodic formalism of mainstream European practice, grounded as it is in a pedagogic tradition which reaches back to Comenius. Comparative analysis of teaching shows that such applications are far from fanciful – and there are many more – for pedagogy is an aspect of the wider development of culture and ideas, not separate from these (Alexander 2001a: 306–19).]

Back to Douglas Brown. For our group, a defining collective experience was a week in the Lake District after A levels, when Douglas booked a cottage at the head of Borrowdale and we shared the chores, read, talked and, of course walked. Too much of the latter, one day: after an immense hike, without Douglas, which took in Scafell, Scafell Pike, Great Gable and Glaramara, most of us, understandably but unprecedentedly, fell asleep while Douglas was reading aloud (the location demanded Wordsworth but it was probably Conrad). For once, but for once only, Douglas's quiet vocal intensity lulled rather than engaged.

After all this, the outcome was not what Douglas wanted or expected. Cambridge it had to be, but 'I've got you down for Downing', he cheerfully announced one day, when I had hoped to follow other members of my family to St John's College. But never mind: Downing meant Leavis, and to be thus redirected was probably an accolade of sorts. Once there, I joined a much larger group who had converged on Downing College from all over Britain to sit at the master's feet. But not long into my first year I decided I could no longer take the cowed or submissive silence of those weekly seminars in Leavis's chilly room on D staircase, his at times vitriolic attacks on contemporary writers and critics – 'Forster [or was it T.S. Eliot?] is nasty down there . . .' – culminating in his public tirade against C.P. Snow, and the sense that we were being dragooned into literary responses we had neither the knowledge nor the experience to venture for ourselves.

For here was the rub. How, validly, could boys or girls emerging from adolescence apply that stern Leavisite test of artistic integrity, psychological acuity and moral authenticity that Douglas had so frequently rehearsed with us – 'This is so, isn't it?', 'Yes, but . . .' – without seeming, like those E.M. Forster youths, callow and affected? Leavis and Brown had seen active service in world wars. They had experienced Life as well as Art. True, there were other tests available to us and at least – so we thought – we knew the difference between art and artifice, but now we had moved from the security of exploration to the bald exposure of absolute judgement. With this shift, that fog that had always drifted in and out of my studies with Douglas – of comprehension no sooner glimpsed than lost, of hard-won insight crumbling into banality – became suddenly denser. Now, as for Stephen Blackpool in *Hard Times* (a novel that had provided one of Douglas's most electrifying opening chapter readings) it was 'A muddle! Aw a muddle!'.

What I couldn't realise then, being too young and impatient, was that this was precisely the point. Great art may certainly move as readily as works that set out with no end other than to manipulate such a response – Jonathan Miller confesses to weeping each time he hears the crystalline 'Erbarme dich' from Bach's sublime St Matthew Passion, and he is surely not alone – but it also demands effort. True educational dialogue is a demanding discipline. The fog is still there, and, the world being as it is, why should we expect it to lift, except fleetingly? The person who sees everything with unbending clarity is either a true visionary or is fit for nothing but high political office.

Leavis was gracious about my decision to switch courses from English to another subject. He merely asked whether I really knew what I was doing, which of course I didn't, though I nodded gamely enough. Douglas, when I met him for the next and last time, at an alumnus gathering where he, Leavis and Peter Hall – all three of them former Perse pupils – were guests of honour, muttered 'Incomprehensible' and walked away. He was probably right. It was a kind of betrayal and I should have persisted rather than given up. Yet this was an uncharacteristic comment, not just in the way he let his guard drop for once, but also because he at least had seemed to understand the adolescent psyche.

But as Douglas surely knew, teaching of that commitment and power leaves its mark and establishes lifelong habits of thought and action, or at least ways of thinking and acting to which one struggles to aspire. His manner of engaging with language and literature, and his close attention to words written and spoken, are with me to this day. His intellect, insight, skill and independence make today's ministerial accolades for politically compliant 'best practice' look utterly tawdry. His moral but never moralistic engagement with literature, music and life render irresponsible as well as contemptible the UK government's injunction to use the dismal pragmatism of 'what works' as the sole touchstone for defining good teaching. His high educational ambitions for his pupils were quite unlike today's teaching 'targets' because we made them our own, gladly, willingly and without the crude panoply of pressures, threats and sanctions upon which the post-1997 target-setting apparatus has depended. In any case, targets may be intended to raise horizons but actually they impose limits and Douglas's aspirations certainly did not. Indeed, they probably far exceeded any targets or attainment levels that might have been thought appropriate to students of the ages he taught – not that we achieved them: aiming high was what mattered. And there's some justice in the fact that after many twists and turns I ended up exploring pedagogy in educational and cultural contexts as far removed from 1950s/1960s Cambridge as it is possible to imagine. For it is that experience that gives me the confidence to assert with more than mere conviction that Douglas Brown was indeed a rare and remarkable teacher.

With Douglas, moreover, there was not one teacher but four: language, literature, music and the man through whom the power of these was unlocked. Not for him the self-important strutting of those teachers whose authority resides in position rather than talent, and whose educational vocabulary neither liberates nor ignites but instead fawns on the clichéd eduspeak of the latest government initiative. He knew, and he wanted us to know, that the words and music mattered much more than he, and in this he displayed the humility of genius and the artistry of teaching at their best.

NOTE

1   Dreyfus and Dreyfus (1986) propose five stages in teacher development: 'novice', 'advanced beginner', 'competent', 'proficient' and 'expert'. Berliner (1994) prefers to collapse the last two categories on the grounds that in teaching it is hard to discriminate proficiency from expertise. Glaser (1996) identifies three cognitive stages generalisable across a wide range of professional activities: 'externally supported', 'transitional' and 'self-regulatory'. Glaser's model pinpoints the essence: the transition from dependence to autonomy. Exceptional teaching, or exceptional performance in any sphere, lies beyond expertise and adds a high degree of artistry, flexibility and originality whose precise features may be hard to pin down as measurable indicators; but we certainly know it when we see it. Bond *et al.* (2000), after a validation exercise endorsed by Berliner, summarise 13 'prototypic characteristics' of expert teachers in areas such as subject knowledge, problem-solving, improvisation, classroom climate, task challenge, sensitivity to context, monitoring, feedback, respect for students and ability to 'read' the cues they provide.

Chapter 8

Conclusion

We started with problems of definition and scope. In Anglophone countries unused to or even embarrassed by the term, what exactly *is* pedagogy? Is pedagogy just teaching by another name? Is this mere linguistic snobbery, with aristocratic Greek supplanting honest Old English?

Teaching, as I hope is now clear, is certainly at the heart of pedagogy but the two are not synonymous. Teaching is a deliberate cultural intervention in individual human development that is deeply saturated with the values and history of the society and community in which it is located. Teaching is not, and even in the most technicist and centralising political regime never can be, a mindless act. Practice, as they say, is 'theory-soaked'. If that is so, we need a separate word to connote the combination of the act of teaching and the values, evidence, theories and collective histories that inform, shape and explain it, a word that will lead us away from the blinkered pragmatism of 'what works' into the realm of ideas and argument. That word, for centuries in common use elsewhere, is pedagogy.

The move towards acceptance of the word and a broader apprehension of its meaning appears to be gathering pace – up to a point. In 2003/4, in the public lecture and subsequent article that formed the basis for this book's third chapter, I offered this:

> Pedagogy is the act of teaching together with its attendant discourse. It is what one needs to know, and the skills one needs to command, in order to make and justify the many different kinds of decisions of which teaching is constituted.
>
> (Alexander 2004a: 11)

This was adapted in a 2007 document from the UK government's National Primary and Secondary Strategies:

> The National Strategies have developed the following working definition: pedagogy is the act of teaching, and the rationale that supports the

actions that teachers take. It is what a teacher needs to know and the range of skills that a teacher needs to use in order to make effective teaching decisions.

(DfES 2007b: 1)

The obvious plagiarism (habitual with the UK government's national education strategies) is in one sense symptomatic of the centralising urge: the emperor's power is secure only as long as nobody spots that his clothes are stolen. However, what is more interesting is the way that the government's modification of my definition implies the bigger picture without really meaning it. The 'many kinds of decisions of which teaching is constituted' are cut back to 'effective teaching decisions'. Since effectiveness is elsewhere defined as no less and especially no more than it takes to deliver government-prescribed strategies and meet government-ordained targets, the wide range of decisions implied by my formulation is reduced to those particular decisions that are necessary in order to ensure these outcomes. On that basis, 'the rationale that supports the actions that teachers take' and the rationale for the government's National Strategies become synonymous, and we are back with Michael Barber's era of 'informed professional judgement' and the culture of compliance (Chapter 3).

Further, the document quoted above is a classic example of the post hoc invention of a rationale to justify a policy that as presented does not actually possess one. In Chapter 3 we saw that process at work in the National Literacy Strategy, which sought to buy evidential respectability some time after it had been published and implemented. In the same chapter we examined the 'principles' in which the 2003 Primary National Strategy was supposedly grounded and found them platitudinous and in most cases meaningless. Four years later, the booklet quoted above 'provides a theoretical yet practical view of the pedagogical principles embedded in the National Strategies' (DfES 2007b). Since not one shred of evidence is cited in support of the booklet's re-statement of the 2003 Primary Strategy 'principles', and the arguments in their support are assertions rather than justifications, 'theoretical yet practical' can be added to the burgeoning heap of official meaninglessness.

No bigger picture there, then, notwithstanding the belated coining of the term 'pedagogy'. Such accounts of pedagogy are as far removed from the larger questions touched on in this book's previous chapters as it is possible to imagine. Fortunately, the growth of British interest in pedagogy is not limited to opportunistic National Strategies (or perhaps that should be national strategic opportunism). Four other initiatives provide rather more encouraging examples of the quickening trend.

The first, about which at this stage little can be said, is the intention to find ways to take forward the important project on conceptualising and mapping pedagogy that Donald McIntyre initiated for the British Educational Research Association and the General Teaching Council for

England, but which was cut short by his untimely death in 2007 (see Chapter 1). It is not yet clear how this will proceed, and without Donald's vision, rigour and compendious knowledge it could fall short of his aspirations, but it deserves every encouragement.

The second, about which we do have a clear picture, is the massive programme of commissioned research that goes by the name of the Teaching and Learning Research Programme (TLRP). This programme, funded by the Economic and Social Research Council (ESRC) comprises nearly 70 separate projects, 22 of them relating to schools. It was launched in 2000 and is due to be completed in 2008, with some outliers continuing until 2011.

TLRP's bigger picture is framed, as its name indicates, by the activities of teaching and learning and the task of finding ways to maximise their potential. However, its take on these is full and diverse, as to both education phase – it spans the gamut from early years to adult and life-long learning – and pedagogical focus. Of particular interest in relation to this book's concern with the world outside the school, one of its major cross-project themes is 'The political, economic and cultural context', although that context tends to be national rather than – as urged in this book – international.

From TLRP's school-based activity have come two helpful frameworks. The first is a post hoc placing of the programme's contributory projects in the following categories:

- Learning in specific curriculum areas (for example, English, mathematics, science).
- Learning across the curriculum.
- Learning through ICT.
- Environments for better learning (for example, group work, home–school knowledge exchange, provision for gifted and talented pupils, effective pre-school provision).
- School conditions for the improvement of teaching and learning (for example, consulting pupils about teaching, learning and assessment, developing inclusive school practices, learning how to learn).

(James and Pollard 2008)

The other framework is a set of ten 'evidence-informed principles to guide policy and practice', which have been distilled from the full range of TLRP projects. Each of these starts with a proposition that is then expanded as a description of practices that enact the principle. Thus:

Effective teaching and learning:

1 Equips learners for life in its broadest sense.
2 Engages with valued forms of knowledge.

   3 Recognises the importance of prior experience and learning.
   4 Requires the teacher to scaffold learning.
   5 Needs assessment to be congruent with learning.
   6 Promotes the active engagement of the learner.
   7 Fosters both individual and social processes and outcomes.
   8 Recognises the significance of informal learning.
   9 Depends on teacher learning.
   10 Demands consistent policy frameworks with support for teaching
      and learning as their primary focus.

(TLRP 2007)

In this form the principles look somewhat anodyne, but their elaboration and backing by evidence from the TLRP contributory projects gives them both solidity and real authority. It is not difficult, even from the ten principle 'stems' listed above, to see how they resonate with some of the ideas explored in earlier chapters, especially in Chapter 5 'Talking, teaching, learning'.

However, in the light of this book's running theme of concern about the impact of the UK government's education policies on the scope and probity of pedagogical discourse, the final principle begs an important question: what kinds of framework provide genuine support without counter-productive intervention?

The next example of an encouraging pedagogical initiative is rather different. It is an ambitious and radical attempt to rethink the pedagogy of secondary schooling, which has been masterminded by David Hargreaves and sponsored by the Specialist Schools and Academies Trust (SSAT). Hargreaves subtly reconfigures the UK government's notion of 'personalised learning' from done deal to work permanently in progress – 'personalising learning' – with the aim of rethinking the nature of school learning, the relationship of teacher and student, and the contexts in which learning takes place. Hargreaves identifies a sequence of nine 'gateways' to personalising learning:

1 student voice
2 assessment for learning
3 learning to learn
4 the new technologies
5 curriculum
6 advice and guidance
7 mentoring and coaching
8 workforce development
9 school organisation and design.

(Hargreaves 2004c)

Each of these is developed by reference both to recent research and examples from schools, thus giving the framework a double validatory onward nudge. Most are well-worked ideas from other contexts. The originality here lies in what Hargreaves has chosen to identify as the key gateways, and how he explores their applications and relationships. As with all of Hargreaves' work, the material, which is presented in booklet form, is clearly written, cogently argued and well referenced – in sharp contrast to documentation from the National Strategies, which can be commended for clarity but not for cogency or evidence.

Cutting across the nine 'gateways' are six core themes predicated on the belief that student engagement is the key to successful learning:

- engagement with learning and life
- responsibility for learning and behaviour
- independence in and control over learning
- confidence in oneself as a learner
- maturity in relationships with staff and fellow students
- co-construction in the design, delivery and assessment of learning.

(Hargreaves 2006b)

The theory – for theory of learning it is – is extended further in booklets that explore the interactions between the gateways in pursuit of the 'four deeps':

1 deep learning
2 deep experience
3 deep support
4 deep leadership.

(Hargreaves 2006a)

So, for example, 'deep learning' brings together the gateways *student voice, assessment for learning* and *learning to learn*, and among the conditions for deep learning proposed are 'meta-cognitive control', 'growing learner autonomy' and 'learning conversations' (Hargreaves 2004b; Sims 2006). The latter condition is adumbrated as 'dialogue', using this author's theory of dialogic teaching and its underpinning principles of collectivity, reciprocity, support, cumulation and purposefulness (Chapter 5 and Alexander 2006a).

This, as I say, is extremely ambitious: not just in terms of an aspiration that encompasses nothing less than the root and branch reform of the culture of British secondary schooling, but also theoretically. Like TLRP, its 'bigger picture' is bounded mainly by school and classroom, though, also like TLRP, it is prepared to look outwards at the contexts of national policy, the economy and society. Neither project has much to say about the global context. TLRP comprises an array of research projects out of whose findings a set of general teaching and learning 'principles' has been constructed. The SSAT Personalising Learning initiative proposes a theory of teaching, learning and indeed schooling that is governed by a single goal – the personalisation of learning – and sets out both principles and strategies through which the goal may be achieved.

The final example is closer to home. Following three years of planning, a comprehensive independent enquiry into English primary education – the biggest for 40 years – was launched in October 2006 and is due to publish its final report in late 2008 or early 2009. It comprises a matrix of four kinds of evidence, three overarching perspectives and ten themes, and aims:

> to identify the purposes which the primary phase of education should serve, the values which it should espouse, the curriculum and learning environment which it should provide, and the conditions which are necessary in order to ensure both that these are of the highest and most consistent quality possible, and that they address the needs of children and society over the coming decades.
>
> (www.primaryreview.org.uk)

The four kinds of evidence are:

- written submissions from all who wish to provide them;
- regional and national face-to-face soundings with specific communities and organisations;
- commissioned surveys of published research; and
- searches of official data.

The various kinds of evidence are all brought to bear on the Review's ten themes:

Core themes: purposes, content, processes and outcomes of primary education

- purposes and values
- learning and teaching
- curriculum and assessment
- quality and standards
- diversity and inclusion
- settings and professionals.

Contingent themes: contexts and conditions for primary education

- parenting, caring and educating
- children's lives beyond school

- structures and phases
- funding and governance.

Each of these is developed as a set of detailed questions that fall into the categories of 'evidence' (What is happening and how good is it?) and 'vision' ('Where should the system be heading, and how can it be improved?'). Overarching them is a group of three broad perspectives, which are cited here complete with their questions, as they constitute the core of the Review's concerns:

> *Children and childhood.* What do we know about young children's lives in and out of school, and about the nature of childhood, at the start of the 21st century? How do children of primary school age develop, think, feel, act and learn? To which of the myriad individual and collective differences between children should educators and related professionals particularly respond? What do children most fundamentally need from those charged with providing their primary education?

> *Culture, society and the global context.* In what kind of society and world are today's children growing up and being educated? In what do England's (and Britain's) cultural differences and commonalities reside? What is the country's likely economic, social and political future? Is there a consensus about the 'good society' and education's role in helping to shape and secure it? What can we predict about the future – social, economic, environmental, moral, political – of the wider world with which Britain is interdependent? What, too, does this imply for children and primary education?

> *Education.* Taking the system as a whole, from national policy and overall structure to the fine detail of school and classroom practice, what are the current characteristics, strengths and weaknesses of the English state system of primary education? To what needs and purposes should it be chiefly directed over the coming decades? What values should it espouse? What learning experiences should it provide? By what means can its quality be secured and sustained?

> (www.primaryreview.org.uk)

At the time of going to press, the Review is just past its half-way point and has begun to publish, at three-weekly intervals, its 32 interim reports in order to promote discussion and debate. These include the 30 surveys of published research commissioned from the Review's 70 academic consultants, and reports on the written submissions and the regional 'community soundings' from the first and second strands of evidence. To date, 12 of these reports have been published; by the time this book appears, all of them will be available. Already they have provoked considerable and somewhat sensational media interest (Alexander 2007b).

However, the issue here is not so much the Review process, or the relationship between the Review, the media and national government. These matters will be more fully explored later (though see Alexander 2007b for a preliminary account). The Primary Review features here because it illustrates the full gamut of versions of pedagogy from the narrow (Theme 2, *Learning and Teaching*), through the somewhat broader (Themes 1, 2 and 3, *Purposes and Values, Learning and Teaching, Curriculum and Assessment*), to the comprehensive. The bigger picture in this case encompasses not just important contingent questions about the professional knowledge, skills and roles on which successful teaching and learning depend (Themes 4 and 6, *Quality and Standards* and *Settings and Professionals*), the relationship between children's experience and learning inside and outside school (Theme 8, *Children's Lives Outside School*), and how pedagogy accommodates difference and diversity (Theme 5, *Diversity and Inclusion*). It also encompasses those larger questions about the nature of knowledge and the national and global contexts that we touched on in Chapter 6 (Perspective 2, *Culture, Society and the Global Context*) and the condition of childhood itself (Perspective 1, *Children and Childhood*).

These four projects alone indicate that things are stirring, and the last three above are all on a grand scale. Although during the half-century (almost) covered by my professional career thus far I can recall phases of intense interest in reconceptualising the curriculum (notably during the 1970s), there has been nothing comparable in the domain of pedagogy to what has built up since 2000 or so.

During the course of this book I have proposed a number of frameworks for conceptualising pedagogy, starting from the proposition (above) that pedagogy is both the act of teaching and its attendant discourse. Chapter 3 mapped the elements in that discourse, tidied up somewhat in Figure 8.1.

Here, *pedagogy as discourse* is conceived as three levels of ideas – classroom, system/policy and culture/society – which in turn enable, formalise and locate the act of teaching.

Then, in Chapter 4, I turned to *pedagogy as act*. This framework, which was developed for the international classroom data from the *Culture and Pedagogy* research, and which needed to be equally valid and workable in five very different cultural contexts, started with two irreducible propositions:

- Teaching, in any setting, is the act of using method x to enable students to learn y.
- Teaching has structure and form; it is situated in, and governed by, space, time and patterns of student organisation; and it is undertaken for a purpose.

Classroom level: ideas that enable teaching

- *Students*   characteristics, development, motivation, needs, differences
- *Learning*   nature, facilitation, achievement and assessment
- *Teaching*   nature, scope, planning, execution and evaluation
- *Curriculum*   ways of knowing, doing, creating, investigating and making sense.

System/policy level: ideas that formalise and legitimate teaching

- *School*   e.g. infrastructure, staffing, training
- *Curriculum*   e.g. aims, content
- *Assessment*   e.g. formal tests, qualifications, entry requirements
- *Other policies* e.g. teacher recruitment and training, equity and inclusion.

Cultural/societal level: ideas that locate teaching

- *Community*   the familial and local attitudes, expectations and mores that shape learners' outlooks
- *Culture*   the collective ideas, values, customs and relationships that shape a society's view of itself, of the world and of education
- *Self*   what it is to be a person; how identity is acquired.

Figure 8.1 Pedagogy as discourse (theories, values, evidence and justifications)
Source: Alexander 2007a

These translated into a model containing three broad analytical categories – the immediate context or *frame* within which the act of teaching is set, the *act* itself, and its *form* – and a set of elements within each such category. The core acts of teaching (*task, activity, interaction* and *judgement*) are framed by *space, student organisation, time* and *curriculum*, and by *routines, rules and rituals*. They are given form, and are bounded temporally and conceptually, by the *lesson* or teaching session (Figure 8.2).

By way of discouraging the reduction of teaching to naive dichotomies, I drew on the same research to identify not two but five versions of teaching that have common currency internationally:

- Teaching as *transmission*
- Teaching as *initiation*
- Teaching as *negotiation*
- Teaching as *facilitation*
- Teaching as *acceleration*

Our discussion of these showed how they can be identified as readily observable tendencies in contemporary classrooms in Britain and elsewhere, but also how each can be traced back to founding ideas and influences in the history of national education systems and movements: to elementary school minimalism for a view of teaching at its most basic (transmission); and to the views of teaching crystallised by figures such as Matthew Arnold (initiation), John Dewey (negotiation), Jean Piaget (facilitation) and Lev Vygotsky (acceleration).

In Chapter 4 I also suggested, again drawing on the international data, that buttressing these specifically pedagogical positions are three 'primordial values' which are concerned with that most fundamental human question, the relationship of humans to each other and to the communities and societies they inhabit:

- Individualism
- Community
- Collectivism

Chapter 4 showed how, far from being abstractions, such values map directly onto classroom practice. I suggested that individualism, community and collectivism – or child, group and class – are the organisational nodes of pedagogy not just for reasons of practical exigency but because they are the social and indeed political nodes of human relations. Individualism, community and collectivism arise inside the classroom not as a clinical choice between alternative teaching strategies so much as a value-dilemma that may be fundamental to a society's history and culture.

This final framework enabled sense to be made not just of the strongly collective spirit and practice of the pedagogy of countries in Central and Eastern Europe, but also of tensions and even contradictions observable in classrooms in the US and England, where the value-orientation was much less clear and secure.

Frame	Form	Act
Space		Task
Student organisation		Activity
Time	Lesson	
Curriculum		Interaction
Routine, rule and ritual		Judgement

Figure 8.2 Pedagogy as act: a generic model of teaching
Source: From Alexander 2001a: 325

One might go further, and add curriculum frameworks such as those discussed in Chapter 6 – *realms of knowledge, generic skills, forms of intelligence* and *versions of learning* – and, picking out just the 'interaction' component from the model of teaching in Figure 8.2, the various repertoires for learning talk, teaching talk and classroom organisation from the theory of dialogic teaching. In its insistence on reciprocity and collectivity in classroom transactions this theory links to two of the primordial values above. There is currently some concern that the proper interest in students' individual needs and educational progress represented by 'personalised learning' will limit such learning by failing to exploit the collective potential of classroom activity and interaction. Hargreaves' model of 'personalising learning', by emphasising mentoring, coaching and 'learning conversations' (or dialogic teaching) appears to avoid this danger, but in other contexts this problematic aspect of personalised learning has yet to be properly worked through.

Each of these frameworks exhibits the inevitable limitations of any attempt to impose tabulated order on the complexities of human affairs. Yet alongside the ideas emerging from projects such as TLRP, the SSAT Personalising Learning initiative and the Primary Review, the frameworks exemplified above and discussed more fully elsewhere in this book serve four important purposes.

First, they confirm the extraordinary richness of pedagogy as a field of intellectual exploration and empirical enquiry. Second, they show that even the narrower definition of pedagogy as the act of teaching has an impressively broad array of dimensions that in planning and execution must be attended to (consider, for example, the professional agenda that is implied by Figure 8.2). Third, they remind us that pedagogy as discourse is not an optional extra, and for the sake of the students whose interests we claim to serve we have an obligation to make explicit and debate those ideas, values, beliefs and theories that may be hidden even from ourselves yet powerfully shape what both teachers and students do. Finally, the frameworks command our urgent attention to that larger canvas of culture, history, language, politics, justice and even survival with which this book has been preoccupied. Pedagogy has a purpose. It mediates learning, knowledge, culture and identity. It enshrines – or ought to enshrine – visions of human empowerment, the good society and a better world.

Appendix

Dialogic teaching

This should be read in conjunction with Chapter 5. It is adapted from Alexander 2006b: 37–43. The dialogic teaching framework, developed in association with schools and local authorities, comprises four elements:

- justifications
- principles
- repertoires
- indicators.

JUSTIFICATIONS

There are seven powerful arguments for making talk central to an empowering pedagogy:

- *Communicative*: talk is humankind's principal means of communication, especially in an era when children are becoming more familiar with visual images than the written word.
- *Social*: talk builds relationships, confidence and a sense of self.
- *Cultural*: talk creates and sustains individual and collective identities.
- *Neuroscientific*: language, and especially spoken language, builds connections in the brain; during the early and pre-adolescent years pre-eminently so.
- *Psychological*: language and the development of thought are inseparable. Learning is a social process, and high-quality talk helps to scaffold the pupil's understanding from what is currently known to what has yet to be known.
- *Pedagogical*: process and process-product research show that cognitively enriching talk engages pupils' attention and motivation, increases time on task and produces measurable learning gains.
- *Political*: democracies need citizens who can argue, reason, challenge, question, present cases and evaluate them. Democracies decline when citizens listen rather than talk, and when they comply rather than debate.

PRINCIPLES

Starting from the justifications above, we argue not for more of the same kind of classroom talk that children already encounter, but for a particular kind of interactive experience that we call dialogic teaching. Dialogic teaching harnesses the power of talk to engage children, stimulate and extend their thinking, and advance their learning and understanding. Not all classroom talk secures these outcomes, and some may even discourage them. Dialogic teaching is:

- *collective*: teachers and children address learning tasks together, whether as a group or as a class;
- *reciprocal*: teachers and children listen to each other, share ideas and consider alternative viewpoints;
- *supportive*: children articulate their ideas freely, without fear of embarrassment over 'wrong' answers; and they help each other to reach common understandings;
- *cumulative*: teachers and children build on their own and each other's ideas and chain them into coherent lines of thinking and enquiry;
- *purposeful*: teachers plan and steer classroom talk with specific educational goals in view.

These five principles are by far the most important component of this theory or framework of dialogic teaching. Talk is an idiosyncratic activity, and a mechanistic approach to its development in classrooms is to be avoided. But if in broad terms classroom talk does not meet the five conditions above, whatever form it takes, it is not dialogic.

REPERTOIRE (I): TALK FOR EVERYDAY LIFE

We can identify six broad categories of talk to empower and support everyday interaction. Whatever else schools do, they should ensure that children are given ample opportunities to develop and explore each of these:

- *Transactional talk* – to manage a wide range of social encounters and to convey and exchange meaning and intention.
- *Expository talk* – to expound, narrate and explain.
- *Interrogatory talk* – to ask questions of different kinds and in diverse contexts.
- *Exploratory talk* – to explore ideas and probe others' thinking.
- *Expressive talk* – to articulate feelings and personal responses.
- *Evaluative talk* – to deliver opinions and make judgements.

REPERTOIRE (II): TALK FOR TEACHING

Alongside the six kinds of everyday talk above, each of which also has its place in the classroom, we can note that most teaching draws on a more distinctive repertoire of three kinds of classroom talk:

- *Rote* (teacher-class): the drilling of facts, ideas and routines through repetition.
- *Recitation* (teacher–class or teacher–group): the accumulation of knowledge and understanding through questions designed to test or stimulate recall of what has been previously encountered, or to cue pupils to work out the answer from clues provided in the question.
- *Instruction/exposition* (teacher–class, teacher–group or teacher–individual): telling the pupil what to do, and/or imparting information, and/or explaining facts, principles or procedures.

These provide the familiar and traditional bedrock of teaching by direct instruction. Less universally, some teachers also use:

- *Discussion* (teacher–class, teacher–group or pupil–pupil): the exchange of ideas with a view to sharing information and solving problems.
- *Dialogue* (teacher–class, teacher–group, teacher–pupil, or pupil–pupil): achieving common understanding through structured and cumulative questioning and discussion which guide and prompt, reduce choices, minimise risk and error, and expedite 'handover' of concepts and principles.

The two groups are not mutually exclusive, and we are not arguing that rote, recitation and exposition should be abandoned. All five have their place. Dialogue, therefore, is part of the larger oral repertoire that is needed in order that schools may meet the diverse objectives of a broad curriculum, and so that children may be empowered both in their learning now and later as adult members of society.

REPERTOIRE (III): TALK FOR LEARNING

Alongside expanded repertoires of everyday talk and teaching talk we should work no less assiduously at helping children to develop their repertoire of learning talk. This should enable them to:

- *narrate*
- *explain*
- *instruct*
- *ask different kinds of question*

- *receive, act and build upon answers*
- *analyse and solve problems*
- *speculate and imagine*
- *explore and evaluate ideas*
- *discuss*
- *argue, reason and justify*
- *negotiate*

and, in order that they can do this effectively with others:

- *listen*
- *be receptive to alternative viewpoints*
- *think about what they hear*
- *give others time to think.*

REPERTOIRE (IV): ORGANISATIONAL CONTEXTS

We have argued against the assumptions embedded in the term 'interactive whole class teaching', for the term itself is a tautology (how can whole class teaching not be interactive?) and it is the *quality* of interaction, regardless of organisational context, that matters most. Nevertheless, organisation can shape interactive opportunities and dynamics, so it too should form part of our repertoire. We distinguish five main ways of organising interaction:

- *whole class teaching (teacher and class)*
- *collective group work (teacher led)*
- *collaborative group work (pupil led)*
- *one-to-one (teacher and pupil)*
- *one-to-one (pupil pairs).*

The discursive potential of each of these needs to be thought about carefully in the planning of talk, but all of them provide opportunities for dialogue. Note that there is not one kind of group work but two. The purposes, dynamics and outcomes of group work led by the teacher are very different from group work that is managed by the pupils themselves.

INDICATORS

The quality of classroom talk depends on many factors: the speaking and listening skills of children and teachers, teachers' subject knowledge (for taking children's thinking forward requires understanding of the directions which that thinking might take), classroom climate, classroom organisation, and so on. The indicators below are placed in two groups. The first group deals with the wider context within which dialogic teaching is placed and the conditions that encourage and support it. The second group lists some of the main properties of the talk, which provides the core of dialogic teaching.

It has been suggested the indicators might be coded to show which of the five dialogic teaching principles each of them enacts. Thus, for example, the first three (starting with 'Questions are structured so as to provide thoughtful answers . . .') are principally concerned with cumulation, though the first one also attends to the need for a supportive classroom culture. However, whereas some – such as 'all parties speak clearly, audibly and expressively' – have a single focus, in this case on the principle of collectivity, others – for example, 'children build on their own and each other's contributions' – simultaneously attend to two or more principles, in this case reciprocity, support and cumulation.

So the exercise of coding the indicators may actually confuse rather clarify, and for this reason I have left them unadorned. What follows is intended to serve a heuristic purpose, not to be translated into a checklist to which teachers are required to conform. If that were to happen, its dialogic intention would be defeated.

Contexts and conditions

Dialogic teaching is facilitated and supported when:

- different organisational settings and tasks – whole class, collective group, collaborative group, and individual – are deployed to meet different educational goals;
- teachers are prepared to change classroom layout to meet the requirements of different kinds of learning task and different kinds of learning talk;
- to aid concentration, distractions and interruptions are kept to a minimum;
- lesson introductions, transitions and conclusions are economically managed, and care is taken to avoid letting lesson episodes (especially writing tasks) extend beyond (a) the time they require and (b) the children's concentration span;
- lesson introductions and conclusions are long enough to make a difference, and, as far as possible, are concerned with ideas rather than procedures;
- tasks are planned with an eye to their potential to provoke and benefit from talk-based as well as text-based and written activities; and 'now let's talk about it' becomes as familiar as 'now let's write about it';
- time is viewed as a precious resource and there is close attention to time on task;

- teaching demonstrates pace in terms of the cognitive ground it enables pupils to cover, not merely in the speed of its organisation or interaction;
- teachers seek to shift from interactions that are brief and random to those which are longer and more sustained;
- the traditional ratio of written to oral tasks and activities is adjusted to give greater prominence to the latter than hitherto;
- relatedly, more and better use is made of oral assessment, and teachers become as skilled in assessing children's understanding on the basis of what they say as by checking what they write;
- teachers are sensitive to the way their expression, gesture, body language, physical stance and location in the classroom can affect the type and quality of classroom talk;
- teachers work with their pupils to develop: a rich and discriminating vocabulary; the ability to speak confidently, clearly, informatively, expressively and succinctly; the capacity to engage with, and communicate in, different registers and genres; the ability – and will – to listen;
- teachers recognise that in all aspects of classroom talk they themselves are influential models.

Characteristics

Dialogic teaching is indicated by:

- Teacher-pupil interaction (for example in whole class teaching and teacher-led group work) in which:
    - questions are structured so as to provoke thoughtful answers;
    - answers provoke further questions and are seen as the building blocks of dialogue rather than its terminal point;
    - individual teacher–pupil and pupil–pupil exchanges are chained into coherent lines of enquiry rather than left stranded and disconnected;
    - there is an appropriate balance between the social and the cognitive purposes of talk, or between encouraging participation and extending understanding;
    - pupils – not just teachers – ask questions and provide explanations, and they are encouraged to do so;
    - turns are managed by shared routines rather than through high-stakes competitive (or reluctant) bidding;
    - those who are not speaking at a given time participate no less actively by listening, looking, reflecting and evaluating, and the classroom is arranged so as to encourage this;

- all parties speak clearly, audibly and expressively;
- children understand that different school subjects and social circumstances demand different registers, and they learn how to use them;
- children have the confidence to make mistakes, and understand that mistakes are viewed as something to learn from rather than be ashamed of;

- Pupil–pupil interaction (for example, in collaborative group settings) in which:

  - children listen carefully to each other;
  - they encourage each other to participate and share ideas;
  - they build on their own and each other's contributions;
  - they strive to reach common understanding and agreed conclusions, yet
  - they respect minority viewpoints.

- Teacher–pupil one-to-one monitoring, which:

  - lasts for long enough to make a difference;
  - is instructional rather than merely supervisory;
  - provides diagnostic feedback on which children can build.

- Questioning (whether in whole class, group or individual interactions), which:

  - is anchored in the context and content of the lesson;
  - builds on previous knowledge;
  - elicits evidence of children's understanding;
  - appropriately combines invitations for closed/narrow and open/discursive/speculative responses ('what is?' and 'what might be?' questions);
  - combines the routine and the probing;
  - uses cued elicitations and leading questions sparingly rather than habitually;
  - prompts and challenges thinking and reasoning;
  - balances open-endedness with guidance and structure in order to reduce the possibility for error;
  - achieves consistency between form and intent (e.g. where questions are questions rather than instructions, and open questions are genuinely open, rather than invitations to guess the one 'right' answer);
  - gives children time to think.

- Responses to questioning, which:

  - address the question in the depth it invites rather than worry about spotting the 'correct' answer;

- move beyond yes/no or simple recall to extended answers involving reasoning, hypothesising and 'thinking aloud';
- are, where appropriate, considered and discursive rather than brief and prematurely curtailed.

- Feedback on responses, which:

  - replaces the simple positive, negative or non-committal judgement, or mere repetition of the respondent's answer, by informative diagnostic feedback on which pupils can build;
  - uses reformulation in a way that avoids ambiguity about whether the reformulation signals approval or disapproval;
  - uses praise discriminatingly and appropriately, and filters out the habitual or phatic 'good boy', 'good girl', 'very good', 'excellent', 'fantastic', 'brilliant', etc;
  - keeps lines of enquiry open rather than closes them down;
  - encourages children to articulate their ideas openly and confidently, without fear of embarrassment or retribution if they are wrong.

- Pupil talk through which children:

  - narrate
  - explain
  - instruct
  - ask different kinds of question
  - receive, act and build upon answers
  - analyse and solve problems
  - speculate and imagine
  - explore and evaluate ideas
  - discuss
  - argue, reason and justify
  - negotiate.

References

Adams, R.J. (2003) 'Response to "Cautions on OECD's recent educational survey (PISA)"', *Oxford Review of Education*, 29(2): 377–89.

Adey, P. and Shayer, M. (1994) *Really Raising Standards: cognitive intervention and academic achievement*, London: Routledge.

Adonis, A. (2001) *High Challenge, High Support*, London: Policy Network.

Alexander, R.J. (1984) *Primary Teaching*, London: Cassell.

Alexander, R.J. (1988) 'Garden or jungle: teacher development and informal primary education' in W.A.L. Blyth (ed.) *Informal Primary Education Today: essays and studies*: 148–188, London: Falmer Press: (reprinted in Alexander 1995).

Alexander, R.J. (1992) 'Holding the middle ground', *Times Educational Supplement*, 31 January.

Alexander, R.J. (1995) *Versions of Primary Education*, London: Routledge.

Alexander, R.J. (1996, rev. 2000) *Other Primary Schools and Ours: hazards of international comparison*, Warwick: University of Warwick Centre for Research in Elementary and Primary Education.

Alexander, R.J. (1997a) *Policy and Practice in Primary Education: local initiative, national agenda*, London: Routledge.

Alexander, R.J. (1997b) 'Basics, cores and choices: towards a new primary curriculum', SCAA Conference on Developing the School Curriculum, June.

Alexander, R.J. (1998a) 'Reinventing pedagogy, rewriting history', *Parliamentary Brief*, November.

Alexander, R.J. (1998b) (ed.) *Time for Change? Primary curriculum managers at work*, Warwick and Oxford: University of Warwick with the National Primary Centre.

Alexander, R.J. (2001a) *Culture and Pedagogy: international comparisons in primary education*, Oxford: Blackwell.

Alexander, R.J. (2001b) 'Border crossings: towards a comparative pedagogy', *Comparative Eduation*, 37(4): 507–23.

Alexander, R.J. (2003) *Talk for Learning: the first year*, Northallerton: North Yorkshire County Council.

Alexander, R.J. (2004a) 'Still no pedagogy? Principle, pragmatism and compliance in primary education', *Cambridge Journal of Education*, 34(1): 7–34.

Alexander, R.J. (2004b) *Talk for Learning: the second year*, Northallerton: North Yorkshire County Council.

Alexander, R.J. (2005) *Teaching Through Dialogue: the first year*, London: London Borough of Barking and Dagenham.

Alexander, R.J. (2006a) 'Dichotomous pedagogies and the promise of cross-cultural comparison' in H. Lauder, P. Brown, J-A. Dillabough and A.H. Halsey (eds)

Education, Globalization and Social Change, pp. 722–33, Oxford: Oxford University Press.

Alexander, R.J. (2006b) *Towards Dialogic Teaching: rethinking classroom talk*, York: Dialogos.

Alexander, R.J. (2006c) *Education as Dialogue: moral and pedagogical choices for a runaway world*, Hong Kong: Hong Kong Institute of Education, and York: Dialogos.

Alexander, R.J. (2007a) *Education for All, the Quality Imperative and the Problem of Pedagogy*, New Delhi: Department for International Development.

Alexander, R.J. (2007b) 'Towards a New Vision For Primary Education? Midway through the Primary Review', invitational lecture presented by the Worshipful Company of Weavers at Church House, Westminster on 20 November 2007, Cambridge: University of Cambridge Faculty of Education, www.primaryreview.org.uk.

Alexander, R.J. and Willcocks, J. (1991) *Primary Education in Leeds*, Leeds: University of Leeds.

Alexander, R.J. and Hargeaves, L. (2007) *Community Soundings: the Primary Review regional witness sessions* (Primary Review Interim Report), Cambridge: University of Cambridge Faculty of Education, www.primaryreview.org.uk.

Alexander, R.J., Rose, A.J. and Woodhead, C. (1992) *Curriculum Organisation and Classroom Practice in Primary Schools: a discussion paper*, London: DES.

Alexander, R.J., Willcocks, J. and Nelson, N. (1996) Discourse, pedagogy and the National Curriculum: change and continuity in primary schools, *Research Papers in Education*, 11(1): 81–120.

Alexander, R.J., Broadfoot, P. and Phillips, D. (eds) (1999) *Learning from Comparing: new directions in comparative educational research. Vol. 1: Contexts, Classrooms and Outcomes*, Oxford: Symposium Books.

Alexander, R.J., Osborn, M. and Phillips, D. (eds) (2000) *Learning from Comparing: new directions in comparative educational research. Vol. 2: Policy, Professionals and Development*, Oxford: Symposium Books, pp. 149–80.

Altbach, P.G. and Kelly, G.P. (eds) (1986) *New Approaches to Comparative Education*, Chicago, IL: University of Chicago Press.

Althusser, L. (1972) 'Ideology and ideological state apparatuses' in B.R. Cosin (ed.) *Education, Structure and Society*, pp. 242–80, London, Penguin Books.

Anderson-Levitt, K. (2001) 'Teaching culture as national and transnational', *Educational Researcher*, 31(3): 19–21.

Apple, M. (1995) *Education and Power* (2nd edn), London: Routledge.

Argyris, C. and Schön, D. (1974) *Theory in Practice: increasing professional effectiveness*, San Francisco, CA: Jossey-Bass.

Arnold, M. [1869] ed. S. Collini (1993) *Culture and Anarchy and Other Writings*, Cambridge: Cambridge University Press.

Bakhtin, M.M. (1981) ed. M. Holquist, *The Dialogic Imagination*, Austin, TX: University of Texas Press.

Bakhtin, M. (1986) *Speech Genres and Other Essays*, Austin, TX: University of Texas Press.

Ball, S.J. (ed) (1990a) *Foucault and Education: disciplines and knowledge*, London: Routledge.

Ball, S.J. (1990b) *Politics and Policy-making in Education*, London: Routledge.

Barber, M. (2001) 'Large-scale education reform in England: a work in progress', paper for the Managing Education Reform Conference, Moscow, 29–30 October. The paper was also presented, with small modifications, to the Federal Reserve Bank of Boston 47th Economic Conference, 19–21 June 2002, and the

Technology Colleges Trust *Vision 2020* Second International Conference, October/November/December (in which form it is available on the Internet).

Barnes, D. (1969) 'Language in the secondary classroom' in D. Barnes, J. Britton and, H. Rosen (eds) *Language, the Learner and the School*, Harmondsworth: Penguin Books.

Barnes, D. (1976) *From Communication to Curriculum*, Portsmouth, NH: Boynton/ Cook.

Barnes, D. and Todd, F. (1995) *Communication and Learning Revisited*, Portsmouth, NH: Heinemann.

Bayliss, V. (1999) *Opening Minds: education for the 21st century*, London: RSA.

BBC (1998) 'The downward spiral of the Asian Tigers', BBC News release, 31 March.

Beard, R. (1998) *National Literacy Strategy: review of research and other related evidence*, London: DfES.

Bempechat, J. and Drago-Severson, E. (1999) 'Cross-cultural differences in academic achievement: beyond etic conceptions of children's understanding', *Review of Educational Research*, 69(3): 287–314.

Benavot, A., Cha, Y-K., Kames, D., Meyer, J.W. and Wong, S-Y (1991) 'Knowledge for the masses: world models and national curricula, 1920–1986', *American Sociological Review*, 56: 85-100.

Bennett, N., Desforges, C., Cockburn, A. and Wilkinson, A (1984) *The Quality of Pupil Learning Experiences*, London: Lawrence Erlbaum.

Berlak, A. and Berlak, H. (1981) *Dilemmas of Schooling: teaching and social change*, London: Methuen.

Berliner, D.C. (1994) 'Expertise: the wonder of exemplary performance' in J.M. Mangieri and C.C. Block (eds) *Creating Powerful Thinking in Teachers and Students*, pp. 141–86, Fort Worth, TX: Holt, Rinehart and Winston.

Berliner, D.C. and Biddle, B.J. (1995) *The Manufactured Crisis: myths, fraud and the attack on America's public schools*, Cambridge, MA: Perseus Books.

Bernstein, B. (1990) *The Structuring of Pedagogical Discourse. Vol. 4: Class, Codes and Control*, London: Routledge.

Black, P. and Wiliam, D. (1998) 'Assessment and classroom learning', *Assessment in Education*, 5(1): 7–71.

Black, P. and Wiliam, D. (1999) *Inside the Black Box: raising standards through assessment*, London: School of Education, King's College.

Black, P., Harrison, C., Lee, C., Marshall, B. and Wiliam, D. (2002) *Working Inside the Black Box: assessment for learning in the classroom*, London: School of Education, King's College.

Black, P., Harrison, C., Lee, C., Marshall, B. and Wiliam, D. (2003) *Assessment for Learning: putting it into practice*, Maidenhead: Open University Press.

Board of Education (1921) *The Teaching of English in England* (the Newbolt Report), London: HMSO.

Board of Education (1931) *Report of the Consultative Committee on the Primary School* (1931 Hadow Report), London: HSMO.

Bond, L., Smith, T., Baker, W.K. and Hattie, J.A. (2000) *The Certification System for the National Board for Professional Teaching Standards: a construct and consequential validity study*, Greensborough: University of Greensborough.

Bonnet, G. (2002) 'Reflections in a critical eye: on the pitfalls of international assessment', *Assessment in Education*, 9(3): 387–99.

Bourdieu, P. and Passeron, J.-C. (1970) *Reproduction in Education, Society and Culture*, London: Sage.

Bowles, S. and Gintis, H. (1976) *Schooling in Capitalist America: educational reform and the contradictions of American life*, London: Routledge and Kegan Paul.

Broadfoot, P. (1999) 'Comparative research on pupil achievement: in search of validity, reliability and utility' in R.J. Alexander, P. Broadfoot and D. Phillips (eds) *Learning from Comparing: new directions in comparative educational research, Vol. I*, pp. 237–60, Oxford: Symposium.

Broadfoot, P., Osborn, M., Planel, C. and Sharpe, K. (2000) *Promoting Quality in Learning: does England have the answer?* London: Cassell.

Bronfenbrenner, U. (1974) *Two Worlds of Childhood: US and USSR*, London: Penguin Books.

Brown, M., Askew, M., Rhodes, V., Denvir, H., Ranson, E. and Wiliam, D. (2003a) 'Characterising individual and cohort progression in learning literacy: results from the Leverhulme 5-year longitudinal study', American Educational Research Association Annual Conference, Chicago, Il, April.

Brown, M., Askew, M., Millett, A. and Rhodes, M. (2003b) 'The key role of educational research in the development and evaluation of the National Numeracy Strategy', *British Journal of Educational Research*, 29(5): 655–72.

Brown, M.D. (1960) *Selected Poems of George Herbert*, London: Hutchinson.

Brown, M.D. (1962) *Thomas Hardy*, London: Longman.

Brown, M.D. (1969a) *Antigone, by Sophocles: a version slightly abridged*, Cambridge: Cambridge University Press.

Brown, M.D. (1969b) *Philoctetes, by Sophocles: a version slightly abridged*, Cambridge: Cambridge University Press.

Brown, P. and Lauder, H. (1997) 'Education, globalisation and economic development' in A.H. Halsey, H. Lauder, P. Brown and A.S. Wells (eds) *Education: culture, economy, society*, pp. 172–92, Oxford: Oxford University Press.

Brown, S. and McIntyre, D. (1993) *Making Sense of Teaching*, Buckingham: Open University Press.

Bruner, J.S. (1966) *Toward a Theory of Instruction*, New York: W.W. Norton.

Bruner, J.S. (1983) *Child's Talk: learning to use language*, Oxford: Oxford University Press.

Bruner, J.S. (1987) 'The transactional self' in J.S. Bruner and H.E. Haste (eds) *Making Sense: the child's construction of the world*, pp. 81–97, London: Routledge.

Bruner, J.S. (1996) *The Culture of Education*, Cambridge, MA: Harvard University Press.

Bruner, J.S. and Haste J.E. (eds) (1987) *Making Sense: the child's construction of the world*, London: Routledge.

Calderhead, J. (1984) *Teachers' Classroom Decision-making*, London: Holt, Rinehart and Winston.

Castells, M. (1996) *The Rise of the Network Society. Vol. 1: The Information Age: economy, society and culture*, Oxford: Blackwell.

Castells, M. (1997) *The Power of Identity. Vol II: The Information Age: economy, society and culture*, Oxford: Blackwell.

Castells, M. (1998) *End of Millennium. Vol. III: The Information Age: economy, society and culture*, Oxford: Blackwell.

Cazden, C.B. (2001) *Classroom Discourse: the language of teaching and learning*, Portsmouth, NH: Heinemann.

Cazden, C.B. (2005) 'The value of eclecticism in education reform', paper presented at the 2005 AERA Annual Meeting.

Central Advisory Council for Education (England) (CACE) (1967) *Children and Their Primary Schools* (Plowden Report), London: HMSO.

Cheung, C-K. and Leung, M. (1998) 'From civic education to general studies: the implementation of political education into the primary curriculum', *Compare* 28(1): 47–56.

Chinese University of Hong Kong (2005) *Analysing the Quality of Education in Hong Kong from an international perspective*, 31(2) and 32(1) (special issue).

Clark, C.M. and Peterson, P.L. (1986) 'Teachers' thought processes' in M.C. Whitrock (ed.) *Handbook of Research on Teaching*, pp. 255-96, New York: Macmillan.

Clarke, P. (2001) *Teaching and Learning: the culture of pedagogy*, New Delhi: Sage.

Confederation of British Industry (2006) *Working on the Three Rs: employers' priorities for functional skills in maths and English*, London: DfES.

Confucius, trans. A. Waley (2000) *The Analects*, New York: Knopf/Everyman.

Cook, H.C. (1917) *The Play Way: an essay in educational method*, London: Heinemann.

Creemers, B.P.M. (1997) *Effective Schools and Effective Teachers: an international perspective*, Warwick: University of Warwick Centre for research in Elementary and Primary Education.

Creemers, B.P.M., Reynolds, D., Stringfield, S. and Teddlie, C. (1996) 'World class schools: some further findings', paper presented at the Annual Conference of the American Educational Research Association, New York.

Daniels, H. (2001) *Vygotsky and Pedagogy*, London: Routledge-Falmer.

Davie, D. (1982) *These the Companions: recollections*, Cambridge: Cambridge University Press.

Deakin Crick, R., Taylor, M., Ritchie, S., Samuel, E. and Durant, K. (2005) *A Systematic Review of the impact of Citizenship Education on Student Learning and Achievement*, London: EPPI-Centre, Social Science Research Unit, Institute of Education.

Department for Education and Employment (1998a) *The National Literacy Strategy: framework for teaching*, London: DfEE.

Department for Education and Employment (1998b) 'Blunkett strengthens curriculum focus on the basics', *DfEE News 006/98* and accompanying letter from the Secretary of State to head teachers of primary schools in England, 13 January.

Department for Education and Employment (1998c) *The Learning Age: a renaissance for a new Britain*, London: TSO.

Department for Education and Employment (1999a) *The National Numeracy Strategy: framework for teaching mathematics from Reception to Year 6*, London: DfEE.

Department for Education and Employment (1999b) *The National Curriculum*, London: DfEE/QCA.

Department for Education and Employment (2001) *Schools: building on success*, London: The Stationery Office, Chapter 1.

Department for Education and Employment/Qualifications and Curriculum Authority (1999) *The National Curriculum: handbook for primary teachers in England and Wales*, London: DfEE/QCA.

Department for Education and Skills (2002a) *A Primary Strategy 2002–2007*, London: DfES Primary Education Programme Board, 27 May.

Department for Education and Skills (2002b) 'Press release', 26 May, London: DfES.

Department for Education and Skills (2002c) published job specification for the Primary Strategy National Director, London: DfES.

Department for Education and Skills (2003a) *Excellence and Enjoyment: a strategy for primary schools*, London: DfES.

Department for Education and Skills (2003b) *The Core Principles: teaching and learning; school improvement; system wide reform* (consultation paper), London: DfES.

Department for Education and Skills (2003c) *Primary Leadership Programme Presenter's File, Part 1: focusing on expectations* (DfES 0475/2003), London: DfES.

Department for Education and Skills (2004) *Excellence and Enjoyment: learning and teaching in the primary years* (Primary National Strategy CD-ROM), London: DfES.

Department for Education and Skills (2005) *Secondary National Strategy for School Improvement*, London: DfES.

Department for Education and Skills (2007a) *Teaching Speaking and Listening* (Secondary National Strategy CD-ROM), London: DfES.

Department for Education and Skills (2007b) *Pedagogy and Personalisation*, London: DfES.

Department for Education and Skills/Qualifications and Curriculum Authority (2003) *Speaking, listening, learning: working with children in Key Stages 1 and 2* (Primary Strategy training handbook for primary teachers and headteachers, DfES 0626/2003), London: DfES.

Department for Education and Skills/Teacher Training Agency (2002) *Qualifying to Teach: professional standards for qualified teacher status and requirements for initial teacher training*, London: TTA.

Department for International Development, with H.M. Treasury (2005) *From Commitment to Action: acting now to improve living standards, health and education for all*, London: DfID.

Department of Education and Science (1978) *Primary Education in England: a survey by HM Inspectors of Schools*, London: HMSO.

Department of Education and Science (1984) *Initial Teacher Training: approval of courses (Circular 3/84)*, London: DES.

Department of Education and Science (1991) *Primary Education: a statement by the Secretary of State for Education and Science*, London: DES.

Desforges, C. (1995) *An Introduction to Teaching: psychological perspectives*, Oxford: Blackwell.

Dewey, J. (1900) *The School and Society*, Chicago, IL: Chicago University Press.

Dewey, J. (1916) *Democracy and Education*, New York: Collier Macmillan.

Dewey, J., ed. P. Jackson (1990) *The Child and the Curriculum*, Chicago, IL: University of Chicago Press.

Downing Street (2003) *Primary Schools Strategy Launched* (press release), 20 May.

Dreyfus, H.L. and Dreyfus, S.E. (1986) *Mind Over Machine*, New York: Free Press.

Drèze, J. and Sen, A. (2002) *India: development and participation*, Oxford: Oxford University Press.

Earl, L., Levin, B., Leithwood, K., Fullan, M. and Watson, N. (2001) *Watching and Learning 2: OISE/UT evaluation of the implementation of the National Literacy and Numeracy Strategies*, Toronto: Ontorio Institute for Studies in Education.

Earl, L., Watson, N., Levin, B., Leithwood, K. and Fullan, M. (2003) *Watching and Learning 3: final report of the external evaluation of England's National Literacy and Numeracy Strategies*, Toronto: Ontorio Institute for Studies in Education.

Education and Manpower Bureau, Hong Kong Special Administrative Region (2005) *Learning to Learn*, Hong Kong: Government Information Centre.

Edwards, A.D. and Westgate, D.P.G. (1994) *Investigating Classroom Talk*, 2nd edn, London: Falmer Press.

Eisner, E.W. (1979) *The Educational Imagination*, London: Macmillan.

Eke, R. and Lee, J. (2004) 'Pace and differentiation in the Literacy Hour: some outcomes of an analysis of transcripts', *Curriculum Journal*, 15(3): 219–32.

Elbaz, F. (1983) *Teacher Thinking: a study of practical knowledge*, New York: Nichols.

Engeström, Y. (1996) *Perspectives on Activity Theory*, Cambridge: Cambridge University Press.

English, E., Hargreaves, L. and Hislam, J. (2002) Pedagogical dilemmas in the National Literacy Strategy: primary teachers' perceptions, reflections and classroom behaviour, *Cambridge Journal of Education*, (32)1: 9–26.

Entwistle, H. (1970) *Child-centred Education*. London: Methuen.

Equalities Review (2007) *Fairness and Freedom: the final report of the Equalities Review*, Wetherby: Communities and Local Government Publications.

Eurydice (1994) *Pre-school and Primary Education in the European Union*, Brussels: Eurydice.

Fisher, R. (1998) *Teaching Thinking*, London: Cassell.

Flanders, N. (1970) *Analysing Teacher Behaviour*, Reading, MA: Addison-Wesley.

Flutter, J. and Rudduck, J. (2004) *Pupil Consultation: what's in it for schools?* London: Routledge.

Foster, M. (1997) *Black Teachers on Teaching*, New York: The New Press.

Fredriksson, P. (2006) 'What is so special about education in Finland? An outsider's view', paper prepared for the EU Presidency Conference, Helsinki, 28–29 September.

Freire, P. (1973) *Pedagogy of the Oppressed*, New York: Seabury Press.

Gage, N. (ed.) (1967) *Handbook of Research on Teaching*, Chicago, IL: Rand McNally.

Gage, N. (1978) *The Scientific Basis of the Art of Teaching*, New York: Teachers College Press.

Galton, M. (2007) *Learning and Teaching in the Primary Classroom*, London: Sage.

Galton, M. and Simon, B. (eds) (1980) *Progress and Performance in the Primary Classroom*, London: Routledge.

Galton, M., Simon, B. and Croll, P. (1980) *Inside the Primary Classroom*, London: Routledge.

Galton, M., Hargreaves, L., Comber, C., Wall, D. and Pell, A. (1999) *Inside the Primary Classroom: 20 years on*, London: Routledge.

Gardner, H. (1983) *Frames of Mind: the theory of multiple intelligences*, New York: Basic Books.

Gardner, H. (1999) *Intelligence Reframed: multiple intelligences for the 21st century*, New York: Basic Books.

Glaser, R. (1996) 'Changing the agency for learning: acquiring expert performance' in K.A. Ericsson (ed.) *The Road to Excellence: the acquisition of expert performance in the arts and sciences, sports and games*, pp. 303-11, Hillsdale, NJ: Lawrence Erlbaum.

Goldstein, H. (2000) 'The National Literacy and Numeracy Strategies: some comments on an evaluation report from the University of Toronto', published communication from Professor Goldstein to the OISE evaluation report's principal author, Lorna Earl, July, www.cmm.bristol.ac.uk/team/HG_Personal/national_literacy_and_numeracy_s.htm.

Goody, J. (1993) *The Interface Between the Written and the Oral*, Cambridge: Cambridge University Press.

Gray, J. (1998) *False Dawn: the delusions of global capitalism*, London: Granta Books.

Green, A. and Steedman, H. (1997) *Into the 21st Century: an assessment of British skill profiles and prospects*, London: Centre for Economic Performance.

Grice, H.P. (1975) 'Logic and conversation' in P. Cole and J. Morgan (eds) *Syntax and Semantics. Vol. 3: Speech Acts*, New York: Academic Press.

Halliday, M. (1989) *Spoken and Written Language*, Oxford: Oxford University Press.

Halliday, M.A.K. (1993) 'Towards a language-based theory of learning', *Linguistics in Education*, 5(2): 93–116.

Hamilton, D. (1995) '*Peddling Feel-good Fictions: reflections on "Key characteristics of effective schools"* ', Liverpool: University of Liverpool School of Education.

Hamilton, D. (1999) 'The pedagogic paradox (or Why no didactics in England?)', *Pedagogy, Culture and Society*, 7(1): 135–52.

Hamlyn, D.W. (1970) 'The logical and psychological aspects of learning' in R.S. Peters (ed.) *The Concept of Education*, pp. 24–43, London: Routledge and Kegan Paul.

Hardman, F., Smith, F. and Wall, K. (2003) ' "Interactive whole class teaching" in the National Literacy Strategy', *Cambridge Journal of Education*, 33(2): 197–215.

Hargreaves, D.H. (2004a) *Learning for Life: the foundations for lifelong learning*, Bristol: Policy Press.

Hargreaves, D.H. (2004b) *Personalising Learning 2: student voice and assessment for learning*, London: Specialist Schools and Academics Trust.

Hargreaves, D.H. (2004c) *Personalising Learning 1: next steps in working laterally*, London: Specialist Schools and Academies Trust.

Hargreaves, D.H. (2005) *Personalising Learning 5: mentoring and coaching, and workforce development*, London: Specialist Schools and Academies Trust.

Hargreaves, D.H. (2006a) *A New Shape for Schooling?* London: Specialist Schools and Academies Trust.

Hargreaves, D.H. (2006b) *Personalising Learning 6: school design and organisation*, London: Specialist Schools and Academies Trust.

Harlen, W. (2007) *Assessment alternatives for primary education* (Primary Review Research Survey 3/4), Cambridge: University of Cambridge Faculty of Education, www.primaryreview.org.uk.

Harris, S., Keys, W. and Fernandes, C. (1997) *Third International Mathematics and Science Study, Second National Report, Part 1*. Slough: NFER.

Hart, S., Dixon, A., Drummond, M.J. and McIntyre, D.I. (2004) *Learning Without Limits*, Maidenhead: Open University Press.

Hatim, B. and Mason, I. (1990) *Discourse and the Translator*, London: Longman.

Hayhoe, R. (ed.) (1984) *Contemporary Chinese Education*, Beckenham: Croom Helm.

Heath, S.B. (1983) *Ways With Words: language, life and work in communities and classrooms*, Cambridge: Cambridge University Press.

Hirst, P.H. (1965) 'Liberal education and the nature of knowledge' in R.D. Archambault (ed.) *Philosophical Analysis and Education*, pp. 113–38, London: Routledge and Kegan Paul.

Hirst, P.H. (1979) 'Professional studies in initial teacher education: some conceptual issues' in R.J. Alexander and E. Wormald (eds) *Professional Studies for Teaching*, pp.15–29, Guildford: SRHE.

HMI (1985) *The Curriculum From 5 to 16*, London: HMSO.

H.M. Treasury (2006) *Prosperity for All in the Global Economy: world class skills*, London: HMSO.

Ho, S-C. (2005) 'Accomplishment and challenges of Hong Kong education system: what we have learned from PISA', *Education Journal* (Chinese University of Hong Kong), 31(2): 1–30.

Hobsbawm, E. (1995) *Age of Extremes: the short twentieth century 1914–91*, London: Abacus.

Hobsbawm, E. (2007) *Globalisation, Democracy and Terrorism*, London: Little, Brown.

Hoggart, R. (1957) *The Uses of Literacy*, London: Chatto and Windus.

Holmes, B. (1981) *Comparative Education: some considerations of method*, London: Allen and Unwin.

Holquist, M. (2002) *Dialogism: Bakhtin and his world*, London: Routledge.

Holt, J. (1964) *How Children Fail*, London: Pitman.

Hopkins, D. (2003) 'Strategies based on real research' (letter), *Times Educational Supplement*, 3 October.

House of Commons (1986) *Achievement in Primary Schools: third report from the Education, Science and Arts Committee*, London: HMSO.

House of Commons (1994a) *The Disparity in Funding Between Primary and Secondary Schools: Education Committee Second Report*, London: HMSO.

House of Commons (1994b) *Government Response to the Second Report from the Committee (The Disparity in Funding Between Primary and Secondary Schools)*, London: HMSO.

House of Commons (1999) *The Work of Ofsted: fourth report of the Education and Employment Committee. Session 1998–9, Vol. 3*, London: The Stationery Office.

Howard-Jones, P. (2007) *Neuroscience and Education: issues and opportunities*, London and Swindon: TLRP and ESRC.

Hull, R. (1985) *The Language Gap*, London: Methuen.

IEA/ISC (2003) *PIRLS 2001 International Report: IEA's study of reading literacy achievement in primary school in 35 countries*, Chester Hill, MA: Boston College.

IndianNGOs.com (1997) *National Programme of Nutritional Support to Primary Education*, http://www.indianngos.com/issue/education/govt/centralprog2.htm.

Jackson, P.W. (1968) *Life in Classrooms*, New York: Holt, Rinehart and Winston.

James, M. and Pollard, A.J. (2008) *Learning and teaching in primary schools: insights from TLRP* (Primary Review Research Survey 2/4), Cambridge: University of Cambridge Faculty of Education.

Johnson, M. (2004) *Developmental Cognitive Neuroscience*, Oxford: Blackwell.

Joseph Rowntree Foundation (2007) 'Experiences of poverty and disadvantage' (synthesis report from the Education and Poverty programme), York: Joseph Rowntree Foundation

Keatinge, M.W. (1896) *The Great Didactic of John Amos Comenius*, London: A. and C. Black.

Keys, W. (1996) 'Take care when you compare', *Times Educational Supplement*, 14 June.

Keys, W., Harris, S. and Fernandes, C. (1996) *Third International Mathematics and Science Study: First National Report, Part 1*, Slough: NFER.

King, E.J. (1979) *Other Schools and Ours: comparative studies for today*, London: Holt, Rinehart and Winston.

Klein, N. (2000) *No Logo*, London: Flamingo.

Kumar, K. (1991) *Political Agenda of Education: a study of colonialist and nationalist ideas*, Delhi: Sage.

Ladson-Billings, G. (1991) *The Dreamkeepers: successful teachers of African-American Children*, San Francisco, CA: Jossey-Bass.

Landes, D.S. (1998) *The Wealth and Poverty of Nations: why some are so rich and some so poor*, London: Little, Brown.

Lawton, D. (1989) *Education, Culture and the National Curriculum*, London: Hodder and Stoughton.

Leavis, F.R. (1960) *The Great Tradition: George Eliot, Henry James, Joseph Conrad*, London: Chatto and Windus.

Leavis, F.R. (1972) 'Two Cultures? The significance of Lord Snow' in F.R. Leavis, *Nor Shall My Sword: discourses on pluralism, compassion and social hope*, London: Chatto and Windus.

Leavis, F.R. and Thompson, D. (1933) *Culture and Environment*, London: Chatto and Windus.

Le Tendre, G., Baker, D.P., Akiba, M., Goesling, B. and Wiseman, A. (2001) 'Teachers' work: institutional isomorphism and cultural variation in the US, Germany and Japan', *Educational Researcher*, 30(6): 3–15.

Levin, H.M. and Kelly. C. (1997) 'Can education do it alone?' in A.H. Halsey, H. Lauder, P. Brown and A.S. Wells (eds) *Education: culture, economy, society*, 240–52, Oxford: Oxford University Press.

Li, J. (2003) 'US and Chinese cultural beliefs about learning', *Journal of Educational Psychology*, 95(2): 258–67.

Lindfors, J.W. (1999) *Children's Inquiry: using language to make sense of the world*, New York: Teachers College, Columbia University.

Linnell, P. (1998) *Approaching Dialogue: talk, interaction and contexts in dialogical perspective*, Philadelphia, PA: John Benjamins Publishing.

Lipman, M., Sharp, A.M. and Oscanyan, F.S. (1980) *Philosophy in the Classroom*, Philadelphia, PA: Temple University Press.

Loades, D. (ed.) (2005) *Douglas Brown: teacher and man of letters*, Cambridge: the Old Persean Society.

Lockheed, M.E. and Verspoor, A.M. (1991) *Improving Primary Education in Developing Countries*, Washington: World Bank in conjunction with Oxford University Press.

Lovelock, J. (2006) *The Revenge of Gaia: why the Earth is fighting back, and how we can still save humanity*, London: Allen Lane.

Luke, A. and Carrington, V. (2002) 'Globalisation, literacy, curriculum practice' in R. Fisher, M. Lewis and G. Brooks (eds) *Language and Literacy in Action*, London: Routledge Falmer.

Luxton, R. (2000) *Interactive Whole Class Teaching: a briefing note*, London: London Borough of Barking and Dagenham.

Luxton, R. and Last, G. (1997) *Underachievement and Pedagogy*, London: National Institute of Economic and Social Research.

Lyytinen, H.K. (2002) 'Why are Finnish students doing so well in PISA?' Paris: OECD.

Macedo, D. (1999) 'Our common culture: a poisonous pedagogy' in M. Castells, R. Flecha, P. Freire, H.A. Giroux and P. Willis (eds) *Critical Information in the New Information Age*, pp. 117–38, Lanham: Rowman and Littlefield.

McGuiness, C. (1999) *From Thinking Skills to Thinking Classrooms*, London: DfES.

McIntyre, D.I. (2007a) 'Pedagogy: a review of key literature. First interim report', Cambridge: University of Cambridge Faculty of Education.

McIntyre, D.I. (2007b) 'Pedagogy for the UK: a useful project?' Cambridge: University of Cambridge Faculty of Education.

McKay, D. (1994) *American Politics and Society*. Malden, MA: Blackwell

Madge, N. and Barker, J. (2007) *Risk and Childhood*, London: RSA.

Major, J. (1991) speech to the Conservative Party Conference, October.

Mansell, W. (2007) *Education By Numbers: the tyranny of testing*, London: Politico's.

Mercer, N. (2000) *Words and Minds: how we use language to think together*, London: Routledge.

Micklewright, J. and Schnepf, S.V. (2006) *Response Bias in England in PISA 2000 and 2003*, London: DfES.

Miliband, D. (2004) *Personalised Learning: building a new relationship with schools*, speech to the North of England Education Conference, 8 January.

Millard, E. (2003) 'Towards a literacy of fusion: new times, new teaching, new learning', *Reading: literacy and language*, April: 3–8.

Millett, A. (1999) 'Why we need to raise our game', *The Independent*, 11 February.

Ministère de l'Éducation Nationale (2002) *Qu'apprend-on à l'école élémentaire?* Paris: CNDP.

Moon, B. (1998) *The English Exception: international perspectives on the initial education and training of teachers*, London: UCET.

Moore, M. (2001) *Stupid White Men*, London: Penguin Books.

Morris, P. (1988) 'The effect on the school curriculum of Hong Kong's return to Chinese sovereignty in 1997', *Journal of Curriculum Studies*, 20: 509–20.

Morrison, A. and McIntyre, D.I. (1973) *Teachers and Teaching*, Harmondsworth: Penguin.

Mortimer, E.F. and Scott, P.H. (2003) *Meaning Making in Science Classrooms*, Maidenhead: Open University Press.

Mortimore, P., Sammons, P., Stoll, L., Lewis, D. and Ecob, R. (1988) *School Matters: the junior years*, London: Open Books.

Moyles, J., Hargreaves, L., Merry, R., Paterson, F. and Esarte-Sarries, V. (2003) *Interactive Teaching in the Primary School*, Maidenhead: Open University Press.

Murphy, C. (2004) 'Little patriots', *The Standard* (Hong Kong), 9–10 October.

Myhill, D. (2005) *'Teaching and Learning in Whole Class Discourse'*, Exeter: University of Exeter School of Education.

National Research Council (2003) *Understanding Others, Educating Ourselves: getting more from international comparative studies in education*, Washington, DC: The National Academies Press.

Neuberger, J. (2005) *The Moral State We're In: a manifesto for the 21st century*, London: Harper Collins.

Nichols, S. and Berliner, D.C. (2007) *How High-stakes Testing Corrupts America's Schools*, Cambridge, MA: Harvard Educational Press.

Noah, H.J. (1986) 'The use and abuse of comparative education' in P.G. Altbach and G.P. Kelly (eds) *New Approaches to Comparative Education*, Chicago, IL: University of Chicago Press.

North Yorkshire County Council, with Robin Alexander (consultant and script) (2006) *Talk for Learning: teaching and learning through dialogue*, Northallerton: North Yorkshire County Council (DVD/CD pack: for ordering details go to www.robinalexander.org.uk/dialogos.htm).

Nystrand, M. with Gamoran, A., Kachur, R. and Prendergast, C. (1997) *Opening Dialogue: understanding the dynamics of learning and teaching in the English classroom*, New York: Teachers College Press.

Office for Standards in Education (1996) 'Look East for new ideas, say educational researchers', News release PN24/96, London: Ofsted.

Office for Standards in Education (2002a) *The National Literacy Strategy: the first four years 1998–2002*, London: Ofsted.

Office for Standards in Education (2002b) *The National Numeracy Strategy: the first three years 1999–2002*, London: Ofsted.

Office for Standards in Education (2002c) *The Curriculum in Successful Primary Schools*, London: Ofsted.

Office for Standards in Education (2002d) *Handbook for the Inspection of Initial Teacher Training (2002–2008)*, London: Ofsted.

Office for Standards in Education (2003a) *The Education of Six Year Olds in England, Denmark and Finland: an international comparative study*, London: Ofsted.

Office for Standards in Education (2003b) *Inspecting Schools: framework for inspecting schools, effective from September 2003*, London: Ofsted.

Office for Standards in Education/Department for Education and Employment (1997) *National Curriculum Assessment Results and the Wider Curriculum at Key Stage 2: some evidence from the Ofsted database*, London: Ofsted.

Organisation for Economic Co-operation and Development (OECD) (1994) *Quality in Teaching*, Paris: OECD.

Organisation for Economic Co-operation and Development (1995a) *Measuring the Quality of Schools*, Paris: OECD.

Organisation for Economic Co-operation and Development (1995b) *Measuring What Students Learn*, Paris: OECD.

Organisation for Economic Co-operation and Development (1995c) *Education at a Glance: OECD Indicators*, Paris: OECD.

Organisation for Economic Co-operation and Development (1995d) *OECD Education Statistics 1985–1992*, Paris: OECD.

Organisation for Economic Co-operation and Development (1998) *Education at a Glance: OECD Indicators 1998*, Paris: OECD.

Organisation for Economic Co-operation and Development (2004a) *Education at a Glance: OECD Indicators 2004*, Paris: OECD.

Organisation for Economic Co-operation and Development (2004b) 'Top-performer Finland improves further in PISA survey as gap between countries widens', OECD press release, 6 December.

Organisation for Economic Co-operation and Development (2005a) *Education at a Glance: OECD Indicators 2005*, Paris: OECD.

Organisation for Economic Co-operation and Development (2005b) *Economic Survey of China*, Brussels: OECD.

Organisation for Economic Co-operation and Development (2006) *Education at a Glance: OECD Indicators 2006*, Paris: OECD.

Osborn, M. and Planel, C. (1999) 'Comparing children's learning, attitude and performance in French and English primary schools' in R.J. Alexander, P. Broadfoot and D. Phillips (eds) *Learning from Comparing: new directions in comparative educational research, Vol. I*, Oxford: Symposium Books, pp. 261–94.

Palincsar, A.S. and Brown, A.L. (1984) *Reciprocal Teaching of Comprehension Fostering and Monitoring Activities: cognition and instruction*, Hillsdale, NJ: Lawrence Erlbaum.

Parmenter, L., Lam, C., Seto, F. and Tomital, Y. (2000) 'Locating self in the world: elementary school children in Japan, Macau and Hong Kong', *Compare*, 30(2): 133–44.

Phenix, P.H. (1964) *Realms of Meaning: a philosophy of the curriculum for general education*, New York: McGraw-Hill.

Pilger, J. (2002) *The New Rulers of the World*, London: Verso.

Popper, K. (1972) *Objective Knowledge: an evolutionary approach*, Oxford: Oxford University Press.

Potts, P. (2003) *Modernising Education in Britain and China: comparative perspectives on excellence and social inclusion*, London: Routledge Falmer.

Prais, S.J. (1997) *School Readiness, Whole Class Teaching and Pupils' Mathematical Achievement*, London: National Institute of Social and Economic Research.

Prais, S.J. (2003) 'Cautions on OECD's recent educational survey (PISA)', *Oxford Review of Education*, 29(2): 139–63.

Qualifications and Curriculum Authority (2000) *Curriculum Guidance for the Foundation Stage*, London: QCA/DfES.

Qualifications and Curriculum Authority (ed.) (2003) *New Perspectives on Spoken English in the Classroom*, London: QCA.

Qualifications and Curriculum Authority (2007) *The Curriculum: taking stock of progress*, London: QCA.

Qualifications and Curriculum Authority/Department for Education and Skills (2003a) *Speaking, Listening, Learning: working with children in KS1 and 2, Handbook*, London: QCA and DfES.

Qualifications and Curriculum Authority/Department for Education and Skills (2003b) *Speaking, Listening, Learning: working with children in KS1 and 2, teaching objectives and classroom activities*, London: QCA and DfES.

Reboul-Scherrer, F. (1989) *Les Premiers Instituteurs, 1833–1882*, Paris: Hachette.

Reynolds, D. and Teddlie, C. (1995) *World Class Schools: a preliminary analysis from the International School Effectiveness Research Project (ISERP)*, Newcastle upon Tyne: University of Newcastle upon Tyne Department of Education.

Reynolds, D. and Farrell, S. (1996) *Worlds Apart? A review of international surveys of educational achievement involving England*, London: Ofsted.

Reynolds, D., Creemers, B.P.M., Nesselrodt, P.S., Schaffer, E.C., Stringfield, S. and Teddlie, C. (1994) *Advances in School Effectiveness Research and Practice*, Oxford: Pergamon.

Reynolds, D., Creemers, B., Stringfield, S., Teddlie, C. and Schaffer, G. (2002) *World Class Schools: international perspectives on school effectiveness*, London: Routledge.

Richards, I.A. (1929) *Practical Criticism: a study in literary judgement*, London: Kegan Paul.

Richardson, V. (2001) *Handbook of Research on Teaching* (4th edn), Washington DC: American Educational Research Association.

Robinson, C. and Fielding, M. (2007) *Children and their Primary Schools: pupils' voices* (Primary Review Research Survey 5/3), Cambridge: University of Cambridge Faculty of Education.

Robinson, P. (1999) 'The tyranny of league tables: international comparisons of educational attainment and economic performance', in R.J. Alexander, P. Broadfoot and D. Phillips (eds) *Learning from Comparing: new directions in comparative educational research. Vol. 1, Contexts, Classrooms and Outcomes*, Oxford: Symposium Books: 217–236.

Rogoff, B. (1990) *Apprenticeship in Thinking: cognitive development in social context*, Oxford: Oxford University Press.

Rosenshine, B.V. (1979) 'Content, time and direct instruction' in P.L Peterson and H.J. Walberg (eds) *Research on Teaching: concepts, findings and implications*, Berkeley, MA: McCutchan.

Ruddock, G., Clausen-May, T., Purple, C. and Ager, R. (2006) *Validation Study of the PISA 2000, PISA 2003 and TIMSS 2003 International Studies of Pupil Attainment*, Slough: NFER.

Rudduck, J. and Flutter, J. (2003) *How to Improve your School: giving pupils a voice*, London and New York: Continuum Press.

Rudduck, J. and McIntyre, D.I. (2007) *Improving Learning Through Consulting Pupils*, London: Routledge.

Ruzzi, B.B. (2006) 'International Education Tests: an overview, 2005', Washington: NCEE.

Sadler, M. (1900) 'How can we learn anything of practical value from the study of foreign systems of education?' in J.H. Higginson (ed.) *Selections from Michael Sadler: studies in world citizenship*, Liverpool: Dejall & Meyorre.

Sadler, M. (1902) 'The unrest in secondary education in Germany and elsewhere' in Board of Education, *Education in Germany: special reports on education subjects, Vol. 9*, London: HMSO.

Said, E. (1979) *Orientalism*, London: Vintage.

Said, E.W. (1994) *Culture and Imperialism*, London: Vintage Books.

Sammons, P., Hillman, J. and Mortimore, P. (1995) *Key Characteristics of Effective Schools: a review of school effectiveness research*, London: Ofsted.

Sammons, P., Sylva, K., Melhuish, E., Siraj-Blatchford, I., Taggart, B., Brabbe, Y. and Barreau, S. (2007) *Effective Pre-school and Primary Education 3–11 Project (EPPE 3–11): influences on children's attainment and progress in Key Stage 2: cognitive outcomes in Year 5*, London: Institute of Education.

Sands, P. (2005) *Lawless World: America and the breaking of global rules*, London: Allen Lane.

Sardar, Z. and Davies, M.W. (2002) *Why Do People Hate America?* Cambridge: Icon Books.

Scheffler, I. (1971) *The Language of Education*, Springfield, Il: Thomas.

Schellnhuber, J., Cramer, W., Nakicenovic, N., Wigley, T. and Yohe, G. (eds) (2006) *Avoiding Dangerous Climate Change*, Cambridge: Cambridge University Press.

Schön, D.A. (1982) *The Reflective Practitioner: how professionals think in action*, London: Temple Smith.

Scruton, R. (2002) *The West and the Rest: globalization and the terrorist threat*, London: Continuum.

Sharpe, K. and Ning, Q. (1998) 'The training of secondary modern language teachers in England and China: a comparative analysis', *Compare*, 28(1): 57–74.

Shulman, L.S. (1987) 'Knowledge and teaching: foundations of the new reform', *Harvard Educational Review*, 57(1): 1–22.

Shweder, R.A. (1991) *Thinking Through Cultures*, Cambridge, MA: Harvard University Press.

Simon, B. (1981) Why no pedagogy in England? in B. Simon and W. Taylor (eds) *Education in the Eighties: the central issues*, pp. 121–45, London: Batsford.

Simon, B. (1992) Review of 'Curriculum organisation and classroom practice in primary schools: a discussion paper', *Curriculum Journal* 3(1).

Simon, B. (1994) *The State and Educational Change: essays in the history of education and pedagogy*, London: Lawrence and Wishart.

Simon, B. (2000) 'Blair on education', *Forum*, 42(3): 91–3.

Simon, J. (1987) 'Vygotsky and the Vygotskians', *American Journal of Education*, August: 609–13.

Sims, E. (2006) *Deep Learning 1*, London: Specialist Schools and Academies Trust.

Sinclair, J. McH. and Coulthard, R.M. (1975) *Towards an Analysis of Discourse*, Oxford: Oxford University Press.

Sinclair, J. McH. and Coulthard, R.M. (1992) 'Towards an analysis of discourse' in M. Coulthard (ed.) *Advances in Spoken Discourse Analysis*, pp. 1–34, London: Routledge.

Skidmore, D. (2002) 'Teacher–Pupil Dialogue and the Comprehension of Literary Texts' (unpublished paper), Reading: University of Reading.

Skidmore, D. (2006) 'Pedagogy and dialogue', *Cambridge Journal of Education*, 36(4): 503–14.

Skidmore, D., Perez-Parent, M. and Arnfield, S. (2003) 'Teacher–pupil dialogue in the guided reading session', *Reading: Literacy and Language*, 37(2): 47–53.

Smith, F., Hardman, F., Wall, K. and Mroz, M. (2004) 'Interactive whole class teaching in the National Literacy and Numeracy Strategies', *British Educational Research Journal*, 30(3): 395–412.

Steedman, H. (1999) 'Measuring the quality of educational outputs: some unresolved problems' in R.J. Alexander, P. Broadfoot and D. Phillips (eds) *Learning from Comparing: new directions in comparative educational research. Vol 1, Contexts, Classrooms and Outcomes*, pp. 201–16, Oxford: Symposium Books.

Stenhouse, L. (1975) *An Introduction to Curriculum Research and Development*, London: Heinemann.

Stern, N. (2007) *The Economics of Climate Change: the Stern Review*, Cambridge: Cambridge University Press.

Sternberg, R.J. (1985) *Beyond IQ: a triarchic theory of intelligence*, New York: Cambridge University Press.

Sternberg, R.J. (1997) *Successful Intelligence*, New York: Plume.

Sternberg, R.J. (2004) 'Individual differences in cognitive development' in U. Goswami (ed.) *Blackwell Handbook of Cognitive Childhood Development*, pp. 600–19, Oxford: Blackwell.

Sternberg, R.J. (2005) 'Culture and intelligence', *American Psychologist*, 59(5): 325–38.

Stevenson, H.W. and Stigler, J.W. (1992) *The Learning Gap: why our schools are failing and what we can learn from Japanese and Chinese education*, New York: Simon and Schuster.

Stigler, J.W. and Hiebert, J. (1999) *The Teaching Gap: best ideas from the world's teachers for improving education in the classroom*. New York: The Free Press.

Stigler, J.W., Gallimore, R., Hiebert, J. (2000) 'Using video surveys to compare classrooms and teaching across cultures: examples and lessons from the TIMSS Video Studies', *Educational Psychologist*, 35(2): 81–100.

Stiglitz, J. (2002) *Globalization and its Discontents*, London: Penguin Books.

Tawney, R.H. (1923) *Secondary Education for All: a policy for labour*, London: Allen and Unwin/The Labour Party.

Teacher Training Agency (TTA) (2005) *Making a difference to every child's life: the TTA's extended remit*, London: TTA.

Teaching and Learning Research Programme (2007) *Principles Into Practice: a teacher's guide to research evidence on teaching and learning*, London: TLRP.

Tharp, R. and Gallimore, R. (1988) *Rousing Minds to Life: teaching, learning and schooling in social context*, New York: Cambridge University Press.

Tobin, J.J. (1999) 'Method and meaning in comparative classroom ethnography' in R.J. Alexander, P. Broadfoot and D. Phillips (eds) *Learning from comparing: new directions in comparative educational research. Vol. I: Contexts, Classrooms and Outcomes*, pp.113–34, Oxford: Symposium Books.

Tobin, J.J., Wu, D.Y. and Davidson, D.H. (1989) *Preschool in Three Cultures: Japan, China and the United States*, New Haven, CT: Yale University Press.

Twist, L., Schagen, I. and Hodgson, C. (2007) *Readers and Reading: the National Report for England 2006* (Progress in International Reading Literacy Study), Slough: NFER.

Tymms, P. (2004) 'Are standards rising in English primary schools?', *British Educational Research Journal*, 30(4): 477–94.

Tymms, P. and Merrell, C. (2007) *Standards and Quality in English Primary Schools over Time: the national evidence* (Primary Review Research Survey 4/1), Cambridge: University of Cambridge Faculty of Education.

UNESCO (2007) *Education For All Development Index (EDI)*, http://portal.unesco.org/education.

United Nations (2005a) *Human Development Report 2005*, New York: United Nations.

United Nations (2005b) *Millennium Development Goals Report 2005*, New York: United Nations.

United Nations Intergovernmental Panel on Climate Change (2001) *Climate Change 2001: synthesis report*, Cambridge: Cambridge University Press.

United Nations Intergovernmental Panel on Climate Change (2005) *Special Report on Safeguarding the Ozone Layer and the Global Climate System*, Cambridge: Cambridge University Press.

United Nations Intergovernmental Panel on Climate Change (2007) *Climate Change 2007: synthesis report of the IPCC Fourth Assessment Report*, New York: United Nations.

United States Congress (1994) *Goals 2000: Educate America Act*, HR 1804, Washington: United States Congress.

United States Department of Education (2007) *American Competitiveness Initiative: a continuing commitment to leading the world in innovation*, Washington: US Department of Education.

Vygotksy, L.S. (1962) *Thought and Language*, Cambridge: MIT Press.

Vygotsky, L.S. (1963) 'Learning and mental development at school age' in B. Simon and J. Simon (eds) *Educational Psychology in the USSR*, pp. 21–34, London: Routledge and Kegan Paul.

Vygotsky, L.S. (1978) *Mind in Society*, Cambridge, MA: Harvard University Press.

Wallace, M. (1993) 'Discourse of derision: the role of the mass media in the educational policy process', *Journal of Educational Policy*, 8(4): 321–37.

Ward, H. (2003) 'Guru attacks "deeply patronising" strategy', *Times Educational Supplement*, 19 September.

Watson, K. (1993) 'Changing emphases in educational aid' in T. Allsop and C. Brock (eds) *Key Issues in Educational Development* (Oxford Studies in Comparative Education, 3:2), Wallingford: Triangle Books.

Wattenberg, B. (1991) *The First Universal Nation*, New York: The Free Press.

Webb, R. and Vulliamy, G. (2007) *Coming Full Circle? The impact of New Labour's education policies on primary school teachers' work*, London: Association of Teachers and Lecturers.

Wells, G. (1999) *Dialogic Enquiry: towards a sociocultural practice and theory of education*, Cambridge: Cambridge University Press.

Wertsch, J.V. (1985) *Culture, Communication and Cognition: Vygotskian perspectives*, Cambridge: Cambridge University Press.

Wertsch, J.V. (1991) *Voices of the Mind: a sociocultural approach to mediated action*, Cambridge, MA: Harvard University Press.

Whetton, C., Ruddock, G. and Twist, L. (2007) *Standards in English Primary Education Over Time: the international evidence* (Primary Review Research Survey 4/2), Cambridge: University of Cambridge Faculty of Education.

Williams, Raymond (1958) *Culture and Society 1780–1950*, London: Chatto and Windus.

Williams, Rowan (2000) *Lost Icons: reflections on cultural bereavement*, London: Continuum.

Williamson, S. (2006) *A New Shape for Schooling: Deep Support – 1*, London: Specialist Schools and Academies Trust.

Wolfe, S. (2006) 'Teaching and learning through dialogue in primary classrooms in England', unpublished PhD thesis, University of Cambridge.

Wood, D. (1998) *How Children Think and Learn* (2nd edn), Oxford: Blackwell.

Wood, D., Bruner, J.S. and Ross, G. (1976) 'The role of tutoring in problem-solving', *Journal of Child Psychology and Child Psychiatry*, 17: 89–100.

Woodhead, C. (1996) Interview in BBC *Panorama* 'Hard Lessons', 3 June.

World Bank (2007) *Cost of Pollution in China: economic estimates of physical damage*, Washington: World Bank.

Wragg, E.C. (1993) *Primary Teaching Skills*, London: Routledge.

Wragg, E.C. (1997) *The Cubic Curriculum*, London: Routledge.

Wyse, D., McCreery, E. and Torrance, H. (2008) *The Trajectory of Reform in Curriculum and Assessment* (Primary Review Research Report 3/2), Cambridge: University of Cambridge Faculty of Education, www.primaryreview.org.uk.

Young, H. (1989) *One of Us: a biography of Margaret Thatcher*, London: Macmillan.

Young, M.F.D. (ed.) (1971) *Knowledge and Control: new directions for the sociology of education*, London: Collier Macmillan.

Zinn, H. (2003) *A People's History of the United States, 1492–Present* (3rd edn), London: Pearson.

Index